The Fisher

ROGER A. POWELL

The Fisher

LIFE HISTORY, ECOLOGY, AND BEHAVIOR

SECOND EDITION

UNIVERSITY OF MINNESOTA PRESS

MINNEAPOLIS / LONDON

Published by the University of Minnesota Press
2037 University Avenue Southeast, Minneapolis, MN 55455-3092

Library of Congress Cataloging-in-Publication Data

Powell, Roger A.
   The fisher : life history, ecology, and behavior / Roger A.
Powell. — 2nd ed.
     p.   cm.
   Includes bibliographical references (p.   ) and index.
   ISBN 0-8166-2265-5 (acid-free paper). — ISBN 0-8166-2266-3 (pbk. : acid-free paper)
   1. Fisher (Animal)   I. Title.
   QL737.C25P66 1993
   599.74′447—dc20
                                       93-3716
                                       CIP

The University of Minnesota is an
equal-opportunity educator and employer.

To ThaCho
    Because I like to think you made it
And to Uskool
    Because I am sorry
I loved you both

Contents

petite, or excessive activity, I would be on the phone to the veteri-
⸱ was exceedingly patient and gave me much wise advice—such as
ectate for the kits' diarrhea. Probably ThaCho's and Uskool's great-
⸱ surviving me!

haCho and Uskool were about three and a half weeks old, we
⸱ir feeding schedule to every four hours. This meant that Consie and
⸱ nights of feeding the kits; one of us could stay in bed all night. The
edings were completely discontinued when the kits were four and a
⸱ld.

⸱nd Uskool taught us many things about themselves and about rais-
⸱mals. Most important, they taught us to pay attention to what they
⸱ to tell us. ThaCho became a very fussy eater when she reached
⸱weeks of age. Was she getting too much to eat? Was she sick? No—
⸱ting ready for food of a more solid consistency than liquid formula.
⸱vould rub ThaCho's and Uskool's tummies with a piece of facial tis-
⸱eeding them. This stimulated them to urinate. By the time they got
⸱weeks older, though, we were going through a lot of tissue. I cannot
⸱ho struck on the idea, Consie or I, but we began holding them over
⸱en we stimulated them. Then all we needed to do was a little bit of

⸱ biggest cleanup came when the kits were weaned. We fed them a
⸱ilac and finely ground raw venison. They loved it. They also made
⸱ of themselves. They were not content with putting the food in
⸱ but insisted on getting it all over their faces, paws, and tummies as
⸱g a squirming fisher kit with a damp washcloth is almost impossi-
⸱ing our female Newfoundland dog clean up the mess was easy.
⸱ Newfoundland, loved the job: she got a rare treat of venison and
⸱. In addition, the kits did not squirm much while being cleaned
⸱gue.

⸱nd Uskool stayed in a variety of places during the time they lived
⸱st, they went through a graduated series of cardboard boxes; then
⸱ to a gable in my upstairs study, and then to our front porch. I set
⸱ on the front porch so that I could train them. ThaCho and Uskool
⸱with their paws on the front door, looking inside the house and
⸱ come out and play with them. They soon learned how to distin-
⸱ I was coming out to play with them or to run them on the tread-
⸱discovered that she could hide in places I had trouble reaching—
⸱ a cage or on top of the curtains in a corner. While the fishers were
⸱front porch, there was more than an occasional "bump in the

Preface and Acknowledgments
to the Second Edition

Since the manuscript for *The Fisher* was finished in late 1980, important research has been completed on fishers and in areas of ecology, animal behavior,
and evolution that relate to fishers. Incorporating that research into a revised
volume has been an enjoyable challenge. No animals fascinate me more than
fishers. By synthesizing the recent research, I have gained yet a greater appre-
ciation for these beautiful creatures.

I thank Bud Heinselman for pushing me to write to Barbara Coffin to pro-
pose a second edition of *The Fisher*. I thank Christopher A. Kline and Mike Don
Carlos for contributing their unpublished data on fisher courtship and growth. I
thank Melanie Hassler for typing the first edition on disk for me to revise. I
thank Bill Krohn for taking several days to review a rough draft of the manuscript for this second edition. His comments have led to significant improve-
ments. I thank Consie, my wife, for contributing the illustrations; they give this
second edition a visual personality. And I thank Consie and Virginia, my daugh-
ter, for tolerating me this past summer while I wrote, revised, and rewrote,
often at odd hours.

On Christmas 1991 I spent yet another day following fisher tracks. I followed
a fisher through old second-growth mixed conifer forest, through young second-
growth aspen forest, and around spruce bogs. I found two resting sites, one
well used. I found where the fisher attacked a snowshoe hare. And I again tried
to meld my mind with a fisher's to understand: Why did it explore this old deer
blind? Why did it cross the spruce bog here? Did it know this hole was here
under the leaning black spruce? I followed the track around an extensive bog
system into an area where I had no maps. I barely found my way back to recognizable country two miles from home before complete darkness fell, which
would have left me to spend the night with the fisher in the woods. The day
could not have been better.

And I cannot help but wonder, Was the fisher a descendant of ThaCho?

30 September 1992

Preface to the First Edit

On 17 April 1974 my wife, Consie, reached
fisher and took out two gray, squirming, little
closed out of her nest box for the removal o
experiences that will stay with me for a life

I remember being scared, excited, ner
the kits from the nest box. We were taking
be much greater than we had imagined. It
take the responsibility, however; I had to h
order to complete my research. Hand raisi
fishers that could be handled and taught to
was the biggest bottleneck in my research
determine the energy expenditure of the r
the woods in Michigan's Upper Peninsula,
fishers running at different speeds. I woul
into a metabolic chamber and running adu
kits were my future adult fishers.

Consie and I named the two kits (a fem
The names mean "fisher" in the Chippewa
and Uskool had been born on 29 or 30 M
with straw. Their mother had been fed a r
mammals and birds and had been taking
the kits in a cardboard box lined with wool
ing pad. They requested their first meal b
hours after being removed from their m
simulated bitch's milk manufactured by B
day, for the next week. It took a while for
and for the fishers to get used to being
fine. Consie and I took turns getting up
of us only had to get up once each night
I was perhaps too worrisome a guardi

reduced a
narian, wh
using Kao
est feat wa

When
changed th
I could tra
nighttime
half weeks

ThaCho
ing baby ar
were tryin
about eight
she was ge
At first we
sue before
to be a few
remember
the toilet w
cleanup.

By far th
puree of Es
total messe
their mouth
well. Cleani
ble, but let
Kaloosit, th
Esbilac pure
with her tor

ThaCho
with us. At
they went o
up a treadm
would perch
hoping I wo
guish wheth
mill. ThaCh
such as unde
living on th
night."

Finally, ThaCho and Uskool moved to the pen where I kept my captive wild fishers. This pen was approximately 6 by 12 meters, had a sagging wire-mesh top, and was out in the woods away from people. ThaCho and Uskool had individual cages with nest boxes. After September 1974, I did not leave them together because of the spats they had over food. I traded access to the big pen back and forth between them every other day, and they learned my ritual. Each day when I came to the pen, both fishers were out of their nest boxes and running back and forth, excited to see me. I climbed into the pen and played with whichever fisher was out and then closed that fisher in his or her cage. That was the trick. They quickly learned to recognize when I had decided it was time to stop playing and to close whoever was out into his or her cage. I learned how to trick them into getting back inside their cages. With both fishers in their cages, I let one fisher out to play. When the playing was finished, I gave the fisher in the pen food when that fisher was to be fed. I sometimes wonder who really played. I believe I played as much as they did, or more.

In early April 1975, my cousin flew ThaCho, Uskool, and me to Dick Taylor's laboratory at Harvard University. It was there that I collected the actual data on metabolic rates and running speeds. ThaCho and Uskool balked on the treadmill and did not like living in concrete runs, and they told me so: Uskool (by this time weighing well over 5 kilograms) gave me a solid warning bite by taking my whole nose firmly between his canines (my cuts healed quickly, but the bruises lasted for weeks and the scars are still there). Nonetheless, the fishers gave me the data I needed, and the results were better than I had hoped.

When I returned to Upper Michigan in mid-May 1975, I was in a quandary. The work for which I had raised ThaCho and Uskool was finished, and yet I did not want to let them go. I continued to make observations of their killing techniques for snowshoe hares, and I collected scats for my work on the fisher's digestive efficiency with different types of prey, as I had done before I went to Harvard for the metabolic studies. I persuaded myself that I needed to keep them in captivity.

On 19 July 1975, Uskool died of an unknown cause. I took his body to one of my favorite places in the woods and left it there. Scavengers came, and so he gave someone a free meal and was put to good use. Still, I wished that I had let him go before he died.

I kept ThaCho, though. In March of 1976, Tom Sterling, a wildlife filmmaker, took many rolls of motion film of ThaCho in her pen. Tom was able to disguise her pen so that ThaCho appeared to be free-living, and ThaCho, in turn, performed like a star. But, like all of us when we have a good thing, Tom wanted more. He pressed me to make a decision about what I would do with ThaCho. I decided to let her go. Then he pressed me to set a date, so that he could film the release. The date was set for 10 April 1976.

In early April, I gave ThaCho a live porcupine in her pen for the first time. Although it took her a few days to get hungry enough to brave the quills, she eventually killed the porcupine. I know of only one other eyewitness account of a fisher killing a porcupine. While he was doing research for his doctorate, Mal Coulter of the University of Maine at Orono once observed a female fisher killing porcupines.

ThaCho did exactly what I had expected from Coulter's account. She circled the porcupine, looking for an opportunity to attack its face. Then she jumped in, bit the face, and jumped back before the porcupine had a chance to hit her with its tail. Killing a porcupine is not easy, and it took ThaCho a long time before she did it. She eventually pulled the top off the porcupine's head with her final, killing bite.

When 10 April came, I was ready to let ThaCho go. I knew that she could kill hares and porcupines, the two main live prey for fishers in Upper Michigan. Tom, Consie, and I took ThaCho to an area in the woods where there is little human activity and let her go. Tom went through more rolls of motion film, and I went through rolls of slide film as ThaCho snooped about in the manner of a well-fed, hand-raised wild animal. We watched her for about three hours. At one point, she loped up to me and climbed up on the top of my head; this had been one of her favorite tricks during the preceding two years. Then ThaCho disappeared into the woods. After waiting about half an hour, we started back toward my truck. Tom decided that he wanted to film a hillside with young aspen and spruce and set up his camera. As though on cue, ThaCho came snooping down the hillside, flushed a snowshoe hare, and took off after it. That was the last I saw of ThaCho, and Tom got it all on film.

For the next two months, I left food for ThaCho, but she only came back to take it once. Either she learned to survive on her own, or she died of an accident soon after her release. I like to believe that she survived, but her death would only have been natural. ThaCho still lives as the finale to Tom's film *Superior, Land of the Woodland Drummer*, which has been shown around the country on Audubon, National Geographic, and other lecture circuits.

I did not mean for this book to be an account of my experiences with, and attachments to, ThaCho and Uskool. I have actually tried to keep their names and personalities out of the body of the book. But they were an important part of my research, and they deserve to be acknowledged.

In writing this book I have tried to walk a fine line. On the one side, there is the public's increasing interest in wildlife and nature. People are interested in knowing about what animals do and how they fit into the scheme of nature, and they are demanding accurate information. The weasels are certainly a fascinating family of mammals. The fisher especially has broad appeal because of its beauty and its ability to deal with porcupines and their quills. But much of the literature about the members of the weasel family has been filled with myths, misinformation, and anthropomorphisms that do not accurately portray these predators. Many people have a very inaccurate image of weasels, minks, martens, fishers, wolverines, and the rest. Therefore, I have tried to write a book that would have appeal to the general public and at the same time accurately deal with the biology of one member of the Mustelidae.

On the other hand, in the scientific literature there is a dearth of information on members of the weasel family, and this is especially true of the fisher. Most of the studies done on the fisher during recent years (since 1950) have been master's and doctoral theses, and most of the knowledge and information gained from these studies has not found its way into the circulating scientific literature. Consequently, in this book I have tried to gather the information included in unpublished theses, the information available in the scientific literature, and the information gained from my own research on fishers. My goal has been to provide the scientific community with a book that covers comprehensively what is known about the fisher. Obviously, as soon as the book is published, it will already be out of date. I hope it will be a source of background information for subsequent work.

My study was done between 1972 and 1976. Most of my fieldwork was done in the Ottawa National Forest, which is located in the far-western tip of Upper Michigan. Although I made observations of fishers' tracks over much of the forest, I concentrated my work in an area a little over 100 square kilometers in size in the southeastern corner of the national forest. I also kept several fishers in captivity for various lengths of time, and I studied the fisher's energetics in the laboratory. My study area is sometimes mentioned in this book, and this reference is to the area of my concentrated fieldwork in the Ottawa National Forest.

Acknowledgments to the First Edition

Numerous people have been of tremendous help to me while I was doing my research and while I was writing this book. It is impossible to name every one of them or to describe how they helped, but I would like to make an attempt. Bob Brander ignited the first spark and made the first contact that initiated the work on this book. Monte Lloyd and Dave Mech provided valuable help with my research, and Monte, because of his editorial experience and ability, deserves much of the credit for anything good that I put in writing.

George Kelly, Mark Clem, Slader Buck, Curt Mullis, and Rich Leonard all provided unpublished data, some of which were incorporated into their own theses and some of which were not. Len Radinsky supplied me with a collection of endocasts of brains for many representatives of all but one genus in the family Mustelidae. T. J. Dunn gave me calm advice on how to deal with the confusing signals I received from ThaCho and Uskool when they were kits.

The Department of Biology at the University of Chicago provided me with office space, library privileges, and a visiting scholar position while I was writing the rough draft for this book.

In addition, the following people provided important help to me at various times and places: Richard Abel, Ron Alderfer, Stuart Altmann, Steve Arnold, Prassede Calabi, the Camp NoBuck trappers Leo and Barney, Bonnie Clements, Rich Earle, Ruth Gronquist, Kim Iles, Phil Jensen, Les Johnson, Ross Kiester, Faye McLamb, Nancy Martin, the students of North Central College, the North Central Forest Experiment Station of the U.S. Forest Service, Lew Ohmann, Catherine Owens, Rick Prestbye, George Rabb, Vicky Rountree, Roy Settgas, Jerry Sutherland, Dick Taylor, Craig Wickman, Walt Winturri, and Phil Wright.

Numerous state agencies generously provided data on the distributions of fishers in response to a survey conducted by Wendell Dodge. Wendell willingly provided me with the results of his survey.

My parents gave me support while I was working on this book, though they did not know that I was writing a book. I regret that my mother did not live long enough to sit back and read this book. She would have loved it, no matter what its quality.

My wife, Consie, has lived through my frustrations and joys as I have worked with fishers and worked on this book. With her has been the responsibility of bringing me up when I am down and keeping me up when I am up. She has done a wonderful job. She has also done a wonderful job with many of the illustrations in this book. Without her artistic ability, this book would have looked very different.

I believe that it is appropriate to acknowledge the contributions of nonhuman animals, too. My Newfoundland dog Valor's Ottawa Kaloosit CD was a priceless help in many aspects of my work, besides cleaning fisher kits. During two winters of fieldwork, Kaloosit hauled all of my gear into and out of the woods on a toboggan and hauled fishers out of and back into the woods. She was a companion while I was tracking fishers, a hand warmer on cold days, a safety factor in the woods, and a listener when I had troubles with my research and writing. At eight years of age, she is still working with me in front of toboggan and travois, and she loves it.

And, of course, nothing would have been the same without ThaCho and Uskool.

Chapter 1

The Fisher Itself

The first time I saw a fisher I was driving a beat-up, army-surplus jeep down an old logging road in the Superior National Forest in northeastern Minnesota. A black animal appeared in the vegetation at the edge of the road, paused, streaked across the road, and then disappeared. I did not even have time to think "fisher." Since then, all of my spontaneous observations of wild fishers have been like the first. I suppose the secretiveness of the fisher has been a factor in my interest: a rare and exceedingly beautiful animal that is relatively unknown can be almost irresistibly fascinating.

But I have not studied the fisher only because of its beauty and allure. Members of the weasel family, like the fisher, are keenly adapted predators that have been very successful. By studying them we gain a better understanding of the ecology and behavior of predatory and prey species. Members of the weasel family have many anatomical and behavioral characteristics that have changed little since the time of the Miacidae, the ancestors of all living carnivores. Thus, the study of these animals can help us to understand how primitive predators may have lived. Fishers are the only predators that consistently prey upon porcupines. Even though fishers live many places where there are no porcupines, they have nonetheless evolved unique killing techniques for porcupines. Studying these techniques provides a better understanding of the evolution of predator-prey relationships. Finally, the social organization, population biology, and energy budgets of fishers lend themselves to mathematical models that can be used to test ecological and behavioral theory. In many ways, the fisher is an excellent predator to study.

Name

No one knows for certain how the fisher acquired its name, a seemingly inappropriate one since it does not fish. Other common names—pekan, pequam, wejack, and Pennant's marten—are more suitable. The names black cat and fisher cat have also been used, but they also are misleading since the fisher is not a member of the cat family. Perhaps the best common name given to the fisher was *tha cho*, which means "big marten" in Chippewayan (Coues 1877). The fisher is very similar to the American marten, but it is much larger. Other American Indian names for the fisher were *uskool* (Wabanaki), *otchoek* (Cree), and *otschilik* (Ojibwa). The last two names were turned into the name wejack by fur traders. The relationships between the various Indian tribes and their languages have been described by Spencer and co-workers (1965).

Some people have concluded that to have acquired the name fisher, fishers must have raided traps baited with fish or taken fish being used as fertilizer in fields (Coues 1877; Hodgson 1937). It is also possible that the fisher was confused with the otter, an expert fish catcher. The most likely possibility is that early settlers noticed the similarity between fishers and European polecats, or fitch ferrets, which are a bit smaller than female fishers but have a dark color phase and the same body build. Trevor Poole (1970) included fitchet, fitche, and fitchew (derived from the Dutch root *visse*, meaning "nasty") among the other names for European polecats. The pelts of polecats are called *fiche*, *ficheux*, or *fichet* in French (Dodge 1977). The similarity of these words to the name fisher is striking. The early American settlers may have believed that fishers were polecats, or they may have called fishers polecats because of physical similarities.

Figure 1. Adult female fisher with snowshoe hare she killed.

Description

The fisher is a medium-size mammal and the largest member of its genus (Anderson 1970). It has the general body build of a stocky weasel and is long, thin, and set low to the ground (Figure 1). Fishers' heads are more elongate with more pronounced muzzles than the weasels' triangular heads but have far less pronounced muzzles than foxes, coyotes, and wolves. Fishers' ears are large but rounded, set close to their heads, and not pronounced. Their eyes are placed facing largely forward, as in other carnivores, indicating well-developed binocular vision. They have horizontal, oval pupils (Douglas and Strickland 1987) and a pale green eyeshine (Pittaway 1978). Adult male fishers generally weigh between 3.5 and 5.5 kilograms, and adult female fishers weigh between 2.0 and 2.5 kilograms (Table 1, Figure 2). A male fisher that weighed over 9 kilograms was reported from Maine (Blanchard 1964) and apparently is the heaviest fisher recorded. Adult males average a little less than twice the weight of adult females (Table 1). The weights of adult females are more constant than those of adult males over the species range (paired t-tests on coefficients of variation, $p < 0.0001$).

The significant sexual dimorphism in body size apparent in weight is also seen in length. Sexual dimorphism in weight is more pronounced, however, because weight increases roughly with the cube of increases in the linear dimen-

Figure 2. Sexual dimorphism in body size of fishers. The fisher on the left is a 2.1-kilogram adult female; the fisher on the right is a 5.7-kilogram adult male. (Both fishers were sedated when the photograph was taken.)

sion. Lengths of male fishers range from 90 to 120 centimeters, and those of females range from 75 to 95 centimeters.

Because of this relationship between weight and linear measures, a measure of an animal's elongation is its length divided by the cube root of its weight. A long, skinny animal will have high values for this measure, but an animal with a chunky or spherical shape, such as a beaver, muskrat, or skunk, will have a low value. The fisher's elongation on this measure is slightly less than that of its near relatives the weasels, but considerably greater than that of other members of the weasel family, such as skunks and badgers (Powell 1979b).

Table 1. Average weights ($\pm$ standard deviation) of fishers
in several states and provinces

Location	Male	N	Female	N	Source
California	4.1±0.64	2	2.3±0.26	3	Grinnell, Dixon, & Linsdale 1937
California	3.5±0.64	14	1.9±0.30	7	Buck, Mullis, & Mossman 1983
California[a]	3.9±0.53	8	2.0±0.39	4	Buck, Mullis, & Mossman 1983
California[b]	3.0±0.23	6	1.9±0.21	3	Buck, Mullis, & Mossman 1983
Maine	4.5	51	2.4	44	Coulter 1966
Maine[a]	4.9±0.78	36	2.4±0.34	32	Coulter 1966
Maine[b]	3.5±0.43	15	2.1±0.24	12	Coulter 1966
Michigan[c]	5.0±0.80[i]	15	2.2±0.28	10	Powell 1977a[d]
Minnesota[e]	4.0±0.57[i]	34	2.2±0.22	13	Irvine 1961, 1962
Minnesota	4.0±0.56	9	2.2±0.21	6	Clements 1975; Mech, pers. comm.
Minnesota[f]	3.9±0.69	50	2.2±0.37	38	Wisconsin Dept. Natural Resources
Minnesota	3.8±0.75	37	2.2±0.18	14	Keuhn 1985
New Hampshire	4.3±0.65	39	2.1±0.18	21	Kelly 1977
New Hampshire	3.3	82	1.6	82	Giuliano, Litvaitis, & Stevens 1989
New Hampshire[a]	3.8	31	1.8	20	Giuliano, Litvaitis, & Stevens 1989
New Hampshire[j]	3.4	19	1.7	32	Giuliano, Litvaitis, & Stevens 1989
New Hampshire[k]	3.3	32	1.8	30	Giuliano, Litvaitis, & Stevens 1989
New York[g]	3.7±0.75	26	2.1±0.40	41	Hamilton & Cook 1955
Ontario[h]	3.9±0.75	147	2.1±0.35	154	Clem 1977
Ontario	4.2	100	2.2	61	Douglas & Strickland 1987
Ontario[a]	4.7±0.80	28	2.4±0.23	22	Douglas & Strickland 1987
Ontario[b]	3.9±0.59	72	2.2±0.29	39	Douglas & Strickland 1987

Note: Males weigh significantly more than females (paired t-tests, $p < 0.0001$), and the weights of males vary significantly more than the weights of females (paired t-tests on coefficients of variation [variance/mean], $p < 0.0001$).

[a] Adults only.

[b] Juveniles only (yearlings + 1-year-old males, yearling females).

[c] Including 3 male fishers captured in adjacent Nicolet National Forest, Wisconsin.

[d] Including 9 fishers from Michigan and Wisconsin departments of natural resources.

[e] Released on the Ottawa National Forest, Michigan, 1961-63.

[f] Released on the Nicolet and Chequamegon national forests, Wisconsin, 1962-63.

[g] Estimated from weights of skinned carcasses.

[h] Estimated from weights of skinned carcasses, according to Hamilton and Cook (1955) and Kelly (1977).

[i] Significantly different, $p < 0.01$, Student's t-test (see chapter 10).

[j] Yearlings only.

[k] 1-year-olds only.

Length divided by the cube root of weight may give counterintuitive results for a slender animal with long, skinny, light legs, such as a red fox or coyote. Hall (1974) found that the hindlimbs of a weasel are barely more than half as long as its body (excluding its head and tail) but that the hindlimbs of a carnivore of average build (such as a raccoon or red fox) are roughly the same length as its body. Calculations made from measurements recorded by Holmes (1980) show that Hall's ratio for long-tailed weasels is actually 0.42 and that for fishers is 0.52. Clearly, fishers are more elongate than raccoons and red foxes but not quite as elongate as weasels. The ratio for American martens, close relatives of fishers, is 0.50, just a little more elongate than fishers. Sokolov and Sokolov (1971) reported that the hindlimbs of European pine martens are also relatively longer than those of weasels.

The fur of fishers differs among individuals, sexes, and seasons. Males have coarser coats than females. On prime, early winter coats the hair is dense and glossy, ranging in length from 30 millimeters on the stomach and chest to 70 millimeters on the back. The color appears almost uniformly black from a distance, especially in contrast to snow, but it actually ranges from deep brown to black, with very light-colored hairs around the face and shoulders. Coulter (1966) reported that young fishers in Maine tended to be darker than adults and that females tended to be darker than males, but there is much individual variation, and these patterns are not found elsewhere (Max Bass, personal communication; Powell, unpublished data). The tail, rump, and legs are glossy black. The face, neck, and shoulders usually have a hoary gold or silver color that comes from tricolored guard hairs (Coulter 1966). These hairs begin at the eyeline on the face and extend backward along the top of the neck to the shoulders and at times as far back as the rump. They are dark brown to black, tipped with a straw-colored, blond, or silver subterminal band. The proximal section of the guard hair from the body to the point where the hair protrudes from the underlying fur is gray. Much of the color variation of fishers is due to the distribution of the tricolored guard hairs. The undersurface of fishers at all seasons is a uniform brown, except for white or cream patches of no predictable size or shape on the chest, in the underarm region, and around the genitals. The white or cream patches on individual fishers do not change in shape over several years (William B. Krohn, unpublished data; Powell, unpublished data) and might be used to identify individuals, as has been done with the ventral color patterns on weasels (King 1989).

Spring and summer pelage is more variable in color than winter pelage. The entire coat may gradually lighten, occasionally so much as to make the fisher almost strawberry blond because of the loss of the terminal part of the tricolored guard hairs (Figure 3). Fishers may begin to shed as early as April, but the single yearly molt generally occurs during late summer and early autumn (Coulter 1966; Grinnell, Dixon, and Linsdale 1937; Powell, unpublished data). I raised two fishers that both lost localized patches of hair during April and May of two successive years (Figure 4). During September and October, the guard hairs are noticeably shorter than during the rest of the year, giving a sleeker than normal appearance. At this time, the fisher's normally bushy tail may be almost ratlike. The molt is finished by November or December (Powell 1985),

Figure 3. Adult female fisher showing light-colored spring pelage. The black tips of the tricolored guard hairs have been lost, giving her a strawberry-blond coloration.

Figure 4. Adult female fisher with a bare patch of skin on her chest in April. Fishers may begin to shed as early as April, though the yearly molt generally occurs during the late summer and early autumn. Sometimes small patches of hair, as shown here, are lost during the early molt.

Figure 5. Juvenile male fisher, five and a half months old, showing adult pelage. Juveniles acquire the general coloration of adults by four months of age.

Figure 6. Fisher showing plantigrade foot posture. Fishers walk on their entire feet, rather than on their toes as canids and felids do. Note the position of the back right foot.

and at this time the fur is very soft and glossy. Juveniles have acquired the general color of adults by four months of age (Figure 5; Coulter 1966; Powell, unpublished data).

A fisher looks most beautiful when its fur is prime, a term used in the fur trade. The hairs have their richest color when the molt has just been completed in the late fall. At this time the fur is glossy and shiny, and all pigment has been absorbed from the skin by the hairs. The inside, the flesh side, of a prime pelt is cream colored or white and at this stage has the greatest value. When prime, a fisher's fur provides maximum insulation: all the hairs are newly grown and healthy, and none have been damaged. As the winter progresses, fishers use their fur coats constantly. Besides insulating them from winter's cold, fishers' fur coats protect their bodies from the branches, brambles, sticks, and rocks that fishers encounter while hunting. Gradually through the winter the guard hairs become abraided, making fishers appear less shiny and glossy. More important to the fishers, the abraided coat is probably less able to deflect snow and to insulate. By the time spring comes and some fishers' coats become reddish to strawberry blond, called "red" or "casty" by fur dealers, the pelts have little value to fur dealers precisely because people value the beauty in the pelts that reflects the functional value of the pelt to its original owner.

Fishers have five toes on all four feet. Their claws are retractable but not sheathed. Fishers are plantigrade animals (walking on the whole foot; see Fig-

Figure 7. Small circular patches of coarse hair on the central pads of the hindpaw of a nine-week-old fisher. These whorls of hair appear to be associated with glands, since the patches on adults carry an odor distinctly different from other fisher odors.

ure 6), and their feet are very large, presumably for walking on snow. There are pads on each toe and four central pads, one each behind digits 1, 2 and 3, 4, and 5, on each foot. From the central pads to the heels of the hindpaws, there are coarse hairs covering tough skin. Retractable claws, pads, and tough furred hindpaws give fishers excellent traction on the ground, in the trees, and on logs, rocks, and other surfaces in their woodland habitat. The small circular patches of very coarse hair on the central pads of the hindpaws appear to be associated with glandular activity and carry an odor distinctly different from other fisher odors (Figure 7). Because these patches enlarge on both males and females during the breeding season (William B. Krohn, unpublished data), they are probably somehow involved in communication for reproduction.

Fishers run in a fashion typical of members of the weasel family. The fore-limbs move together, with one slightly in front of the other; the same is true of the hindlimbs. The forepaws leave the ground slightly before the hindpaws land, allowing the hindpaws to fall into the same place as the forepaws. This leaves a characteristic track in the snow: two footprints right next to each other but slightly out of line. Figure 8 shows a fisher running, and Figure 9 shows a typical fisher track pattern in the snow. In very deep snow, fishers may be forced to walk rather than use their normal gait because they sink so deep in the snow (Cahalane 1947; Grinnell, Dixon, and Linsdale 1937; Leonard 1980b, 1986;

Figure 8. Fisher running. The fisher's running gait is typical of members of the weasel family. The front legs move together as do the back legs, and the back feet fall into the prints left by the front feet. Note that one front foot is extended slightly in front of the other, which creates the typical track pattern.

Figure 9. Typical fisher track pattern (*upper half of photo*) showing that one foot is slightly in front of the other both front and rear and that the back feet fall into the prints left by the front feet.

Figure 10. Tracks left by a fisher walking on a thin snow crust. Had the fisher run with its typical gait, it would have broken the crust.

Powell, unpublished data; Raine 1983). Fishers may also walk on a thin snow crust, which would break under the force of the normal gait (Figure 10). Where snow is deep and fluffy in midwinter, it restricts fishers' movements and forces them to travel more often along snowshoe hare trails and their own trails than they do during early winter when snow is shallow or during late winter when crusts form (Raine 1983). To avoid sinking into deep snow, fishers sometimes hunt in habitats in which they can travel most easily rather than in habitats that have the most prey and in which they would prefer to hunt were the snow not so deep (Leonard 1980b, Raine 1983).

Trappers' accounts and early scientific reports claimed that it was possible to determine a fisher's sex by its track size. Coulter (1966) measured the hindpaws of 38 male fishers and 27 female fishers. The lengths ranged from 8.6 to 12.5 centimeters in females and from 10.0 to 13.5 centimeters in males. Johnson (1984) measured the pad dimensions of 10 male and 8 female fishers. Lengths of neither forepaw nor hindpaw foot pads differed significantly between the sexes, but widths did. The widths of forepaw pads averaged 4.8 centimeters (range 3.8-5.4) for males and 3.9 centimeters (3.8-4.1) for females; the widths of hindpaw pads averaged 4.7 centimeters (3.8-5.1) for males and 3.9 (3.5-4.5) for females. Even though the distributions of the total length of hindpaws and pad widths of fore- and hindpaws were different for the two sexes, the dimensions overlapped, except at the extremes. Thus, it is not possible to determine positively a fisher's sex from its foot dimensions or track size unless the foot length is less than 10 centimeters or greater than 12.5 centimeters (this occurs in only about 15% of fishers) or unless the width across the pads is less than 3.8 centimeters or greater than 5.4 centimeters.

Classification

The scientific name for the fisher is *Martes pennanti*, a reference to Thomas Pennant, one of the first people to describe the fisher in the scientific literature (Pennant 1771). Pennant's descriptions of the fisher appear, however, to have been the source of about eighty years of confusion. In 1765 Buffon wrote the first scientific description of the fisher, describing it from a specimen in a collection in Paris (Buffon and D'Aubenton 1765); Buffon called the animal the *Pekan*. In 1771 Pennant described Buffon's *Pekan* but gave a new scientific description of what he called the *Fisher*, using the same specimen Buffon had used for the basis of his description. Pennant apparently was unaware that his *Fisher* and Buffon's *Pekan* were descriptions of the very same specimen.

Audubon and Bachman (1845), among others, were responsible for reducing the taxonomic status of the fisher to one species (Hagmeier 1959), although they included it in the genus *Mustela*. Coues (1877) was the first person to determine the root of the classification problems. Nomenclature varied until the late 1800s, when it was acknowledged that the correct species name was *pennanti* (Hagmeier 1959); and by the first part of the twentieth century it was acknowledged to be in the genus *Martes*.

The fisher is classified in the order Carnivora, family Mustelidae, subfamily Mustelinae, and genus *Martes*. There are eight families in the order Carnivora (Wozencraft 1985, 1989): Mustelidae, Canidae (dogs, wolves, foxes), Ursidae (bears, pandas), Procyonidae (raccoons, coatis, ringtails, kinkajou), Herpestidae (mongooses), Viverridae (civets, genets), Hyaenidae (hyenas), and Felidae (cats).

The family Mustelidae is divided into four subfamilies (Holmes 1987; Wozencraft 1985, 1989). Mustelinae includes the weasels, ferrets, polecats, minks, martens, wolverines, grisons, tayra, and ratel. Most closely allied with the Mustelinae is the Mellinae, which includes the true badgers and the stink badgers. Mephitinae includes all the skunks. Because brain morphology of stink badgers is similar to that of skunks, Radinsky (1973) suggested that Mephitinae should also include the stink badgers. Both stink badgers and skunks have relatively primitive brains that are little changed from that of their common ancestors, and other characteristics clearly place the two groups in different subfamilies (Holmes 1987). Lutrinae includes the otters and is most closely allied with the Mephitinae.

Members of the genus *Martes* are distinguished from their nearest relatives, members of the genus *Mustela*, by having four premolars on both sides of both upper and lower jaws (members of *Mustela* have only three) and by the cusp patterns on the first lower molar teeth, the lower carnassials (Anderson, in press). *Martes* has seven extant species, which are divided into three subgenera: *Pekania*, *Charronia*, and *Martes* (Anderson 1970; Holmes 1987). The fisher is the only living member of the subgenus *Pekania*, which includes three, or more likely two, extinct species. The skulls of members of *Pekania* can be distinguished from skulls of other *Martes* because a root of each fourth upper premolar (the external median rootlet of the upper carnassial) can be seen when the skull is viewed from the side (this can be seen in Figure 20 in chapter 2). The subgenus *Charronia* contains the yellow-throated marten, *Martes flavigula* (Figure 11), which is found in eastern Asia and southern India. The population in the Nilgiri Hills of southern India is completely isolated from other yellow-throated marten populations and may be a distinct species, *Martes gwatkinsi* (Anderson, in press). Yellow-throated martens have large yellow throat patches, contrasting light and dark colors on their faces, and dark brown to black feet, legs, and tails. The subgenus *Martes* includes the other five extant martens: the beech, stone, or house marten, *Martes foina*; the European pine marten, *M. martes*; the sable, *M. zibellina*; the Japanese marten, *M. melam-*

Figure 11. Yellow-throated marten. Yellow-throated martens are found in southeastern Asia and southern India. (Brookfield Zoo, Chicago Zoological Society.)

Figure 12. American marten. American martens are in the same subgenus as European pine martens, sables, and Japanese martens, and closely resemble them.

pus; and the American marten, *M. americana*. These five species all have yellow or orange throat patches and are rusty red-brown in color; the color is darker on the tail and legs (Figure 12). They have relatively large rounded ears and bushy tails. The stone marten is the largest (Anderson 1970; Jensen and Jensen 1970), and the American marten is the smallest. There is no question that the stone marten, which is sympatric with the European pine marten, is a distinct species; but Anderson (1970) and Hagmeier (1955, 1961) hypothesized that the other four may be members of a single circumboreal species. They are very similar in morphology, habits, and habitat and are allopatric. The ranges of these four species are shown in Figure 13. Because these species gradually decrease in body size from European pine martens in western Europe through sables and Japanese martens to American martens in eastern North America, and because other characteristics show similar gradual changes, Anderson (in press) recognized these four as sister species (Mayr 1963).

Three subspecies of fishers were recognized by Goldman (1935): *Martes pennanti pennanti*, *M. p. pacifica*, and *M. p. columbiana*. It is questionable whether recognition of subspecies is warranted. Goldman stated that the subspecies were difficult to distinguish, and Hagmeier (1959) concluded from a more extensive study that the subspecies were not separable on the basis of pelage or skull characteristics. Coulter (1966) felt that there are too few specimens from different parts of the fisher's range to determine conclusively whether there are any subspecies. Hall (1981) retained all three subspecies in his compilation, as did Anderson (in press), but failed to address Hagmeier's conclusion. On the basis of Whitaker's (1970) evaluation of the subspecies concept, Hagmeier was undoubtedly correct.

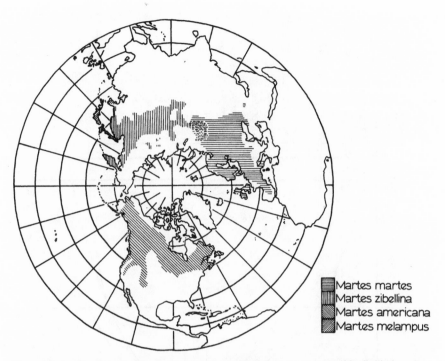

Martes martes
Martes zibellina
Martes americana
Martes melampus

Figure 13. Species ranges of the European pine marten (*M. martes*), sable (*M. zibellina*), American marten (*M. americana*), and Japanese marten (*M. melampus*). These four species are best described as a superspecies, species with a recent common ancestor that have nonoverlapping ranges but differ too much in morphology to be considered a single species (Mayr 1963). Note that the ranges are completely nonoverlapping, except for a small area in northern Asia. This area of possible overlap of European pine marten and sable ranges is in an area that has been little studied and for which there are contradictory statements about species ranges and hybridization. (Adapted by C. B. Powell from Anderson 1970 and Hagmeier 1955.)

Evolution

The evolution of the fisher is difficult to trace because its ancestors appear to have been small, arboreal, forest-dwelling carnivores that did not leave a clear fossil record. All modern carnivores evolved from the Miacidae (Colbert 1969; Ewer 1973; Romer 1966). The miacids were the first mammals to evolve the flesh-shearing dentition characteristic of modern carnivores (Colbert 1969; Ewer 1973; Romer 1966). This dentition, in turn, has allowed the evolution of extreme flesh-eating habits in some modern carnivores. The miacids gave rise to two major groups of carnivores, the Canoidea and the Feloidea, in the late Eocene or early Oligocene (Figure 14). Mustelids may represent a basal lineage of the canoids (Romer 1966), from which the canids, ursids, and procyonids evolved. Although it is difficult to distinguish between the early viverrids, canids, and mustelids in the fossil record, it appears that other canoids quickly

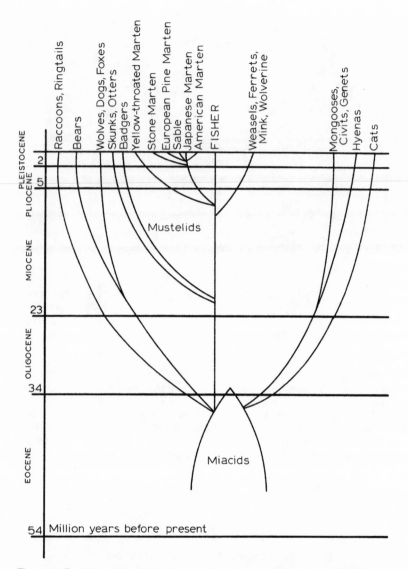

Figure 14. Evolution of the fisher. Also shown are the evolution of the families in the order Carnivora and details on the evolution of members of the weasel family and the genus *Martes*. (Adapted by C. B. Powell from Anderson 1970, in press, and Ewer 1973.)

diverged from the mustelids (Anderson 1970; Ewer 1973). Small, elongate carnivores with short, stocky legs and five toes on each foot, the mustelids have maintained many characteristics of the miacids (Anderson 1970; Colbert 1969; Ewer 1973; Romer 1966). The dentition of the mustelids reflects their carnivorous habits, and their reduced number of molars indicates that they are more carnivorous than were the miacids (Anderson 1970; Colbert 1969).

Between the late Eocene (the time of the divergence of the rest of the Canoidea from the Mustelidae) and the Miocene, the adaptive radiation of the Mustelidae was wide and often short-lived. This gave rise to a confusing fossil record, but by the end of the Miocene the four subfamilies recognized today were distinguishable. Most members of the subfamily Mustelinae have retained primitive features: small size, carnivorous dentition, and forest habitat. Several marten-like fossils from the Miocene have been found, but it is not certain whether they were true martens (Anderson 1970, in press). Some Pliocene mustelids were intermediate between *Mustela* and *Martes*, but by that time there were true martens living in Asia. *Martes palaeosinensis* and *M. anderssoni* lived in China during the Pliocene and were probably ancestral to the fisher. Both species have been placed in the subgenus *Pekania*, along with the fisher (Anderson 1970), but they are probably not two distinct species (Anderson, in press). The fossil specimens probably exhibit age and sex differences found in a single species, *M. palaeosinensis*. All three subgenera of *Martes* are distinguishable in the Pliocene fossil records.

The first true fisher found in North America was *Martes divuliana*, dated from the early Pleistocene (Anderson, in press). It is probable that it came to North America via the Bering Bridge, since relationships to *M. palaeosinensis* and *M. anderssoni* are strongly indicated (Anderson 1970, in press; Kurtén 1971). *M. divuliana* was slightly smaller than *M. pennanti* and was probably semiarboreal. Anderson (1970, in press) hypothesized that *M. divuliana* preyed on squirrels of the genera *Sciurus*, *Glaucomys*, and *Tamias*, and perhaps on porcupines as well, since remains of these animals have been recovered from the same deposits as fossil remains of *M. divuliana*.

Remains of the modern fisher, *Martes pennanti*, are first found in late Pleistocene deposits, and the species is probably closely related to but not directly descended from *M. divuliana*, which is only known from the middle Pleistocene (Anderson 1970, in press). There is no overlap of the fossil record for *M. divuliana* and *M. pennanti*, and no fossil fishers have been dated between the fossils of these two. Present-day fishers show no morphological differences from the late Pleistocene fossil fishers. However, the distribution of fossil sites indicates that fishers once lived in areas farther south than they have occupied during recent times (Anderson 1970). This change is undoubtedly related to the climatic changes associated with glaciation.

The Fisher's Ecological Niche

The food webs of which fishers are a part are complex, and it is a difficult task to identify all the relationships among all the organisms that are somehow associated with fishers. Within all food webs, however, it is possible to identify a small number of trophic levels: the first trophic level contains the producers (the green plants), the second trophic level contains the primary consumers (the herbivores that eat the plants), the third trophic level contains the secondary consumers (the carnivores that eat the herbivores), and the fourth trophic level contains the tertiary consumers (the higher carnivores). It should be noted that the classification of organisms by trophic level is a classification by function and not by species. Therefore, one species can occupy more than one trophic level.

The fisher, as a predator, must be placed predominantly in the third or fourth trophic levels and actually fits in both, as well as in the second. Most of the fisher's prey are herbivores (snowshoe hares, squirrels, mice, porcupines), and so the fisher is a secondary consumer. Occasionally, however, fishers also eat berries and other carnivores, making the fisher both a primary and a tertiary consumer as well.

In the community of organisms living in the northern forests of North America, the fisher most clearly takes the role of a predator on small- to medium-size mammals and often birds. In this role, the fisher is a competitor with other predators. Depending on the specific community, fishers can be in competition with coyotes, bobcats, lynxes, foxes, American martens, wolverines, and weasels. Fishers and American martens are the only medium-sized predators that are agile in trees and also elongate and able to explore hollow logs, brush piles, and holes in the ground for prey. Fishers are larger than American martens, however, and able to kill a larger range of prey. And where fishers and porcupines occur together, fishers have little competition with other predators for porcupines. Thus fishers have a unique role in northern forest communities. As far as is known, adult fishers are not regularly subject to predation. The occasional fishers reported as killed by other predators are probably ill or old or otherwise in poor health, making them easy and not dangerous to kill.

Study Techniques

Techniques used to study the ecology and behavior of mammals fall into two broad categories, which I call direct and indirect study methods. Direct study methods entail the direct observation of a mammal as it goes through its everyday routine. Indirect study involves gaining information from secondary sources, such as tracks in the snow and animals in captivity. There is actually a broad continuum of techniques of which direct and indirect methods are extremes. Direct experimental manipulation of certain aspects of an animal's biology within wild populations utilizes both direct and indirect methods.

Direct observation is the best way to gain accurate information about a mammal, at least as an initial step before experimental manipulation is used to test hypotheses generated by direct observation. Direct observation cannot be used with some mammals, however, because such observations are impossible or would affect the mammals' behavior. Both of these factors limit the direct observation of fishers. Thus, all studies of fishers have used the various means of indirect observation.

Before the studies of deVos (1951, 1952) and Quick (1953a), almost all source material for articles about the ecology and behavior of fishers came from trappers. Trappers were the first white people to spend extensive amounts of time in the forests where fishers were present, and they are still the only people who get into certain areas of Canada. Trappers were and are interested in fishers because of their valuable pelts. Steel traps, devices that when triggered cause a set of steel jaws to spring closed and hold an animal's foot firmly, have been the predominant tool used to trap fishers. Traps are set in those places and baited with those substances that are believed to increase the number of fishers caught. In recent years many trappers have switched to trapping fishers with quick-kill traps such as Conibear traps, which crush a fisher's chest or break its neck to kill it immediately upon capture. New traps have been designed that hold animals' paws firmly but minimize hurt to or do not hurt the paws (Novak 1987). These traps may become generally available in the future.

Trappers have always been interested in making observations about the natural history of the animals they trap. Much of the information gathered is used to increase the number of animals trapped, and all of it is gathered from incidental observations and not through strict data-gathering techniques. Thus, the information provided by trappers has been valuable because it has been the first information gathered, but it has not always been completely accurate. Trappers were the first to report that fishers are the only predators consistently able to prey upon porcupines and that fishers can be very agile in trees. On the other hand trappers have also been the source of misinformation—for example, that fishers flip porcupines over to kill them and can walk along the bottom sides of branches; that fishers are the most agile of all mammals in trees; and that fishers are so strong that they habitually fight with and kill other predators, including bobcats and lynxes. In each of these pieces of misinformation, misunderstanding, misinterpretation, and exaggeration have overcome truth.

DeVos (1951, 1952) and Quick (1953a) used trappers' observations as supplements to information collected from observations of fishers' tracks in the snow and from carcasses of fishers killed by trappers. Since these reports, tracking has become a major source of information about the fisher's natural history. The combination of information obtained from fisher carcasses and information obtained from tracks has provided much of our present knowledge about the distribution, diet, habitat, and reproduction of fishers. One limitation of using information from tracking is that individual fishers cannot usually be identified. Also, tracking and carcasses can provide data only about the fisher's winter habits.

With the development of radiotelemetric techniques in the 1960s and the continued refinement of these techniques since then, new information has been collected on many species, including the fisher. Radiotelemetry involves placing a small radio transmitter on an animal; in studies of fishers, the transmitter has been mounted in a collar placed around a fisher's neck. Each transmitter has a different frequency, allowing individual fishers to be identified. The transmitters' signals are monitored by using a radio receiver tuned to the frequencies of the transmitters on the animals being followed. The transmitters that are most commonly used issue beeping signals with a constant pulse rate and provide location data, but transmitters with variable pulse rates can provide activity data. Other types of transmitters have been used to gather data on activity, body temperature, heart rate, and other physiological functions in animals other than fishers. Different types of transmitters have different limitations, and the transmitters used in a study must fit the questions being asked and the specifications imposed by working conditions. For example, the transmitting range for a transmitter depends not only on its battery power but also on the topography of the animal's environment and the height of the receiving antenna. To increase the transmission range, many workers have mounted receiving antennas on trucks, towers, and small planes. Radiotelemetry has greatly increased the information that can be obtained about an individual's movements and the social organization of a species. Arthur (1988) summarized many of the live-trapping and radiotelemetry techniques used to study fishers.

To outfit a fisher with a transmitter, it must be captured alive and then immobilized. Fishers are usually immobilized with drugs, which opens the door to more research on free-living animals. Blood samples can be drawn from immobilized fishers to study blood chemistry and hormone profiles. Ultrasound scans can be made to study embryo implantation and development. Other new techniques will be applied to research on fishers as they become available and can be applied to questions about fishers. Belant (1991) discussed drugs used to immobilize fishers.

Some studies have used observations and experiments on captive fishers to supplement information gained from tracking, studying carcasses, and radiotelemetry. The secretive nature of fishers captured in the wild and the small number of fishers accustomed to humans have limited the studies. Nonetheless, much information can be obtained from studies on captive fishers. Almost all information on the reproduction and the physiology of fishers has been gained from captive studies, and much of the work on the energetics and the predatory behavior of fishers has depended on captive animals. Future research will combine data from captive studies with data collected using radiotelemetry and data collected using new tools such as hormone assays, ultrasound scans, and DNA fingerprinting. Soon we shall be able to answer questions we did not dream of asking only a few years ago.

Chapter 2

Anatomy

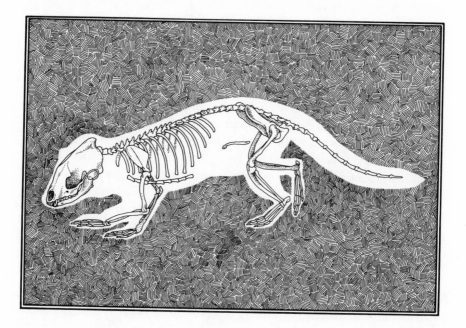

Fishers show no basic skeletal or muscular adaptations not common to the other carnivores. Therefore, this chapter discusses anatomy as it affects fisher ecology and behavior and the study of fishers rather than detailed descriptions of bones, muscles, and systems. A general discussion of the carnivores' anatomy can be found in *The Carnivores* by R. F. Ewer (1973), and more detailed analyses can be found in the works cited in this chapter.

Postcranial Skeletal and Muscular Systems

Because they are predators, fishers must be able to perform a wide variety of movements. Prey must be sought, captured, killed, and eaten; and these activities vary with the type of prey. Therefore, fishers cannot be specialized for only one type of movement but must be able to run for long distances, sprint for short distances, climb trees, and dig. Fishers' skeletons are not extremely specialized (Ewer 1973; Leach 1977a, 1977b). Like other mustelids, fishers have elongate bodies, but their bodies are not as elongate as the bodies of members of the genus *Mustela*. Fishers' limbs are relatively short with respect to their body length when compared to other carnivores such as dogs and cats. Their tails are relatively long and are used for balance in climbing, jumping through ground brush, and turning quickly. King (1989) argued that the elongate shape of the small weasels is a special adaptation for hunting small prey in narrow places. The same argument applies to fishers. Having an elongate body is to a fisher's advantage when it goes through hollow logs or down holes and when it searches for prey under piles of brush and in the tops of fallen trees. The elongation has not been taken to such an extreme, however, that it poses great limitations on running ability or heat conservation.

The comparative morphology of the postcranial skeletons of members of the genus *Martes* has been studied by Anderson (1970), Holmes (1980), Joliceous (1963a, 1963b), Leach (1977b), Leach and Dagg (1976), Ondrias (1960, 1962), and Sokolov and Sokolov (1971). All these researchers concluded that the appendicular skeletons of these mustelids are not specialized in an extreme form for any manner of locomotion. Sokolov and Sokolov (1971) concluded that the postcranial skeleton of the European pine marten is more specialized for arboreality than that of the European polecat. The polecat, however, is more adapted to a ground-dwelling mode of life, is a less generalized mustelid than the European pine marten, and has skeletal morphology and musculature closely resembling that of other members of its genus. Thus, Sokolov and Sokolov had their perspective backwards: European polecats are more specialized for a ground-dwelling, or fossorial (digging), mode of life than are European pine martens.

Leach and his co-workers (1977b; Leach and Dagg 1976; Leach and DeKleer 1978; Leach and Hall 1982) tried to find distinguishing features of the appendicular and axial skeleton bones of fishers and American pine martens that would allow identification of individuals by species, sex, and age. They found that species and sex could be distinguished only from morphometric data. In their samples, no overlap occurred in the measurements taken on fisher and marten bones, and there were several measurements that could be used to distinguish between the sexes within each species. The suprafabellar tubercle, a protection on the femur (thigh bone) could be used to distinguish between juvenile and adult males but not between juvenile and adult females. Their samples came entirely from the Algonquin region of Ontario, however, and Table 1 in chapter 1 shows that there is a considerable range in weights of male fishers across the continent. Consequently, the distinctions they found among their fishers and martens may not hold for other areas of North America, and the usefulness of these measures is limited.

The running gait of mustelids is always associated with a slight strengthening of forelimb muscles due to the shock-absorbing role of these limbs at the end of the suspended phase of the gait (Gambaryan 1974). Leach (1977a) found this strengthening in fishers. During the support phase of the gait, the greatest load on the forelimbs is borne by the extensors of the shoulders and elbow, by the flexors of the carpus (forepaw), and by the muscles of the forelimb joints (Gambaryan 1974). All of these muscles are well developed in the fisher. The serratus ventralis and pectoralis muscles, which act to prevent abduction of the upper limb and to transfer the weight of the body to the limbs during the stance phase, are particularly well developed. In vertical climbing these muscles are used along with the latissimus dorsi, triceps brachii, and biceps brachii, which are also well developed (Leach 1977a). Leach (1977a) concluded that small, agile animals adapted to running over rough ground could use similar modes of progression in trees without extensive changes in limb structure. He believed, therefore, that "the existence of the musculature development needed for cursorial locomotion in marten and fisher potentiates a secondary function of arboreal locomotion" (1977a, 40). Holmes (1980) further explained that arboreal mustelids should not have evolved restrictions on claw or on wrist and ankle mobility that are associated with running. The lack of extreme skeletal specializations in fishers is logical.

Fishers (and other martens) may exhibit a small, specialized adaptation for climbing. This adaptation is taken to extreme form in the Ursidae. The scapula (shoulder blade) of a black bear has a wide flange, the postscapular fossa, on the upper part of the posterior margin (Figure 15). The subscapularis minor muscle arises from this fossa, runs along the scapula, and inserts in the head of the humerus (Davis 1949). The reason for the unusual development of this muscle in bears appears to be that bears climb by pulling their heavy bodies up with their forelimbs. This method of climbing exerts forces that are the exact opposite of those created during normal quadrupedal locomotion and tends to pull the humerus out of the glenoid (shoulder joint). The enlarged subscapularis minor functions to oppose this pull. The scapulae of many carnivores do not have a postscapular fossa (Figure 15), and those animals that do have this fossa are at least partially arboreal. Fishers and other martens (Figure 15) do have this fossa (Leach 1977a). Since fishers are considerably smaller than bears and since much of their arboreal activity is jumping and running along branches, it is to be expected that the development of the postscapular fossa would be less than that occurring in bears. When climbing vertical tree trunks, however, fishers do pull their bodies up with their forelimbs; this activity correlates with the development of the postscapular fossa. The postscapular fossa is larger in fishers than in American martens (Leach 1977b).

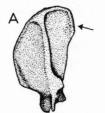
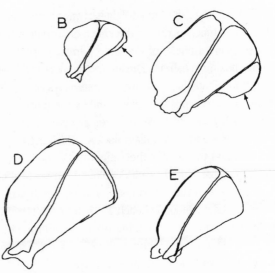

Figure 15. Scapulae of several carnivores. *A*, fisher; *B*, raccoon (*Procyon*); *C*, bear (*Ursus*); *D*, large felid (*Panthera*); and *E*, canid (*Canis*). Note the large postscapular fossa on the scapula of the bear (*arrow*) and the small postscapular fossae on the scapulae of the raccoon and the fisher (*arrows*). The postscapular fossa is an attachment for muscles used in climbing by species that must pull themselves up with their forelimbs. *D* and *E* are shown for comparison. (Redrawn by C. B. Powell from Leach 1977b [*A*] and Davis 1949 [*B-E*].)

In fishers, as in most carnivores, the forelimb is used for a variety of purposes. In contrast, the hindlimb is used almost exclusively for locomotion and has fewer adaptations. Fishers and martens, however, are among the very few carnivores that have tremendous mobility of the ankle joints. They are able to rotate their hindpaws through almost 180 degrees and to grasp branches exceptionally well with their hindpaws. Fishers are able to descend trees head first (Figure 16) and are able to chase prey both up and down trees. If need be, they can hold on to a tree with their hindpaws while hanging head down. Grinnell, Dixon, and Linsdale (1937, 224) made this observation:

> The fisher was up about forty feet. When it saw us it started down, head foremost like a Douglas squirrel. Its hind legs and claws were used in exactly the same manner as a squirrel uses its rear legs and feet in descending a tree. When it got to within fifteen feet of the ground and clear of limbs it stopped and began scolding the dog just as a big gray squirrel would do. Like a squirrel it pounded with one forefoot and then the other on the tree, all the while hanging there head downward.

Holmes (1980) analyzed skeletal adaptations of North American mustelids for different modes of locomotion and lifestyle. From the literature he developed hypotheses for trends that should be found within species groups for adapta-

Figure 16. Twelve-week-old fisher descending a tree headfirst. Fishers are able to turn their hindpaws through almost 180 degrees and to grasp branches with their hindpaws.

tions toward fossorial (digging), aquatic, ambulatory, cursorial (running), and arboreal locomotion. Within the arboreal group, Holmes hypothesized that adaptations should become more extreme starting with the generalized long-tailed weasel, through the American marten and the fisher to the tayra, a Central and South American close relative to the martens. In contrast, skeletal adaptations for arboreal locomotion increased from long-tailed weasels through tayras and fishers to American martens. Recent literature (reviewed by Powell 1984) indicates that American martens are indeed the most arboreal of the group, consistent with skeletal adaptations.

No work has been done on how fishers use their limbs during locomotion, but work has been done on the stone marten (Gambaryan 1974) and members of the genus *Mustela* (Gambaryan 1974; Hildebrand 1974). Because of the elongation and mobility of their vertebral columns, mustelids flex and extend their vertebral columns to accelerate their trunks during locomotion on the ground. "Flexion and extension of the spine is best achieved with simultaneous pushing away or suspension of the limbs, and therefore the Mustelidae developed the bound, in which the hindfeet push away together and the forefeet land together" (Gambaryan 1974, 254). Actually, most mustelids use the halfbound, in which the forepaws land alternately but the hindpaws land more or less in unison (Hildebrand 1974; Hildebrand et al. 1985).

Some of the locomotory characteristics of fishers can be traced from footprints in the snow. The front feet land with one slightly in front of the other, and the back feet land in approximately the same places as the front feet. The forceful extension of the spine as the forepaws are lifted from the ground imparts acceleration to the trunk and promotes extended flight. When mustelids run, their bodies are suspended for a relatively long time while in the extended position. Because the hindpaws land close to, and not in front of, the forepaws, flexion of the spine while the body is supported only by the forepaws is by inertia. Figure 17 shows the stages in the halfbound of the stone marten.

Hildebrand (1974; Hildebrand et al. 1985) explained that animals can evolve potential for greater running speed by evolving longer legs or the ability to use more parts of each leg in running to increase stride length. Because mustelines flex and extend their vertebral columns when bounding, they functionally incorporate their vertebral columns as part of their legs to increase stride length. This allows them to run at greater speeds than would be possible without bending their backs. Hildebrand (1959) calculated that flexion and extension of a cheetah's vertebral column contributed approximately 5% of its speed. Because mustelines have such short legs, an even greater contribution must be gained by them. The energetic costs of running depend, in part, on the weights of limbs, and highly evolved cursorial mammals have light limbs, especially distally. Thus horses, deer, and antelopes have long, slender limbs with reduced numbers of toes. Mustelines all have five toes on each foot, have muscular limbs, and incorporate their entire bodies into each stride. These characteristics make bounding extremely energetically expensive. By and large, small- to medium-sized mammals bound, probably because of the high efficiency of muscles on small mammals. The strength of a muscle is proportional to its cross section, but its weight is proportional to its volume. Thus, muscles must become disproportionately large in large animals to do the same job that small muscles do in small mammals. Few mammals larger than fishers bound, but many smaller mammals do.

Bounding is energetically very expensive for fishers. Sinking in deep snow (Raine 1983) makes bounding even more expensive, enough more expensive that fishers avoid areas with deep snow even when those areas have high prey densities and are used predominantly for hunting when snow is shallow. The added energetic expense of bounding in deep snow is apparently greater than the energetic benefits to be gained from foraging for high-density prey in deep snow. This added expense forces fishers to forage in areas with shallow snow where bounding is less expensive but where there are also fewer prey.

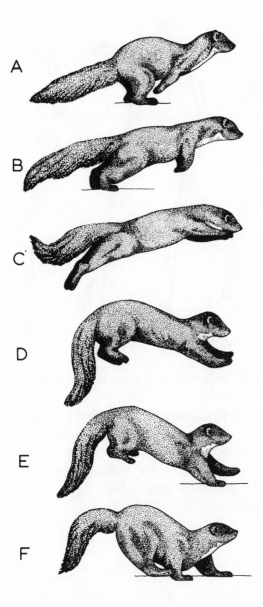

Figure 17. Stone marten going through the stages of the half-bound. *A*, beginning phase of support by back legs; *B*, ending phase of support by back legs; *C*, beginning phase of free flight; *D*, ending phase of free flight; *E*, beginning phase of support by front legs; and *F*, ending phase of support by front legs. (Drawn by C. B. Powell from photos by Gambaryan 1974.)

Baculum

Bacula can be used to classify dead male fishers as adults ($\geq$ 1 yr.) or juveniles (< 1 yr.; Douglas and Strickland 1987; Leonard 1986; Wright and Coulter 1967). Baculum development is stimulated by testosterone in male long-tailed weasels (Wright 1950) and presumably in fishers and other *Martes* species as

Figure 18. Fisher bacula (distal ends upward) showing progressive changes with age. *A* and *B*, bacula from juveniles trapped on 12 October and 5 January, respectively; *C*, baculum from a juvenile fisher trapped in late February or early March, which shows deposition of bone at the basal end; *D*, baculum from an adult fisher, which shows the characteristic oblique ridge near the basal end and the more massive appearance. (Redrawn by C. B. Powell from Wright and Coulter 1967.)

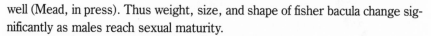

A   B   C   D

well (Mead, in press). Thus weight, size, and shape of fisher bacula change significantly as males reach sexual maturity.

The bacula of adults are more than 10.00 centimeters long, have an enlarged proximal end and a splayed distal tip with a small oval or round foramen, and commonly weigh more than 2.00 grams. Fully mature bacula have an elevated ridge near the proximal end that completely circles the bone in a diagonal fashion when viewed from the side (Figure 18). Baculum shape is species specific, and baculum shape has been hypothesized as a reproductive isolating mechanism in weasel species (Long 1969). The unique shape of the baculum in fishers is probably necessary for proper uterine stimulation during mating to induce ovulation.

Bacula of juvenile fishers weigh significantly less than those of adults and do not show the circular ridge. When male fishers approach one year of age, however, their bacula may weigh as much as 2.00 grams, and their circular ridges begin to form clearly. At this time, the testes of one-year-old males become active. Bacula show progressive weight gain until fishers reach age three and a half or four and a half, but there is too much variation between individuals and by season to categorize dead male fishers beyond being juveniles or adults (Douglas and Strickland 1987; Wright and Coulter 1967).

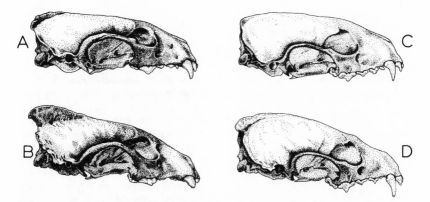

Figure 19. Fisher skulls. *A*, a juvenile male fisher; *B*, an adult male fisher; *C*, a juvenile female fisher; *D*, an adult female fisher. (Drawing by C. B. Powell.)

Teeth, Skull, and Related Musculature

In mammals, skull shape is related in many ways to dentition. The shape of the jaws, the shape of the glenoid articulation (jaw joint), the jaw musculature, and the places of origin and insertion of the jaw muscles are all adaptively correlated. Thus, the skull is more than a housing for the brain and sense organs. Since the anterior neck muscles and temporalis muscles originate on the outer surface of the braincase, the size of the brain affects the shape of the skull in more ways than just the size of the housing. If muscles require larger areas for attachment than the braincase provides, bony crests develop to provide the extra anchoring space. The prominent sagittal and occipital crests on fishers' skulls are examples of this and will be discussed shortly. Fisher skulls are illustrated in Figure 19.

The fisher's dentition is highly adapted to a carnivorous way of life. The incisors are used to hold and to tear small items, such as small pieces of flesh, from bones. The canines are large and sharp and are used for stabbing and holding prey. The premolars are used for holding and softening flesh and for shearing. The molars are used for shearing and crushing. The fisher's carnassials (the fourth and last upper premolar, P^4, and the first lower molar, M_1, on each side of the jaw), characteristic of the Carnivora, are highly developed and efficient for shearing flesh. The dental formula for the fisher is

$$I_3^3, \; C_1^1, \; P_4^4, \; M_2^1$$

making a total of thirty-eight teeth.

Other than being more robust, the fisher's dentition is morphologically similar to that of other martens. The exposed external median rootlet on the upper

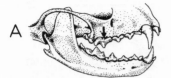

A

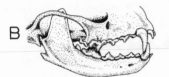

B

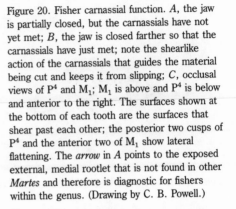

Figure 20. Fisher carnassial function. *A*, the jaw is partially closed, but the carnassials have not yet met; *B*, the jaw is closed farther so that the carnassials have just met; note the shearlike action of the carnassials that guides the material being cut and keeps it from slipping; *C*, occlusal views of P^4 and M_1; M_1 is above and P^4 is below and anterior to the right. The surfaces shown at the bottom of each tooth are the surfaces that shear past each other; the posterior two cusps of P^4 and the anterior two of M_1 show lateral flattening. The *arrow* in *A* points to the exposed external, medial rootlet that is not found in other *Martes* and therefore is diagnostic for fishers within the genus. (Drawing by C. B. Powell.)

C

carnassial, which is diagnostic for the fisher, is the only easily discernable difference (Figure 20; Anderson 1970, in press). The incisors are small and grouped tightly together. There is a small diastema (space) between the third upper incisor and the upper canine into which the lower canine fits when the jaw is closed, allowing the teeth to interlock. The first upper premolar is large and apparently functional (Anderson 1970), which is not the case with many carnivores. The premolars other than P^4 have one major cusp and sometimes small accessory cusps in line before and behind the major cusp.

The carnassial teeth are the most specialized teeth in the fisher's jaw. They are specially adapted for cutting and shearing flesh and work with a scissorlike action. According to Ewer (1973, 36):

> The posterior two cusps of P^4 and the anterior two of M_1 are laterally flattened and, as the jaws close, the blades shear past each other. The two constituent cusps do not form straight lines but are arranged so that each blade has the shape of a wide open V. This increases efficiency by preventing the meat from slipping out forwards and makes the action really more comparable with that of pruning shears than of ordinary scissors.

The shearing and holding functions of the carnassials are shown in Figure 20.

The function of the carnassials is more complex yet (Mellett 1981). Raw flesh is tough and when chewed would force the upper and low carnassials apart if they did not have convex occlusal surfaces (Figure 20C). Think again of the scissors analogy. When cutting tough material, for example, a thin stick, a scissors' blades are forced away from each other laterally. If the blades are not held tightly together, the stick will tend to pivot and push the blades apart. Jaws must be flexible and able to move from side to side and hence cannot be held tightly in place like a well-functioning scissors. They must be more like scissors with a loose screw whose blades can move apart. The convex occlusal surfaces of the carnassials, however, allow flesh to force the teeth together. When the tips of the carnassials meet (a moment between those shown in Figure 20A and B), although the tips of the upper carnassial are lateral (outside) to the tips of the lower carnassial, the notch of the upper carnassial is medial (inside) to the notch on the lower carnassial. The flesh in the notch pushes the upper carnassial medially (inward) and the lower carnassial laterally (outward), each against the other tooth (Mellett 1981).

The molars behind the carnassials are adapted for crushing. However, the upper molar and the second lower molar are not directly above and below each other but are slightly offset. Therefore, the first lower molar is a dual-purpose tooth: its anterior two cusps are the lower brace of the carnassials, and the posterior cusps occlude with M^1 and are part of the crushing apparatus. M_2 occludes with the posterior of M^1. Fishers and other mustelines have fewer molars than most other canoids because of their mostly carnivorous diet. In particular, they are more carnivorous than ursids and procyonids.

When a fisher kills and eats a snowshore hare, for example, all of the different tooth types with their different functions are used. The canines are used for killing and holding the hare until it is dead. The carnassials are used to open the skin and cut off pieces of flesh and skin. The fisher will turn its head sideways to the dead hare so that it can use the carnassials (Figure 21). Incisors are used to pull off or to loosen pieces of flesh or organs and to help manipulate the hare. Premolars and molars, excluding the carnassials, are used to soften and pulverize flesh so that it can be cut more easily by the carnassials and swallowed.

The jaw of a fisher is relatively short compared to that of most other carnivores, although not as short as those of smaller mustelines, such as the weasels and minks. The braincase is long and relatively low and extends far behind the glenoid. There are three sets of muscles responsible for jaw closure, two of which (temporalis and masseter) insert primarily on the outer surface of the mandible (the lower jaw) and one of which (pterygoideus) inserts primarily on the inner surface. The masseter muscle fibers originate along the lower edge of the zygomatic arch and insert on the angle of the lower jaw and on the masseteric fossa (Figure 22). Their action is basically for simple closure when the jaw is not wide open. The zygomatic arch of mustelines is less robust than in other carnivores, which indicates that the masseter muscles are less important in fishers than in other carnivores.

Figure 21. Adult female fisher turning her head sideways to use carnassials to cut into a showshore hare.

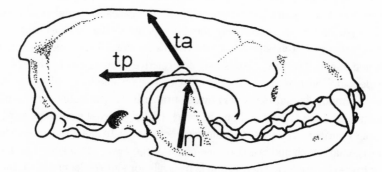

Figure 22. Diagram of a fisher skull showing the direction of the action of the muscles that close the jaw. The *arrows* show the areas of origin and insertion of muscles and the direction of pull. The *m* stands for masseter, the *tp* for posterior temporalis, and the *ta* for anterior temporalis. (Drawing by C. B. Powell.)

The temporalis arises from the lateral surface of the braincase and the sagittal crest and inserts on the coronoid process. When the jaw is wide open, the anterior part of the temporalis pulls upward on the coronoid process to close the jaw. As the jaw closes, more work is done by the posterior part of the temporalis, which pulls the coronoid process backward. Consequently, when a fisher is using its carnassials or exerting strong force when holding and killing prey, the posterior part of the temporalis is being used. In other carnivores, the masseter is used for this function. Thus, much more torque is exerted on the glenoid by fishers and other mustelids than by other carnivores. The glenoid of most mustelids is very elongate, and the preglenoid and postglenoid processes are enlarged almost to encircle the condyle, forming an unusually strong, hinge-like jaw joint. This joint is so extreme in some mustelids, such as the mink and the Canadian otter, that it is difficult to extract the lower jaw from the skull without breaking the processes.

The large temporalis, which takes over much of the function performed by the masseter in most carnivores, explains the large sagittal crests found in mustelids. Normally, small carnivores with their relatively large braincases have ample space for muscle attachment and therefore have no large crests. The development of the temporalis in mustelids is so great, however, that prominent sagittal crests are found even on skulls of the small members of the genus *Mustela*. The sagittal crest on a large male fisher is extremely well developed because its braincase is relatively small compared to that of a smaller musteline. Fishers also have well-developed occipital crests, which function to increase the surface area for the origins of the anterior neck muscles.

Several investigators have attempted to use skulls to age fishers (Boise 1975; Coulter 1966; deVos 1952; Eadie and Hamilton 1958; Wright and Coulter 1967; reviewed by Poole et al., in press). The sex of the fisher being aged must be known, however, because the skulls of males and females differ. Sex can be determined quite accurately from the size and development of the sagittal crest, which is much greater in males (Figure 19); sexual dimorphism in skulls is greater in fishers than in any other American mustelid (Wright and Coulter 1967). The skulls of both male and female fishers change as they mature (Anderson 1970): the sagittal crest forms and increases in size, zygomatic breadth increases, and postorbital breadth decreases. No single measurement, however, clearly distinguishes juvenile from adult skulls in either sex. A few techniques, such as using the development of the temporalis muscles, have been used on American martens, but not on fishers, with mixed success (Poole et al., in press); mixed success is likely for these techniques with fishers as well.

By using development of the sagittal crest and fusion of skull sutures as criteria, fishers can be aged accurately from skulls (Eadie and Hamilton 1958;

Wright and Coulter 1967). In female fishers, the sagittal crest is not developed in juveniles, and distinct temporal lines can be seen on each side of the skull. The crest first develops near the back of the skull by fusion of the temporal lines around the time of first breeding, or one year of age, and grows progressively forward during the succeeding months and years. At one year of age, the sagittal crest is at most just beginning to develop, and naso-maxillary, maxillary-frontal, and maxillary-palatine sutures have not fused. In male fishers, the sagittal crest begins to develop during the first winter, and as soon as it is formed it runs its entire ultimate length along the top of the skull. The sagittal crest is much better developed in adults, however, and extends over 6 millimeters beyond the posterior margin of the skull. In juvenile male fishers, as in females, the naso-maxillary, maxillary-frontal, and maxillary-palatine sutures have not fused.

It is possible to age fishers as juveniles or adults and to sex fishers by using only canine teeth (Dix and Strickland 1986; Jenks et al. 1984, 1986; Keuhn and Berg 1981; Parson, Brown, and Will 1978; Poole et al., in press). No overlap in the maximum width of the root of fresh lower canine teeth was found between 149 female fishers and 98 male fishers captured in northern New York (Parsons, Brown, and Will 1978). The dividing point for lower canine maximum root width between male and female fishers was 5.645 millimeters. This width was 2.6 times the standard deviation from the means for males and females and gave a 99.5% probability of correctly sexing a fisher from one tooth measurement. Jenks and co-workers (1984, 1986) felt that the total length of a chosen standard canine is a more reliable measure for determining fisher sex from a single tooth. They found no overlap in this measure for lower left canines from 197 male and 243 female fishers from Maine; all teeth from females were 21.1 to 21.8 millimeters in length, whereas all teeth from males were 28.0 to 28.8 millimeters. This measure requires undamaged teeth, however, and fishers' canine teeth become worn as fishers age and use their teeth daily. Canine teeth also break sometimes from traumatic but normal use (a fight, perhaps [Arthur et al. 1989a]) and often break when a fisher is captured and bites the trap. Canine wear and breakage limit the use of canine length, but not root width, to sex fishers.

Dix and Strickland (1986), Jenks and co-workers (1984, 1986), and Keuhn and Berg (1981) used the relative width of the pulp cavity in lower canine teeth, seen in X-rays of teeth, to age fishers. Although Jenks and co-workers stated they could differentiate ages 0, 1, 2, and $\geq$ 3 by this technique, Dix and Strickland showed that dependable differentiation could only be made between ages 0 and $\geq$ 1. Pulp cavities of juvenile male fishers are $\leq$ 46.5% of lower canine width; pulp cavities of juvenile females are $\leq$ 39.5% of tooth width.

The best way to estimate a fisher's age is to count teeth cementum annuli. Cementum, a bonelike substance that surrounds the roots of teeth and anchors them to the periodontal ligament and thus anchors them in the jaw, is added on a continuous basis (Lieberman and Meadow 1992). The rate at which cementum is added differs during different seasons or periods with different food availability, giving the cementum of tooth roots a pattern that looks similar to tree rings when the teeth are properly decalcified, sectioned, and dyed. These rings are called annuli. This method has been used successfully to estimate ages in several species of mammals (reviewed by Grue and Jensen 1970; Lieberman and Meadows 1992), including fishers (Arthur et al. 1992; Kelly 1977; Strickland et al. 1981). A distinct advantage of this method is that it can be used with live animals.

Strickland and co-workers (1981) looked at several teeth (C_1, P^1, P_1, P_2) of fishers with known ages ranging from seven months to five years, and Arthur and co-workers (1992) looked at teeth of fishers up to ten and a half years. They and Kelly (1977) also looked at teeth from fishers of unknown ages caught by trappers. Kelly (1977) removed lower right premolars (P_1) from the carcasses of 202 trapped fishers and 11 live fishers. The first premolar is a small tooth whose removal causes little or no functional problem for a live fisher, unlike the removal of a canine or a molar, which have been used to age carcasses of fishers and other mammals (Crowe 1975; Crowe and Strickland 1975; Fogl and Mosby 1978; Nellis, Wetmore, and Keith 1978). The clarity and width of annuli vary with the tooth used and with the position on the tooth. Strickland and co-workers (1981) found annuli to be clearest on canines, which should not be removed from live animals. Kelly (1977) found that live fishers can be aged using a single premolar, and annuli on lower premolars are most easily observed near the root apex in a sagittal (lengthwise) section. He also discussed some technical problems with this method.

From the teeth of fishers of known ages, Strickland and co-workers (1981) found that fishers less than thirteen months old have no cementum annuli (Table 2). A fisher almost sixteen months old had one annulus that was just barely visible, indicating that annuli appear sometime during late spring and early summer. All fishers over one year old had one annulus for each spring after the spring of parturition. From fisher carcasses whose reproductive tracts, skulls, and bacula showed them to be less than one year old, Kelly (1977) found that no annuli were visible. All fishers whose reproductive tracts showed them to be over one year old had annuli, and Kelly also found that annuli appear during the late spring. Arthur and co-workers (1992), however, found that age estimates became less accurate in old fishers and that fishers nearing age ten could have their ages underestimated by a few years. Precision of age estimates (whether different people looking at slides of teeth estimate the same ages and whether

Table 2. Tooth cementum annuli in fishers of known ages

Age (months)	Fisher identification number	Tooth examined	Date extracted	Number annuli
7	1	C_1	November	0
13	2	P_1	May	0
16	3	P_2	19 July 1975	1
31	4	P_1	30 November 1976	2
31	5	P_1	30 November 1976	2
44	6	P_1	28 December 1977	3
44	4	P_1	28 December 1977	3
44	5	P_1	28 December 1977	3
53	6	P_1	7 September 1978	4
53	6	P_1	7 September 1978	4
53	6	C_1	7 September 1978	4
65	5	P^1	17 September 1979	5

Source: M. A. Strickland et al. 1981. Reproduced by permission of the New York State Department of Environmental Conservation.

different teeth from the same animal give the same age estimate) remained high even to old ages. Arthur and co-workers concluded that a fisher's age can be estimated accurately by the number of cementum annuli shown on its teeth through age three but thereafter the estimates may be biased to underestimate age.

Brain

A lateral view of a fisher's brain is shown in Figure 23. The fisher's external brain morphology differs little from that of other martens, except in its size. The lateral and postlateral sulci (grooves) are continuous in fishers whereas they are not in American martens. It is not known whether this pattern has any significance.

Work done by Welker and co-workers (Welker and Compos 1963; Welker and Seidenstein 1959; and references cited in these reports) showed that sulci may result from differential growth and elaboration of adjacent cortical regions of the brain. There is also a fairly accurate mapping of primary somatic sensory cortex and primary motor cortex to particular areas of the body. The approximate areas of somatic sensory cortex mapping to different parts of the body and of primary motor cortex for the fisher are shown in Figure 23. Fishers show fairly typical development of these areas and other parts of the brain. This indicates that fishers are similar to most contemporary carnivores and have less dependence on olfaction and more dependence on vision than fossil mustelids or "primitive" contemporary mustelids such as skunks and stink badgers.

Brain morphology reinforces conclusions drawn from skeletal morphology

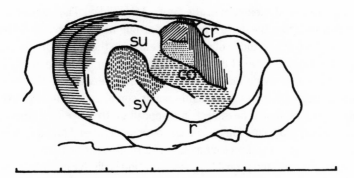

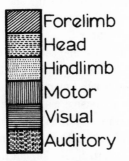

Figure 23. Lateral view of the fisher's brain. The areas indicated control the somatic sensory abilities of the forelimb, head, and hindlimb and control motor, visual, and auditory abilities. The *r* stands for rhinal fissure, the *sy* for sylvan sulcus, the *su* for suprasylvan sulcus, the *co* for coronal sulcus, and the *cr* for cruciate sulcus. Sulci appear as grooves on the brain's surface and externally divide it into the areas labeled. The drawing is taken from an endocast of a fisher's brain. Radinsky (1968a, 1968b, 1971) has shown that such endocasts accurately show external brain morphology. (Drawn by C. B. Powell from a latex endocast of a fisher's brain.)

that fishers have no major locomotory adaptations. There are no outstanding characteristics of fisher brains like those found in some otters (expanded coronal gyrus corresponding to increased sensitivity on the head [vibrissae] in river otters and giant otters; expanded lateral portion of the posterior sigmoid gyrus corresponding to increased forelimb sensitivity in other genera [Radinsky 1968b]), coatimundis (expanded coronal gyrus [Welker and Compos 1963]), and raccoons (expanded lateral portion of the sigmoid gyrus [Welker and Seidenstein 1959]).

Scent Glands and Soft Anatomy

Fishers possess anal glands, or sacs, as do all other members of the subfamily

Mustelinae and most members of the family Mustelidae. The odor of the substances emitted from these sacs is neither strong nor offensive in comparison to that of skunks and to those of small mustelines in the genus *Mustela*. Brinck and co-workers (1983) found that the predominant compound in anal gland secretions of European pine martens was benzaldehyde whereas the secretions of *Mustela* species were predominantly sulfur compounds. The anal gland secretions of fishers should be similar in composition to those of European pine martens and certainly smell more similar to those of other *Martes* species than to those of *Mustela*. The precise function of anal gland secretions has not been determined. An odor and probably some secretion is discharged when wild fishers are frightened, such as when they are handled by humans. Crump (1980a, 1980b) found differences in the anal gland secretions of male and female short-tailed weasels and fitch ferrets and differences between these mammals during and outside the breeding season. It is presumed that the anal gland secretions of fishers provide information to other fishers regarding sex, sexual activity, and perhaps maturity and territorial behavior.

European pine martens, American martens, and sables have well-developed abdominal glands (de Monte and Roeder 1990; Rozhnov 1991), but these are not present in stone martens or yellow-throated martens (Rozhnov 1991) and have not been found in fishers despite extensive inspections of study skins, whole carcasses, and pelts (Hall 1926; Pittaway 1984). Sables have glands on their necks (Petskoi and Kolpovskii 1970), and European pine martens have high concentrations of sebaceous glands on their cheeks, but the glands are not specialized (de Monte and Roeder 1990). The high concentration of the glands and the fact that European pine martens, other martens and sables, and fishers all rub their cheeks, necks, and flanks (necks and flanks of European pine martens also have many sebaceous glands) indicate that these glands have some communication function. It is probable that other neck and chin glands will be found in these species and in other mustelids.

The whorls of hair and associated apparent glands that fishers have on their hind feet have not been reported in other martens. Nothing is known of their histology or function other than that they become enlarged during the breeding season and therefore undoubtedly communicate something about breeding or social status.

Little else is known about the fisher's anatomy. It can be assumed that since the fisher is mainly carnivorous, it has a digestive tract that is relatively short and that it does not have even moderate adaptations for digesting vegetation. Such is the case for most carnivores (Ewer 1973). The fisher's digestive efficiency has been investigated and will be discussed in chapter 10. No other systems have been studied, nor have fishers' special senses been tested. Fishers' green eyeshine suggests excellent night vision, which aids hunting.

An Anatomical Approach to Understanding the Evolution of Sexual Dimorphism

All researchers who have studied the anatomy of fishers and closely related species have documented great sexual dimorphism in size, including sizes of bones and muscles. In a study of arboreal adaptations of fishers and their close relatives, Holmes (1980) used ratios of bone measurements to minimize the effects of sexual dimorphism on his measures of arboreal adaptations and found an unexpected sexual dimorphism in the ratios themselves. Although the postcranial skeletons of male and female mustelines, including fishers, are sexually dimorphic in size, they are proportionally the same. Thus, the skeletons of female fishers are scaled down versions of the skeletons of males. The skulls of the sexes, however, are significantly less dimorphic than the rest of the animals' bodies. Females have relatively larger skulls than males (or males have relatively smaller skulls than females). Holmes (1987; Holmes and Powell, in press) further examined the sexual dimorphism in weasels, fishers, and martens.

Two major hypotheses have been proposed to explain the large sexual dimorphism in body size of mustelines. Brown and Lasiewski (1972) and Yurgenson (1947) suggested that sexual dimorphism permits members of the two sexes to have somewhat different diets (resource partitioning), reducing competition for food. Moors (1974, 1980) and Erlinge (1979) hypothesized that sexual selection favors large size in males, but the energetic costs of reproduction constrain size in females. The hypothesized selective pathways for these two hypotheses are shown in Figure 24. One, the other, or both of these two hypotheses might be correct, or other selective pressures, as of yet not studied, may be involved.

Holmes (1987; Holmes and Powell, in press) examined the resource partitioning hypothesis because if sexual dimorphism is a resource partitioning phenomenon in any mammals, it ought to be in fishers, martens, and their close relatives. Ralls and Harvey (1985) also examined this hypothesis but hindered their analyses by computing sexual dimorphism indices from condylobasal lengths of skulls. Although condylobasal length is highly correlated with head and body length, the facial skulls of carnivores are more variable than their basicrania (Radinsky 1984). Skulls are clearly complex structures whose sizes, shapes, and proportions are the result of myriad selective pressures. Therefore Holmes (1987; Holmes and Powell, in press) analyzed head and body length and thirteen cranial and dental measures that are related to eating and predation.

Tooth measures do not correlate with condylobasal length of skull as well as do other measures, indicating that teeth vary somewhat independently from skull length. Nonetheless, indices of sexual dimorphism based on teeth track those based on skull and body measures. And indices based on teeth are not

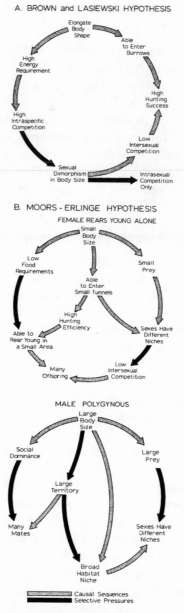

Figure 24. A simplified version of the (A) Brown-Lasiewski (1972) model (adapted from Moors 1980) and the (B) Moors (1974, 1980)-Erlinge (1979) model for the evolution of sexual dimorphism in mustelines. (Drawn by C. B. Powell; used by permission of Cornell University Press.)

different for fishers and American martens found in areas with or without the other species. The same holds for the three North American weasel species. If resource partitioning is important for these species, sexual dimorphism should be most pronounced when competition from closely related species is absent. It should also be affected more by the presence or absence of competitors larger in size than smaller in size (Holmes and Powell, in press; Wilson 1975). These patterns were not seen. Holmes (1987; Holmes and Powell, in press) concluded that the resource partitioning hypothesis was unequivocally refuted as a strong selective force leading to the large sexual dimorphism in bodies of fishers and their close relatives. Evidence on fishers' diets (chapter 6), reproduction (chapter 3), social organization (chapter 9), and energetics (chapter 10) indicates that sexual selection and the energy costs of reproduction have probably directed the evolution of sexual dimorphism.

Life History
and Early Development

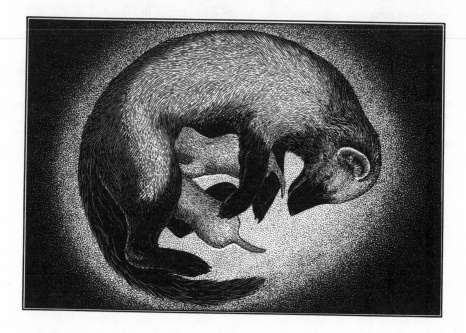

Early information on the reproduction and the life history of fishers came from fur farms. This information established that parturition and the breeding season occur in late winter and early spring and that gestation lasts almost a full year. Laboratory work done on fishers killed by trappers showed that the long gestation resulted from delayed implantation.

Delayed implantation is the interruption of normal development before implantation with a period of embryonic dormancy during the blastocyst stage. Mammals that are characterized by delayed implantation fall into two categories (Daniel 1970): those with *obligate* and those with *facultative* delayed implantation. In the former, delayed implantation is a regular event in the reproductive pattern; in the latter, delayed implantation only occurs when a female breeds before she has ceased lactating for the previous litter. Fishers have obligate delayed implantation.

Breeding Season

The first visible sign of estrus in female fishers is the enlargement of the vulva (Laberee 1941; Mead, in press), and females are in estrus about six to eight days (Laberee claimed only two days) beginning three to nine days following parturition (Hall 1942; Hodgson 1937; Laberee 1941). Matings on fur farms have occurred between 26 March and May (Hall 1942; Hodgson 1937; Laberee 1941). Hodgson (1937) reported that females occasionally mate during a second estrus that follows the first matings by about ten days. A similar condition has been observed in minks (Enders and Enders 1963). An isolated, captive female fisher observed by Douglas and Strickland (1987) exhibited vulval swelling in September, and they hypothesized that she had stayed in estrus because she had not been bred. I did not observe such prolonged estrus in captive female fishers, but it is possible that there is considerable individual variation.

The first information on the breeding season of wild fishers indicated that in Maine fishers breed from late February through mid-April (Coulter 1966). Because the reproductive tracts of two female fishers had tubal embryos in late March and early April, Wright and Coulter (1967) calculated that these females must have bred in mid- to late March. The reproductive tracts of male fishers first showed signs of sexual activity in March (Coulter 1966; Wright and Coulter 1967).

Coulter (1966) noted that fisher tracks indicated a marked increase in activity during March and interpreted this to mean that March was the height of the breeding season for fishers in Maine. Fishers backtracked and circled during their daily activities more in March than they did earlier in the winter. Fishers outfitted with transmitter collars by Arthur and co-workers (1989a) and by Leonard (1980b, 1986) exhibited significant increases in movement rates and distances traveled in March, and the established spacing patterns of males appeared to break down. Adult males trespassed on the territories of other males. Such extensive movement has been documented in other mustelines (Erlinge 1974, 1977; Lockie 1966; Moors 1974). Leonard (1986) observed no male-male interactions but interpreted minor skull injuries (broken zygomatic arches) found in males, but not in females, as evidence for aggression between males. Arthur and co-workers (1989a) found the broken canine of a male fisher embedded in the back of another male that had been trapped. An adult female that Leonard (1980b, 1986) followed during two breeding seasons did not increase activity in March, but a juvenile female did, perhaps as part of dispersal. During March fishers scent mark with urine, feces, and musk on elevated objects such as stumps and rocks (Leonard 1980b, 1986; Powell 1977a). Laberee (1941) noted that male fishers from fur farms marked (with urine) extensively in their pens during the beginning of the mating season. This March surge in male fisher activity appears to mark the beginning of the breeding season and is probably dependent on elevated levels of testosterone (Mead, in press).

The breeding seasons (the range of dates encompassing most breedings) for all martens appear to last some thirty to forty-five days (Mead, in press). The breeding season for fishers has been dated from March (Coulter 1966; Douglas and Strickland 1987) through April (Douglas and Strickland 1987; Hall 1942; Hodgson 1937; Christopher A. Kline and Michael Don Carlos, Minnesota Zoological Society, unpublished records) to May (Laberee 1941). Douglas and Strickland (1987) summarized the breeding season for fishers to be from 27 February to 15 April, based on known birth dates of captive litters, but this ignores the three to nine day delay between parturition and breeding. In general, males of all marten species have completed testicular recrudescence (enlargement) one month prior to estrus (Mead, in press). Most data indicate that male fishers are fully sexually active by early March. If fishers are like other martens, these data indicate that breeding in fishers may not generally occur before early April.

Male Reproductive Biology

In 1937, Hodgson wrote that the testicles of male fishers are enlarged during the breeding season. This was the only information available until the mid-1960s, when Coulter and Wright (Coulter 1966; Wright and Coulter 1967) presented data on the reproductive tracts of ten male fishers trapped by Maine trappers between 5 January and 4 April (Table 3). Douglas and Strickland (1987) and Leonard (1980b, 1986) have subsequently gathered limited additional data, and Mead (in press) summarized data on the reproductive biology of males of all marten species.

Testes of both adult and juvenile male fishers may begin to enlarge (begin recrudescence) as early as December (Leonard 1986), but almost no males have been found with sperm prior to the beginning of March (Table 3; also Douglas and Strickland 1987 [3 of 39 males with sperm prior to March]; Leonard 1986 [0 of 25]). Testes of harvested fishers have been found with sperm as late as May (1 in April, 1 of 2 males checked in May; Wright and Coulter 1967), but few spring data are available because almost all fishers studied were harvested for fur during the winter (Douglas and Strickland 1987). Michael Don Carlos (Minnesota Zoological Society, unpublished records) electroejaculated an adult male fisher on 22 April and found sperm with normal heads and tails and good motility. The weights of combined testes and epididymides and the weights of paired testes are greater for those males that have abundant sperm in the testes and epididymides (Table 3). The timing of the testicular cycle is probably

Table 3. Condition of reproductive tracts of male fishers taken in late winter and early spring

Date (1957)	Weight (g) of combined testes and epididymides	Paired testes weight (g)	Paired epididymides weight (g)	Status of sperm in testes	Status of sperm in epididymides	Baculum weight (g)	Estimated age of animal	Body weight (kg)
5 January	2.7	1.8	0.4	None	None	1.26	Juvenile	3.3
26 February	7.4	5.6	1.4	Active spermatogenesis	None	?	?	?
February or early March	6.3	4.8	1.1	None	None	1.72	Juvenile	4.7
1 March	6.3	4.8	1.0	Active spermatogenesis	Few	1.25	Juvenile	3.8
1 March	8.6	6.9	1.3	Abundant	Abundant	1.55	Juvenile	4.4
1-15 March	10.3	7.6	1.9	Abundant	Abundant	1.56	Adult	–
17 March	11.3	8.6	1.9	Abundant	Abundant	1.52	Adult	5.1
27 March	7.4	5.8	1.2	Abundant	Abundant	1.92	Adult	3.7
27 March	13.0	9.8	2.2	Abundant	Abundant	2.05	Adult	6.5
4 April	9.0	7.0	1.7	Abundant	Abundant	1.80	Adult	4.2

Note: Baculum weights coverted from mg to g to be consistent with text; body weights converted from pounds and ounces to kg.
Source: Table 3 in Wright and Coulter 1967. Reproduced by permission of the Wildlife Society.

dependent on day length (Mead, in press), as is the case in stone martens (Audy 1976) and sables (Song, Tong, and Xiao 1988).

Not all males are in breeding condition by early March, but by mid-March through April all adults appear fully sexually active and have abundant sperm in the epididymides (Table 3). Despite having sperm, one-year-old fishers appear not to be effective breeders, probably because baculum development is incomplete. Bacula require testosterone to complete development, and this can only occur as testes mature and spermatogenesis occurs during males' first breeding season. Strickland and Douglas (1981; Douglas and Strickland 1987) became interested in the reproductive biology of fishers because trapping returns decreased in the early 1970s in the Algonquin region of Ontario. To obtain the data needed to adjust trapping quotas, in 1972 they began a study of carcasses of fishers caught by trappers. When the trapping season in Ontario was four months long and the fisher population was heavily trapped, about 8% of the females trapped had not ovulated and formed corpora lutea in their ovaries. Trapping was allowed as late as March, and the proportion of adult males in the harvest changed from low before January to very high by March. This change corresponded with high movement rates of adult male fishers at the beginning of the breeding season. Douglas and Strickland hypothesized that overharvest of adult males had led to increased female barrenness. Beginning in 1975 the trapping season was restricted to November and December, harvest of adult males declined while total harvest of males did not, and female barrenness dropped to less than 2%. Douglas and Strickland concluded that juvenile males are not effective breeders.

Female Reproductive Biology

The reproductive biology of female fishers is similar to that of other mustelines. Minor differences are due mostly to size differences between species. Mead (in press) reviewed the reproductive biology of females of all marten species. Historically, work on the reproductive system of female fishers has used reproductive tracts from fishers caught by trappers. Only recently has research begun on female reproductive biology using captive female fishers.

Female fishers are sexually mature and breed for the first time at one year of age (Douglas and Strickland 1977; Eadie and Hamilton 1958; Hall 1942; Wright and Coulter 1967). Nipples of adult females who have nursed young are noticeably larger than those of females who have not (Strickland 1978). Most females of the genus *Mustela* breed for the first time during their first summer. Female American martens do not usually reach sexual maturity until they are two years of age (Wright 1963), although some have bred at age fifteen months in captivity (Markley and Bassett 1942).

Female Reproductive Tracts and Embryos

The reproductive tract of a female fisher is similar to those of most other female mustelids (Mead, in press; Wright and Coulter 1967). The ovaries are completely encapsulated, with only a small ostium through which a small portion of the fimbria extends, and the ovaries are encircled by the oviducts. The average combined weights of the ovaries of forty-four adult female fishers in inactive pregnancy (embryos not implanted) studied by Wright and Coulter (1967) was 134.4 milligrams, and the average combined weights of the ovaries of thirty-three immature female fishers was 76.5 milligrams. Fishers were judged immature when they lacked corpora lutea; all immature female fishers were captured during the fall or early winter of their first year. The ovaries of female fishers with implanted embryos are much larger than those of females in inactive pregnancy and averaged 231.9 milligrams (combined weight, $N = 9$). The corpora lutea are markedly enlarged during active pregnancy, as is the case in other mustelids with a long delayed implantation (Wright 1963), but the increased size of ovaries is not due only to the increase in the size of the corpora lutea (Wright and Coulter 1967).

Ovulation is presumed to be induced by copulation. Although this has not been documented in fishers, it has been in sables (Bernatskii, Snytko, and Nosova 1976). The corpora lutea of actively pregnant female fishers can be readily identified (Douglas and Strickland 1987; Wright and Coulter 1967) because their cells are highly vacuolated (Eadie and Hamilton 1958; Wright and Coulter 1967), a condition probably correlated with the secretion of progesterone (Wright and Coulter 1967). The diameters of corpora lutea of fishers in inactive pregnancy average approximately 1.25 millimeters (Eadie and Hamilton 1958; Wright and Coulter 1967), whereas those of fishers in active pregnancy average approximately 2.8 millimeters (Wright and Coulter 1967). Ovaries containing these corpora lutea have much interstitial tissue and numerous small- and medium-size follicles. Corpora albicantia are evident for approximately eight to nine months following parturition but degenerate at highly variable rates (Douglas and Strickland 1987).

The uterus of a female fisher has a common corpus uteri; the uterine horns are 40 to 60 millimeters long and 2.5 to 4.0 millimeters in diameter in adult fishers. The uterine horns of immature females are smaller, about 30 to 40 millimeters long and 1.5 to 2.5 millimeters in diameter (Wright and Coulter 1967).

A fertilized ovum has a diploid number of 38 (Ewer 1973), and cleavage of embryos to the blastocyst stage is probably slow. Wright (1948) found that cleavage in the long-tailed weasel embryo is slow; at day eleven embryos are in the morula stage, and not until day fifteen is the blastocyst stage reached. Using the cleavage rate for long-tailed weasels, Wright and Coulter (1967) calculated that two female fishers whose reproductive tracts had tubal embryos in the

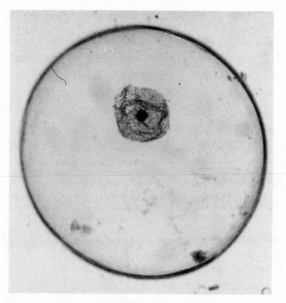

Figure 25. Well-preserved fisher blastocyst. (*Source*: Figure
4 from Douglas and Strickland 1987, used with permission
of Ontario Ministry of Natural Resources. Copyright 1987,
Queen's Printer for Ontario.)

morula stage must have bred approximately eight to ten days before capture.
The condition of the ovaries of these fishers also indicated that ovulation had
occurred about eight to ten days before capture. This finding supports slow
cleavage in the fisher embryo.

The two fisher reproductive tracts with tubal embryos had a total of 5 morulae.
One fisher had 3 morulae, one of which had about 228 nuclei. The 2 morulae in the
other fisher had 12 and 20 nuclei. Embryos become dormant in the blastocyst stage
before implantation (Enders and Pearson 1943) and are enclosed by the acellular
membrane, the zona pellucida. Dormancy is probably related to the proteins in the
uterine environment (Daniel 1970; Mead, in press). Dormant blastocysts found in
the uterus during fall and winter (Figure 25) measure from 0.25 to 1.50 millimeters
in diameter and are clear, transparent spheres with an inner cell mass plainly visible
at one side (Eadie and Hamilton 1958). Enders and Pearson (1943) were able to
count 798, 807, and 844 nuclei in three dormant blastocysts taken from two fishers
trapped in January and February. However, none of these observations were of
well-preserved, well-fixed blastocysts.

Implantation, Gestation, and Parturition

Sometime before implantation there may be transuterine migration of blastocysts. In a sample of twelve reproductive tracts of female fishers in inactive pregnancy, Kelly (1977) found three tracts that had more blastocysts in one uterine horn than corpora lutea in the respective ovary. Wright and Coulter (1967) found only one tract showing transuterine migration in a sample of eleven tracts in inactive pregnancy. However, five of eight tracts in active pregnancy showed transuterine migration. Wright and Coulter believed that transuterine migration may act to space out embryos just prior to implantation when they were asymmetrically derived from the two ovaries.

Implantation of blastocysts of American martens is dependent on day length (Pearson and Enders 1944). Implantation in other mustelids is correlated with prolactin secretion, which leads to elevated progesterone levels; prolactin secretion is influenced by photoperiod in other mammals (Mead, in press; Papke et al. 1980). It is assumed that the same is true for fishers, but the entire hormone cascade required to induce implantation has not been elucidated for any mustelid, and unknown luteal secretions, perhaps a protein, are believed to be involved (Mead, in press). The postimplantation period for American martens is less than twenty-eight days (Jonkel and Weckwerth 1963) and that for long-tailed weasels is about twenty-three to twenty-four days (Wright 1948). Therefore, Wright and Coulter (1967) calculated that the expected postimplantation period of female fishers should be about thirty days. Subtracting thirty days from known parturition dates (Coulter 1966; Hall 1942; Hodgson 1937; Laberee 1941; Leonard 1980b, 1986; Paragi 1990; Powell 1977a; Wright and Coulter 1967) suggests that implantation can occur as early as January and as late as early April.

Little is known of embryo development. Coulter (1966) reported the following crown rump measurements: January, 3 embryos, 18 millimeters; February, 4 embryos, 8 millimeters; 7 February, 3 embryos, 13 millimeters; 21 February, 3 embryos, 18 millimeters; late February, 4 embryos, 26 millimeters; 3 March, 4 fetuses, 55 millimeters; 11 March, 3 fetuses, 71 millimeters; 13 March, 3 early embryos, uterine swellings, 7 millimeters diameter; 20 March, 3 fetuses, 79 millimeters.

Research has begun at the Maine Cooperative Fish and Wildlife Research Unit, University of Maine, Orono, on hormone levels in female fishers during delayed implantation through birth. Ultrasound scans are being used to study implantation and development of embryos (William B. Krohn, personal communication).

Parturition dates as early as February and as late as May have been recorded. Most fur farms have reported parturition in March and April (Douglas 1943; Hall 1942; Hodgson 1937) but Laberee (1941) reported that parturition occurred in April and May. Twenty-two parturition dates from fur farms in British Columbia ranged from 23 March to 7 April (mean date was 31 March;

Hall 1942). Coulter (1966) and Wright and Coulter (1967) reported on twelve female carcasses of fishers that had embryos and fetuses in different stages of development. Estimated parturition dates ranged from mid-February through mid-April. Coulter (1966) listed two known parturition dates as 3 and 20 April, I recorded one parturition date of 29-30 March (Powell 1977a), and Christopher A. Kline and Michael Don Carlos (Minnesota Zoological Society, unpublished records) recorded three dates of 31 March and 2 and 10 April. Hamilton and Cook (1955) reported that a trapper brought home litters of two and three kits in February and mid-March, respectively, and Leonard (1980b) observed a wild female fisher with kits calculated to have been born in early April. Twelve litters were born between 3 March and 1 April to wild female fishers outfitted with transmitter collars in Maine (Paragi 1990); the middle six litters were born between 14 and 29 March with a median date of 21 March. Paragi also stated that nineteen wild-bred captive fishers on fur farms gave birth between 26 February and 6 April, with a median date of 14 March. Because implantation is probably stimulated by changes in day length and day length varies with latitude, implantation, parturition, and breeding may vary by latitude.

The three parturition dates recorded by Kline and Don Carlos at the Minnesota Zoo were for captive bred litters. The first of these females bred on 16 April 1989, gave birth on 31 March 1990, and bred again on 7-9 April 1990. The second female bred on 22 April 1990, gave birth on 2 April 1991, and bred again on 11-12 April 1991. This female then gave birth again on 10 April 1992. The consistency in the parturition and breeding dates for each of these females between years suggests that individual females may tend to implant around the same date every year, and thus give birth and breed around the same date every year. This finding suggests that the spread in dates for parturition and breeding are caused by variation between females and not by individual females giving birth early in some years and late in others.

Litter Size

The average numbers of corpora lutea, unimplanted blastocysts, implanted embryos, placental scars, and kits in a litter reported by different investigators range from 2.7 to 3.9 (Table 4). The average number of corpora lutea reported per female ranges from 2.7 to 3.9, and most reports are close to the mean of 3.35 found for over 1,000 female fishers from Ontario. Juveniles tend to have slightly fewer corpora lutea than adults, but the difference is not significantly different. There are usually fewer unimplanted blastocysts than corpora lutea (Crowley et al. 1990; Kelly 1977; Wright and Coulter 1967). In a special subsample of eleven especially well-preserved reproductive tracts, Wright and Coulter found 35 corpora lutea and 33 unimplanted blastocysts; two tracts

Table 4. Average numbers per female of corpora lutea, blastocysts, implanted embryos, and placental scars and average litter sizes for fishers in several studies

Corpora lutea				Blastocysts				Implanted embryos				Placental scars				Litter sizes				Source
Mean	SD	Range	N	Mean	SD	Range	N	Mean	SD	Range	N	Mean	SD	Range	N	Mean	SD	Range	N	
																3.0	2.8	1-5	2	Kline & Don Carlos (Minn. Zoo unpub. records)
3.7	0.1		50	3.2	1.0		44	3.4	0.5	3-4	11	2.9	0.8	2-4	27	3.0	0	3	2	Coulter 1966
3.6	0.1		57	3.0	1.0		50					2.8	1.3		15					Crowley, Krohn, & Paragi 1990
												2.5	1.3		11					Crowley, Krohn, & Paragi 1990
3.4			1173					3.1			45									Douglas & Strickland 1987
2.7	0.7	2-4	22																	Eadie & Hamilton 1958
																2.7	0.7	1-4	21	Hall 1942
				2.7	1.0	1-4	7									2.5		2-3	2	Hamilton & Cook 1955
																		1-6		Hodgson 1937
3.7	0.3		12																	Kelly 1977
3.9[b]			9	2.9[b]			9													Kelly 1977
																3.0			1	LaBarge, Baker, & Moore 1990
3.5			16																	Leonard 1986
																2.0			5	Paragi, 1990
																2.0			1	Powell 1977a
3.0[c]	1.0	0-5	141	3.0			11	3.3	0.5	3-4	9									Shea et al. 1985
3.4	0.6	2-5	54																	Wright & Coulter 1967
3.3[a]			44																	Wright & Coulter 1967
3.4	0.5	3-4	8																	Wright & Coulter 1967
3.2[a]			11	3.0																Wright & Coulter 1967

[a] Subsample of total sample of 54 reproductive tracts.
[b] Subsample of total sample of 12 reproductive tracts; the deterioration of the carcasses caused the low number of blastocysts in comparison to the number of corpora lutea.
[c] Mean number of corpora lutea per adult female, including barren females; mean for pregnant females = 3.2, $N = 134$.

showed a loss of 1 blastocyst each for an approximate 6% loss of potential embryos. Wright and Coulter also found that the number of corpora lutea in the ovaries of eight females with implanted embryos was the same as the number of embryos. Consequently, they felt that the actual loss of potential embryos was probably more like 3%. Crowley and co-workers (1990), however, found a 14% loss of potential embryos, and Kelly (1977) found an even greater loss. Because several of his tracts were very poorly preserved, Kelly believed that his number of lost embryos was inflated from the actual value.

The average number of unimplanted blastocysts reported ranges from 2.7 to 3.2 (Table 4). The average number of implanted embryos ranges from 3.1 to 3.4, and the average number of placental scars ranges from 2.5 to 2.9. Douglas and Strickland (1987) reported a possible case of twinning in a female who had more embryos than corpora lutea.

The only large samples of actual litter sizes come from fur-farm fishers: an average of 2.7 kits per female fisher from fur farms in British Columbia (Hall 1942). Other studies agree with this number reasonably well (Table 4).

Small sample sizes and other unknown sources of variation probably influenced the results shown in Table 4. For example, it is impossible for the average number of unimplanted embryos to be smaller than the average number of implanted embryos in any one fisher, for any one population, or over the entire continent. Nonetheless, it appears that the average litter size for a female fisher is between two and three kits, with a normal range from one to four and extremes of five or six (Wright and Coulter [1967] reported one fisher with five corpora lutea; Hodgson [1937] reported one litter of six!).

Pregnancy rates for fishers have generally been calculated as the proportion of adult females ($\geq$ 2 yr.) harvested whose ovaries contain corpora lutea (Crowley et al. 1990; Douglas and Strickland 1987; Shea et al. 1985). Placental scars have not been used, even though they should in theory document birth and litter sizes more accurately, because they have been believed not to persist consistently, especially in poorly preserved reproductive tracts typical of samples obtained from harvested fishers (Douglas and Strickland 1987; Wright and Coulter 1967). Corpora lutea generally indicate ovulation rates of greater than or equal to 95% (Douglas and Strickland 1987; Shea et al. 1985), while placental scars indicate much lower birth rates.

Far fewer than 95% of female fishers two years old and older den and produce kits each spring. From 1984 to 1989, twelve female fishers wearing transmitter collars in Maine denned in only 63% of the twenty-five fisher denning opportunities (most fishers were followed for more than one spring; Arthur and Krohn 1991; Paragi 1990). Arthur, Krohn, and Paragi wondered whether placental scars might not actually be a more accurate measure of pregnancy rates than corpora lutea. In a follow-up study, Crowley and co-workers (1990) showed

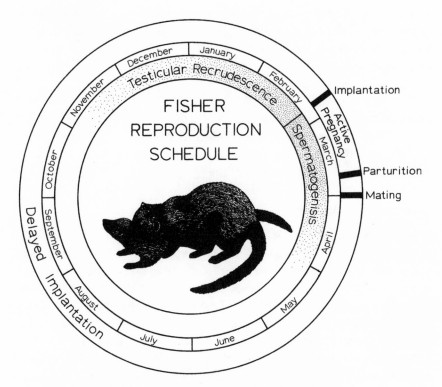

Figure 26. Fisher reproduction schedule. (Drawing by C. B. Powell.)

that an average of 97% of the female fishers from Maine, New Hampshire, Ontario, and Vermont had corpora lutea (range 92 to 100 for any one place in any one year), but only 58% had placental scars (range 22 to 88). This placental scar rate is in close agreement with a denning rate of 63%.

Reproductive Schedule

With the information already given, a general reproductive schedule for fishers can be diagrammed (Figure 26). Female fishers are shown to breed around the first of April. The rate of cleavage of the embryos is probably slow, and the embryos most likely reach the blastocyst stage about fifteen days after fertilization. Embryos become dormant during the blastocyst stage and remain so for approximately ten months. Implantation is induced by the increasing day length during late February, and an approximately thirty-day active gestation ensues. Parturition probably occurs on the average in late March, and females probably breed again within ten days. Thus, an adult female fisher is pregnant almost all the time, except for a brief period following parturition. Healthy females breed for the first time when they are one year old, produce their first litters when they are two years old, and probably breed every year thereafter as long as they are healthy. For fishers with parturition and breeding dates before or after those dates diagrammed in Figure 26, the whole schedule is shifted appropriately.

In at least some male fishers, testicular recrudescence begins in December. Active spermatogenesis starts in February, and by early March males are completely reproductively active and capable. By this time males are traveling well beyond the borders of their territories in search of estrous females. Sometime in April, probably, spermatogenesis ceases. By late May no sperm are in the epididymides, and testes decrease in size.

Courtship and Mating

For an animal like the fisher, it has been difficult to prove whether matings in the wild are monogamous, polygynous, or polyandrous. Use of DNA fingerprinting may change this. Fishers raised on fur farms have been mated monogamously and polygynously (Douglas 1943; Hodgson 1937; Laberee 1941). It is probable that polygamous mating occurs in the wild. Large sexual dimorphism in body size is strongly correlated with polygynous mating systems in mammals (Kleiman 1977), and there is no reason to believe that fishers should be an exception.

During mating, which was first observed on fur farms, the female appears to dominate the male (Hodgson 1937; Laberee 1941). Laberee (1941, 102) stated that when a female "wants to mate, you better provide the necessary facilities and do it promptly." If a female is not receptive, she may act aggressively toward a male; the male's response will not be aggressive, however (Hodgson 1937). Hodgson's (1937, 36-37) most complete description of mating is as follows:

From the fifth to the ninth day following date of arrival of the litter [the female] shows up for the first time. She runs up and down her pen often stopping at the chute leading in to the male. On being let through, if the male is out, there will be a mating in a very short time, but very often he will be in his nest box. In this case she will investigate the pen, finally landing at the opening leading into his nest box. Then she will make a peculiar crooning noise, as if calling to him. He will soon make his appearance and a mating takes place with little delay.

Laberee related (1941, 103) one mating this way:

Soon the love-making began. And if there was anyone within a mile of us who did not think some large animal was being tortured to death, that person must have been deaf. Such noise! Such yowls! Such howling! No thousand cats caterwauling on a backyard fence at midnight ever could make such noise. But that was before copulation began. Once the pair mated there was not a sound. And the moment the mating was over, the female insisted on getting back to her pen immediately. As soon as we had removed the heating pad from the young pekans' nest we let her in—and all was serene. The mating lasted from 10:17 A.M. until 4:27 P.M., six hours and ten minutes. The next day she mated again for four hours and twenty-five minutes.

Unfortunately, neither of these descriptions is precise. Kline and Don Carlos at the Minnesota Zoo made observations of fisher courtship in the 1990 and 1991 breeding seasons (Minnesota Zoological Society, unpublished records). Their observations agreed with those of Hodgson and Laberee that females are dominant over males. When females were not receptive, they were quite aggressive toward males, but males were not overly aggressive back. Courtship involved chasing, vocalization, and tail flagging by females when receptive. Don Carlos (personal communication) felt tail flagging was diagnostic of estrus and readiness to breed. During copulation, males gripped females by the napes of their necks. Males sometimes dragged females by their necks between copulations. Hodgson (1937) noted that this biting sometimes caused noticeable irritation on the necks of females.

The observations of Kline and Don Carlos, Hodgson (1937), and Laberee (1941) are consistent. Courtship can be brief or prolonged, depending on the receptiveness of the female, perhaps. Matings between fishers on Hodgson's and Laberee's fur farms commonly lasted from one to seven hours, averaging around four hours. Copulations at the Minnesota Zoo lasted from twenty minutes to over three hours. From these descriptions, the courtship of fishers appears similar to that of other mustelines (Heidt, Petersen, and Kirkland 1968; Hodgson 1937), which are known for being prolonged and very vigorous (Enders and Enders 1963). Such long copulations are not needed to induce ovulation, but when copulation is interrupted after five to twelve minutes in ferrets and minks, no fertilization occurs (reviewed by Mead, in press).

Denning

All known dens used to raise young fishers have been high up in hollow trees. Thirty-two natal dens used by fishers outfitted with transmitter collars by Arthur (1987) and Paragi (1990) were all in trees, and over half were in aspens. These data are summarized in Table 5. Female fishers routinely moved their litters, and all subsequent dens were also in trees. Female fishers used one to three dens per litter and were more likely to move litters if disturbed (Paragi 1990).

A fisher's natal den found by Leonard (1980b) was approximately 7 meters up in a hollow, living quaking aspen. There were two entrances: a small entrance too small for the female to use at the bottom of the hollow and a larger hole approximately 10 meters up the tree trunk through which the female entered and descended through the inside of the tree to the kits at the bottom of

Table 5. Characteristics of natal dens in trees used by fishers
in southcentral Maine, 1986-89

Tree type	Tree dbh (cm)			Entrance height (m)			Entrance area[a] (cm^2)			% Dead	N
	Median	IQR[b]	N	Median	IQR[b]	N	Median	IQR[b]	N		
Aspen[c]	45	38-45	17	7.0	5.0-10.0	17	78	63-95	14	63	16
Other hardwoods[d]	60	45-75	13	5.1	4.4-7.5	10	108	85-149	8	36	14
Softwoods[e]	43		2	9.9		2	520		1	0	2
All dens	45	39-60	32	6.3	4.6-9.0	29	95	70-110	23	48	31
Range	25-92 cm			0.9-12 m			140-1,570 cm^2				

Note: dbh (cm), height (m), and area (cm^2) of cavity entrance were not different between aspens and other hardwoods (Mann-Whitney U, $p > 0.20$).

[a] Area of entrance = $(\pi \cdot \text{length} \cdot \text{width})/4$

[b] Interquartile range (25th-75th percentiles)

[c] Balsam poplar, bigtooth aspen

[d] Red maple, sugar maple, yellow birch, red oak, American basswood, American elm

Source: Paragi 1990. Reproduced by permission of the author.

the hollow. The nest area was on flat, rough wood, and there was no nesting material at all. The nest was extremely neat after the kits left, with no sign that fisher kits had been raised there—no excrement, no regurgitated food, and no food remains. Natal nests of captive fishers are similarly spartan with no lining of fur (Hodgson 1937; Powell, unpublished data). Other reports of natal dens conform to these descriptions (Hamilton and Cook 1955).

Except during mating, female fishers raised on fur farms spend little time outside maternal nest boxes after parturition (Hodgson 1937; Laberee 1941). Although mating may keep a female away from her young for several hours when the young are only a few days old, she returns quickly to her young when she has finished mating. Fur farmers sometimes artificially warmed nests with young in them during the female's absence (Hodgson 1937; Laberee 1941), but it is not known whether this increased the survivorship of the young.

The female fisher with young observed and radiotracked by Leonard (1980a, 1986) spent very little time away from her kits at first. When the kits were less than a week old, the female spent no more than two or three hours of twenty-four away from the kits. During the following eight weeks, she spent more and more time away from the kits, so that just before the kits left the natal den the female was spending only about an hour in the early morning with them. As the kits grew, the female was under increasing pressure to hunt in order to meet the energy and nutritional demands of lactation. This pressure undoubtedly explains the increased time spent away from the kits longer and longer after parturition. Arthur and Krohn (1991) also found that female fishers with kits increased activity through the spring.

The four females monitored by Paragi (1990) raised five litters over two years and did not exhibit the neat behavior pattern shown by the female monitored by Leonard (1980a, 1986). These females showed tremendous individual variation in activity patterns both before and after weaning their kits. One female with three kits was more active than females with two kits, but in another year when this same female had a litter of only two kits, she was also more active than other females.

Evidence suggests that female fishers raise their young with no help from males. On fur farms some male fishers have entered nest boxes with kits and done no harm (Hodgson 1937; Laberee 1941), but other males have seriously injured young (Hodgson 1937). In addition, the young a wild female raises were conceived a year earlier and may have been fathered by more than one male. There is no reason to believe that male fishers can remember with which females they mated the previous year. Therefore, a male who helps raise young could be helping to raise the offspring of another male, while his own offspring are being raised by another female without assistance. These circumstances should lead to little care of young by males (Grafen 1980). In no close relatives of fishers do males help raise kits.

During the time that the female fisher radiotracked by Leonard (1980b) had kits in her maternal den, her activities and hunting periods were oriented toward parts of her home range distant from the den. This female traveled rapidly in roughly a straight line from her maternal den to the outer edges of her home range each day. She stayed at long distances from the den until returning, again roughly in a straight line. This female bred on at least one of these active periods away from the den (her ovaries, collected during the trapping season the following winter, had corpora lutea [Leonard 1980b]). Breeding took place far from the maternal den, and her activity patterns may also have oriented the activities of male fishers away from her natal den (Leonard 1980b).

Use of the natal den by the female fisher and her young ceased when the young were approximately eight weeks old (Leonard 1980b). The female probably took the young to another den. Duration of denning by the females monitored by Paragi (1990) ranged from fifty-eight to seventy-one days. Grinnell, Dixon, and Linsdale (1937) reported the den-oriented activities of three-month-old fishers.

Delayed Implantation

Delayed implantation has evolved independently several times (Heidt 1970;

Wright 1963; reviewed by Sandell 1990), and many placental mammals exhibit delayed implantation (Table 6). Many species not yet studied will undoubtedly be found to delay implantation, such as unstudied *Mustela* species, *Martes* species, and pinnipeds (seals and sea lions). Delayed implantation also occurs in several marsupials.

Six, or seven, basic hypotheses have been developed to explain the origin of delayed implantation. Fries (1880, 1902) suggested that delayed implantation in roe deer and European badgers is an adaptation that benefits the young. He argued that young need to be born as early in the spring as possible to be able to survive the next winter. Without delayed implantation, mating would have to occur during the winter, which he presumed would be unfavorable to adults. Thus, delayed implantation uncouples the normal temporal relation between mating and parturition, allows both events to occur at the most favorable times, and therefore is an adaptation that actually benefits both young and adults. Fries did not generalize his ideas beyond roe deer and European badgers.

Prell (1927, 1930) argued that delayed implantation developed in "old genera" that were exposed to glaciation and that harsh climatic conditions forced a modification in embryonic development. Prell was not consistent in his aging of "old" and "new" genera, however, and the occurrence of delayed implantation and delayed fertilization in tropical species nullifies his hypothesis (Murr 1929, 1931).

Murr (1929, 1931) believed that delayed implantation arose as a direct effect of environmental temperature on embryonic development. For example, he thought that the delay could be caused by the alleged drop in body temperature of bears and badgers and the chilling of organs and glands in martens and roe deer. The obvious argument nullifying this theory is that delay in most species begins or occurs during the summer.

Hamlett (1935) reviewed these three hypotheses and concluded that Fries's was the only one that held any merit. He further concluded, however, that delayed implantation is a "useless character" that has no value for a species' survival. There is little question today that delayed implantation is not a "useless character" and that it does have survival value in those species that exhibit it (Ealey 1963; Heidt 1970; Sandell 1990; Wright 1963).

Ealey (1963, 46) presented a good argument for the evolution of delayed implantation in the euro, a species of kangaroo:

A seasonal variation in the nutritional state of the euro population has been demonstrated. An increase in reproductive activity occurs at such a time that the young are becoming large when the parents are best able to supply adequate milk. However, this reproductive activity occurs before the main rain

Table 6. Placental mammals that display
delayed implantation

Order, family, and species	Delay (months)
Cingulata	
Dasypodidae	
nine-banded armadillo	3½-4½
Mulita armadillo	?
Chiroptera	
Pteropodidae	
equatorial fruit bat	3-5
Jamaican fruit bat	2½
Vespertilionidae	
lesser long-fingered bat	3-6
Schreiber's long-finger bat	2½
Soricomorpha	
Talpidae	
Siberian mole	8-9
Carnivora	
Ursidae	
sloth bear	?
spectacled bear	?
black bear	5-6½
brown/grizzly bear	6+
polar bear	8+
Asiatic black bear	?
Mustelidae	
short-tailed weasel	8½-10
long-tailed weasel	7-9
mink	⅓-1⅔
American marten	7-8
European pine marten	7-9
sable	7-9
house marten	7
yellow-throated marten	?
fisher	10-11
wolverine	6-8
American badger	6
Eurasian badger	6-10
hog-badger	?
river otter	9-11
sea otter	?
striped skunk	?
western spotted skunk	5-7½
Otariidae	
Afro-Australian fur seal	4
northern fur seal	3½-4
South American fur seal	4
southern sea lion	11½-12
Steller sea lion	3½
California sea lion	3-3½

Odobenidae	
walrus	3-4
Phocidae	
harbor seal	2-3
largha seal	2-3
ringed seal	3-4
harp seal	3-4
gray seal	5-6
hooded seal	3-4
bearded seal	2-3
crabeater seal	2
Weddell seal	2-3
southern elephant seal	$3\frac{1}{2}$-4
Artiodactyla	
Cervidae	
roe deer	4-5

has fallen, and there is considerable mortality among the young. Many of the young that die can be replaced by others from quiescent blastocysts. Time is saved, and the replacing young have a better chance of obtaining enough milk for survival when they are larger than if they had been born about a month later, as they would have been if the mothers had gone through another estrous cycle and been fertilized. When there is a prolonged good season, the mechanism of delayed implantation insures that the maximum number of pouch young are produced in the shortest time.

Although this theory nicely fits delayed implantation for many marsupials, especially those in unpredictable environments, it cannot be applied to fishers or most other placentals. Fishers are unable to regulate implantation directly with availability of food.

Heidt (1970) believed that Fries's theory for the origin of delayed implantation should apply to mustelids that live in northern climates. In addition, Heidt suggested that species at high trophic levels need no more than one litter per year (which is often necessitated by delayed implantation) and that delayed implantation may be a factor designed to limit populations. There are many problems with Heidt's suggestions. First, the three species of North American weasels are at trophic levels lower than Heidt assumed (Errington 1943, 1967; Powell 1975, 1978b, 1982a). Thus, Heidt's suggestion could only apply to larger mustelids. Second, minks do have delayed implantation, but this in itself does not limit litters to one per year because the delay is very short (as little as ten days). Third, there are no adequate explanations for the evolution of population self-limitation.

Wright (1963) noted that some female mustelids breed while lactating, which could result in a temporary family relationship at the time the young are being weaned. Growing young require much food, and if a courting male actively cooperated in bringing food to a female and her young, this might increase their survival. Newborn fishers need extended attendance by their mothers, and a male bringing food would reduce the amount of time mothers must be away from kits. Neither Leonard (1980b, 1986) nor Paragi (1990) recorded such behavior by males and, in contrast, found that females appeared to keep males away from natal dens. The young a female raises were conceived a year earlier, and there is no reason to believe that a male fisher can know with which females he bred the previous year or which of those females have born him offspring. There is no advantage for a male to feed offspring that are not his own.

I believed in 1982 (Powell 1982b) that the best explanation for the origin of delayed implantation was still to come and that this explanation would deal with advantages of uncoupling normal temporal relations between mating and parturition so that each can occur at an optimal time. For the fisher, mating occurs in late winter because at this time both sexes range widely for food and are most likely to be in olfactory contact. Parturition must occur in late winter for young fishers to have time to develop to independence by the following winter. I proposed that delayed implantation had a common origin among the Mustelidae—if not in a common ancestor, then at least in a common selective agent. Given that all the extant mustelids acquired delayed implantation for the same reason, I proposed that each species has tuned the evolution of delayed implantation to its own specific requirements. Therefore, to understand the evolution of delayed implantation I proposed that we look more broadly than at each species' individual use of delayed implantation.

Such a broad view was recently developed by Sandell (1990). He started with Fries's (1880, 1902) understanding that the importance of delayed implantation lies in the uncoupling of mating and parturition times, and thus Sandell's hypothesis might be considered an extension of Fries's. But Sandell has hypothesized a workable mechanism by which delayed implantation, and delayed fertilization and delayed development found in some bats, can evolve. Thus Sandell's can be considered a seventh major hypothesis.

The most common reproductive pattern in mammals has mating and parturition separated by a fixed time, the length of gestation. There is no reason to believe, however, that the optimum times for mating and parturition are always separated by the optimum gestation length. Although gestation length can be varied through evolution, such changes also involve changes in how developed neonates are at birth: shortening gestation leads to less developed young whereas lengthening gestation leads to more developed young. Evolution has generally led to parturition occurring at roughly the optimal time, whereas mating occurs a gestation length before parturition. If this is not the optimum time for mating, survivorship of males, for example, might be low because of excess energy expenditure during the breeding season when food supplies are low, or sexual selection might be limited.

Sandell (1990) started with the assumption that parturition times and gestation lengths evolved to their optima in ancestral mammals. If mating was not at its optimum time but having an immediately earlier mating date would not have been better, the potential for delayed implantation to evolve did not exist. If, however, mating was not at its optimum time and having an immediately earlier mating date would have been better, then the potential for delayed implantation to evolve did exist. A species that evolved a short delay before implantation would be able to mate at a better time. If even earlier dates were better for mating, then a longer delay might evolve. Longer and longer delays could evolve until mating reached its optimum time. A delay can potentially evolve that backs mating time to right after parturition, as occurs in fishers.

Unlike other hypotheses for the origin of delayed implantation, which attempt to explain existing reproductive patterns, Sandell's hypothesis includes a mechanism for the evolution of delayed implantation and is able to make predictions: for species with delayed implantation, all dates between the time of mating and a gestation length before the time of parturition are in some way poorer times for mating; dates earlier than the present mating time are also poorer; and for those species that have not evolved delayed implantation, earlier dates for mating are not better than the date set by gestation length. If these predictions can be proven wrong, Sandell's hypothesis will be proven wrong.

In the presentation of his hypothesis, Sandell (1990) gave many examples of species that delay implantation for which later mating dates appear to be poorer than the dates set through delay. His examples do not prove his hypothesis correct because they are taken from information Sandell used in generating the hypothesis. The examples do support the hypothesis, however. Future research will show whether predictions from the hypothesis are upheld, including the predictions that (1) a later breeding season for fishers is disadvantageous (shorter delay, parturition still in late winter), (2) shorter and shorter delays are more and more disadvantageous, and (3) no delay is the most disadvantageous of all.

Neonates and Early Development

Neonates

Newborn fishers are completely helpless (Coulter 1966; Hodgson 1937), and their eyes and ears are tightly closed (Coulter 1966). Coulter (1966) and La-Barge and co-workers (1990) observed the development of a litter of two females and one male and a litter of two males and one female born in captivity. LaBarge and co-workers (1990) made only occasional observations of their kits until they separated them from their mother at age 34 days. Although Coulter (1966) left his kits with their mother throughout development, he was able to observe them almost from their birth but did not handle them until they were 37 days old. His description (1966, 81-82) of 1- to 4-day-old fisher kits can be paraphrased as follows:

> Fishers are altricial. Neonates are blind, helpless and only partially covered with a sparse growth of fine, light gray hair over the mid-dorsal area. From the first day, they utter short, high-pitched cries somewhat similar to those of domestic kittens.
>
> Growth and development is rapid during the first few days. By the third and fourth days, almost the entire body has a growth of fine, fawn-gray hair up to 6 millimeters long along the mid-dorsal line and extending partway down the tail. Even at this early stage, young fishers show several characteristics typical of adults: long and slender bodies, rounded heads and rather flat faces, dark feet, curved claws, and relatively long, tapering tails. The male and female 3-day-old kits from a litter I did not observe closely weighed 39.0 grams and 41.2 grams, respectively.

Similar observations were made by LaBarge and co-workers (1990) and Leonard (1986), and on fur farms (Hodgson 1937). Leonard (1986) noted that both captive and wild kits cease mewing when their mothers leave the nest.

Leonard (1980b) suggested that being so altricial may be adaptive in fishers because little developmental or physiological damage would be done to neonates if their temperatures were to drop during their mother's absence for hunting or mating shortly after their birth. Giving birth to altricial young also allows female fishers to hunt unburdened with heavy fetuses.

Other mustelines are born in a similar condition. Newborn least weasels are naked and acquire only fine white hair during their first day of life (Heidt 1970; Heidt, Petersen, and Kirkland 1968). At 1 day of age, short-tailed weasels and long-tailed weasels are covered with only fine white hair (East and Lockie 1965; Hamilton 1933). In all three species, the hair is most profuse along the back. Newborn least weasels weigh about 1.4 grams (Heidt 1970), and newborn short-tailed weasels weigh about 1.7 grams (Hamilton 1933).

Pelage

At 2 weeks of age, the kits observed by LaBarge and co-workers (1990) were light silver-gray. My two kits were completely covered with downy gray hair at 18 days of age.* When 25 days old, they were still gray in color, but a

---

*Some of the observations I made in my research journals about my two hand-raised fisher kits have only been reported in the first edition of this book (Powell 1982b). In this section (Neonates and Early Development), such information about my kits is not followed by a citation.

small light-colored mark was detectable on the chest of the female. That mark later developed into a white chest patch. At 3 weeks of age, the litter Coulter (1966) observed had changed to a chocolate-brown color over the back, with sparse light straw-colored hair on the flanks and sparse fawn-gray hair 2 to 4 millimeters long on the chest and stomach. At that age the kits LaBarge and co-workers observed had begun to turn dark brown, mostly on their heads and underparts. In Coulter's and my litters, hair around the mammae in both sexes and around the penis of the males was distinctly light gray colored.

Coulter (1966) was first able to detect a white patch in the genital region of a kit at 7 weeks; the white patch was completely developed by the time the kit was 10 weeks old. At about 10 to 12 weeks my kits changed to the chocolate-brown color Coulter's had acquired when several weeks younger. From this age on, the tricolored guard hairs characteristically found on the head, neck, and shoulders of adults could be seen but with a restricted distribution. Thus, through the summer and the early autumn, young fishers are the same general color as adults but are more uniform in color.

The white hair on least weasels, short-tailed weasels, and long-tailed weasels persists until they are about 2½ to 3 weeks old. By this time, some darker pigmentation can be found leading down from the back, and some brown hairs have appeared on the back. By shortly after 3 weeks of age, least weasels have acquired adult pelage. The black tail tip on long-tailed weasels can be distinguished by 3 weeks of age, and by 5 weeks long-tailed weasels have acquired pelage closely resembling that of adults. Short-tailed weasels do not acquire adult pelage until they are approximately 6 to 7 weeks old (East and Lockie 1965; Hamilton 1933; Heidt 1970; Heidt, Petersen, and Kirkland 1968). Thus, it appears that fishers retain distinguishable juvenile pelage to an older age than do the three species of weasels.

Weight and Other Measurements

The kits observed by LaBarge and co-workers (1990) were 34 to 36 centimeters in total length at 34 to 36 days. At 43 days they had chest girths (at the heart) of 12.5 to 15.5 centimeters. These increased as follows: 51 days, 14.0 to 15.5 centimeters; 58 days, 15.0 to 16.0 centimeters; 66 days 15.5 to 16.0 centimeters; 71 days, 17.0 to 17.5 centimeters.

Coulter (1966) obtained the weights of two dead 3-day-old fisher kits, the weights of two female kits as they grew from 40 through 96 days of age, the weight of one male kit 44 days old, and the weight of a wild kit aged approximately 4 months. LaBarge and co-workers (1990) obtained weights for two males and one female kit for ages 34 to 82 days. Christopher A. Kline and

Michael Don Carlos (Minnesota Zoological Society, unpublished records) obtained the weight of one stillborn kit shortly after birth and the weights of three males and two females from ages 7 days to over 200 days. I was able to follow the weight gain of my two kits from 18 through 177 days of age. The lightest kits of each sex (Coulter's) and the heaviest (Kline and Don Carlos's) were raised by their mothers in captivity. The kits hand raised by LaBarge and co-workers and by me were intermediate in weight. Thus, whether kits were hand raised or raised by their mothers did not appear to affect weight gain. Figure 27 shows growth curves (approximate Gompertz growth curves) fitted to all data for males and females.

Growth continues later in male fishers than in females, and there is probably geographic variability in growth. The epiphyses of all long bones of juvenile male fishers from Maine are open in November, indicating continued growth, whereas the epiphyses of the long bones of females are partially fused (Wright and Coulter 1967). In contrast, only about 17% of juvenile male fishers from Ontario have open epiphyses in their femurs in November, and the epiphyses of females' femurs are completely fused (Dagg, Leach, and Sumner-Smith 1975).

Sexual dimorphism in weight is pronounced by late autumn (Coulter 1966; Hodgson 1937). Although the male kit in my litter was heavier than his sister from the time they were first weighed, the male in the litter observed by Coulter (1966) weighed less than his sisters at 44 days of age. Unfortunately, that male kit died at 44 days of age, so a comparison of the male's weight to the females' weights at later ages could not be made. Noticeable differences in weight are not apparent until around age 3 months (Figure 27). At that age the female in my litter weighed slightly more than 75% as much as the male. The captured wild kit weighed by Coulter (1966) weighed approximately the same as the kits in his litter at 4 months of age.

Sexual dimorphism develops much faster in the smaller mustelines. American martens reach full size at about 3 months of age and, therefore, have shown sexual dimorphism for some time before reaching maturity (Markley and Bassett 1942). Sexual dimorphism in body size begins to become pronounced sometime after the fourth week of age in least weasels (East and Lockie 1965; Heidt 1970) and after the eighth week in minks (Travis and Schaible 1961). At these ages, these species have reached 50% to 75% of their full size. Sexual dimorphism in weight of European fitch ferrets of laboratory stock may be apparent at birth (Hahn and Wester 1969).

Other Physical Development

Fishers stay quite helpless for weeks following birth (Coulter 1966; Hodgson 1937), and at 18 days of age, my kits were only able to grasp awkwardly with

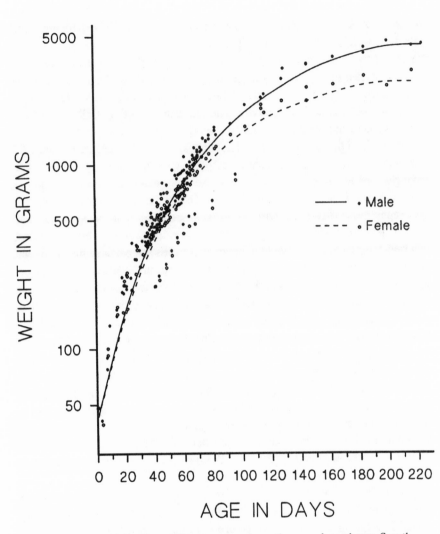

Figure 27. Weights of fisher kits at different ages, and growth curves for each sex. Growth curves approximating Gompertz curves were fitted to all weight data provided by Coulter (1966), Kline and Don Carlos (Minnesota Zoological Society, unpublished reports), and LaBarge and co-workers (1990) and from my unpublished records.

their claws. By 21 days, they were able to crawl around on the wool rags in their box and crawl up the sides (approximately 15 centimeters high) well enough to put their heads over the edge. At 21 days of age, the male stood up to defecate, but he was very unstable. My kits did not make consistent attempts to hold themselves up until they were about 7 weeks old. By 7½ weeks, they walked clumsily. At about 8 weeks, they began uncoordinated climbing on the branches propped in their enclosure. Even though by 10 weeks both of them could run with the typical fisher gait, they still crawled frequently. At 12 weeks of age, the female kit climbed 3 meters up a tree.

In contrast, the kits Coulter (1966) observed did not begin their awkward crawling until they were 8 weeks old, and they did not walk until they were over 9 weeks old. Grinnell and co-workers (1937, 226-227) mentioned that fisher kits about 3 months old could "scamper about as young squirrels do" on the rocks surrounding their den.

One of my kits began to open one eye on day 45, and both kits had both eyes open by day 49. Coulter (1966) noted that his kits had their eyes open when they were 53 days old, and the kits LaBarge and co-workers (1990) observed opened their eyes on days 48, 54, and 55. These ages are consistent with Hodgson's (1937, 41) description of fishers raised on fur farms: "They are about seven weeks old before their eyes open."

My kits' teeth began to break through when they were about 40 days old. The deciduous premolars came first. The canines had completely broken through at 7 weeks. LaBarge and co-workers also noted eruption of premolars on day 40. They could feel deciduous canines through their kits' gums at that time, but the canines were not fully erupted until 7 weeks (50 days). In Coulter's kits, the canines did not completely erupt until 9 weeks of age.

Fisher kits are completely dependent on milk until they are 8 to 10 weeks old. Starting at 8 weeks, my kits became fussy about taking formula (Esbilac) from a bottle, so I introduced them to a mash made from pureed venison (white-tailed deer) and formula. By 10 weeks they were completely weaned to whole road-killed mammals and birds. LaBarge and co-workers weaned their kits from formula to a mixture of strained chicken baby food and formula. Over 3 weeks they gradually introduced a horse-meat base canine food until the kits were on this diet entirely. Coulter first noticed his mother fisher taking meat to the kits when they were 62 days old: "During the following few days the kits ate small portions of meat, but were unable to tear pieces from larger chunks. By the 83rd day they were eating much meat regularly, although the only visible teeth were the canines and first premolars" (Coulter 1966, 91). Weaning of Coulter's kits took place at around 4 months, but the kits still occasionally nursed up to 114 days of age.

Like fishers, least weasels, short-tailed weasels, and long-tailed weasels are all born with their eyes and ears closed. Eyes open at 26 to 30 days in least weasels and at around 35 days of age in the other two species. Sound can probably first be heard between 3 and 4 weeks of age, depending on the species. The deciduous canines and premolars erupt at about 10 to 14 days of age in least weasels, but not until 21 to 25 days of age in short-tailed and long-tailed weasels. The young of all three species begin ingesting solid food at around 3 weeks of age, and weaning occurs when they are between 5 and 8 weeks old

(East and Lockie 1965; Hamilton 1933; Heidt 1970; Heidt, Petersen, and Kirkland 1968). American martens are weaned at about 6 to 7 weeks of age (Markley and Bassett 1942). It appears that fishers may be relatively older than these other mustelines when they begin to take solid food; for example, the weasels take solid food before their eyes are open.

Behavioral Development

Most observations of the behavioral development of fishers have been made of behaviors related to prey catching and feeding. At about 53 days old, my hand-raised female fisher kit began grabbing and shaking pieces of bedding material in play. She did this frequently by day 55; the male did it occasionally. After being fed puree on day 55, the female kit rubbed her chin back and forth on the towel in my lap. I have observed adult fishers, American martens, long-tailed weasels, short-tailed weasels, and European polecats rubbing their chins back and forth on the ground after eating and during play. These species probably all have glands on their chins and necks (see chapter 2).

Coulter (1966, 92) described the development of killing behavior in growing fisher kits:

> Beginning at age 90 days, dead Coturnix quail were placed in the pen. At the first trial the kits sniffed the strange object and began to play with it. In a few minutes they dragged it into the nest box where the adult began to tear it up. The young became increasingly excited on the second and third trials at intervals of three days. On the third trial they pounced upon the dead bird and began to eat it. After the fifth trial with dead birds a live one was introduced. The larger, dominant kit immediately seized it, carried it to shelter, and both young began to eat from it, but without killing it. It was obvious that they did not know how to kill at 106 days. In later trials the kits attacked live birds, crippled mice and red squirrels. They were about 125 days old before the dominant kit began to attack the head and neck region of small prey as is typically done by adults.

I presented my fisher kits with their first live prey—a wild baby snowshoe hare—when they were 93 days old. They generally ignored it. The male did chase the hare a bit in what appeared to be play. At this same age, he began to play pounce on objects within his enclosure.

When they were 121 days old, I again presented my hand-raised kits with a young snowshoe hare. The male cautiously nipped at the hare's rump and neck while both he and the hare were confined in a small cage. The hare then escaped into the kits' enclosure and was chased by the male kit. When the hare was again confined, the male kit made a directed bite to the back of the hare's neck. He was surprised by an accidental disturbance in the enclosure, however, and released his grip on the hare. After this age, both kits killed hares in the same manner as adults.

Young American martens are able to kill proficiently by 2½ months of age (Remington 1952), a considerably younger age than fishers. This ability is probably related to their rapid attainment of full adult weight.

Young least weasels show aggressive behavior toward live mice as early as 32 days of age, but until about their 38th day they will only play with dead mice (Heidt 1970). When a litter of least weasels was 40 days old, Heidt and his co-workers (Heidt 1970; Heidt, Petersen, and Kirkland 1968) observed their mother presenting them with one dead mouse and one immobilized live mouse. The young played with the immobilized mouse. Gillingham (1978) observed similar behavior in a family of short-tailed weasels when the kits were 51 days old. Heidt and co-workers (Heidt 1970; Heidt, Petersen, and Kirkland 1968) interpreted this behavior to be parental instruction of the kits on how to kill. Young least weasels are adept at killing by 42 to 45 days of age (Heidt 1970; Heidt, Petersen, and Kirkland 1968). Short-tailed weasels begin to show interest in live mice at around 9 weeks of age and may kill as early as 10 weeks of age (Gillingham 1978), but killing may not begin until 11 or 12 weeks of age (East and Lockie 1965; Gillingham 1978). By 12 weeks of age, short-tailed weasels can kill proficiently (Gillingham 1978). Young short-tailed weasels will not kill mice until they have become proficient at seizing and securing mice (Gillingham 1978). The weasels do this by wrapping themselves around the mice and holding them with all four paws.

Fishers do not require parental instruction to learn proper killing techniques (Powell 1977a; Kelly 1977). My hand-raised kits killed snowshoe hares, red squirrels, and porcupines with the proper techniques even though a live porcupine was first presented to the female when she was two years old (Powell 1977a). Kelly gave live red squirrels to two hand-raised female fishers who were several years old (they were believed to be littermates). According to him (1977, 164), "both fishers killed squirrels quickly by biting the base of the head." To Kelly's knowledge, neither of these fishers had been given live prey before that time.

Intraspecific aggression in fishers begins to appear when the kits are around 3 months old. Coulter (1966) and I took special care to see that both kits in our respective litters obtained enough food when they reached that age. I separated my kits at age 5½ months because of aggressive behavior over food (Powell 1977a). The mother fisher observed by Coulter (1966) became increasingly hostile toward her kits beginning late in their fourth month. The kits began sleeping in a nest box separate from their mother at that time and shortly thereafter began sleeping in individual nest boxes. At age 5½ months, one kit was killed and the other injured by the mother. Hodgson (1937, 42) said of fishers raised on fur farms:

They should be separated from their mother when about ten weeks of age up to twelve weeks. By this time they have learned to eat well and like some children have learned to scrap as well. It is necessary to feed them in separate pens. They are best placed two in a pen at three months of age and it may be necessary in a short time to place them in individual pens.

Coulter (1966, 85) speculated that a delay in the development of the pronounced sexual dimorphism in body size may be "an adaptation of definite advantage to the growth and survival of females." Because of aggression between littermates, differences in weight could place small littermates at a distinct disadvantage when food is not provided regularly and in good quantity. This is a kin selection argument.

Wild kits followed by Paragi (1990) using radiotelemetry remained in their mothers' territories into the winter. The kits, now juveniles, appeared to avoid somewhat the areas in which their mothers spent the most time. This could have been to avoid aggressive interactions or to avoid areas most heavily hunted by their mothers. By age 9 months, a third of the male juveniles but no female juveniles had dispersed and established their own home ranges. By age 1 year, juveniles had established their own home ranges (Arthur 1987; Paragi 1990).

One final behavior of interest has been noted. Up until they were about 5 months old, my hand-raised kits readily accepted the presence of strange people in their enclosures. After 6 or 7 months, however, both acted very aggressively toward strangers in their enclosures and attacked people who entered. Don Carlos (personal communication) and Laberee (1941) also made this observation, but Laberee stated that adult fishers could be tamed to accept new people when properly handled. Similar behavior has been identified in other solitary carnivores (Fox 1978).

Longevity, Disease, Parasites, and Mortality

Fishers have lived longer than 10 years in zoos (unpublished records, Bronx Zoo, New York Zoological Society), but their longevity in the wild is not well known. Arthur and co-workers (1992) recorded a wild fisher living for 10½ years. Weckwerth and Wright (1968) provided data on seven fishers released in Montana in 1959 and 1960 and subsequently trapped in sets for other furbearers. One female fisher was recovered in February 1966, at least 6 years after her release. Because all the fishers were at least yearlings when they were released, this female was at least 7 years old. By counting cementum annuli, Kelly (1977) calculated that of 202 fishers caught by trappers in New Hampshire, 1 female and 2 males were 6 years old and 4 males were 7 years old. Because age estimates from cementum annuli tend to underestimate ages of fishers 3 years old and older (Arthur et al. 1992), some of these fishers were probably older. Data on the recovery of tagged fishers from Wisconsin and Michigan releases are even less extensive than those from Montana and New Hampshire (Irvine and Brander 1971). However, I captured no tagged fishers during intensive trapping near one of the Michigan release sites between 1973 and 1976. Thus, approximately 10 years may be an upper limit to the life expectancy of wild fishers.

Fishers exhibit a low incidence of diseases, but enough carcasses of harvested fishers have been studied and enough fishers have been live-trapped to document sarcoptic mange (Coulter 1966; O'Meara, Payne, and Witter 1960), Aleutian disease, leptospirosis, toxoplasmosis, and trichinosis (Douglas and Strickland 1987). Fishers and American martens appear to be the main vectors for sylvatic trichinosis in the boreal regions of Canada (Dick et al. 1986).

Fishers in the Algonquin region of Ontario have detectable levels of DDT, chlordane, dieldrin, mirex, and PCBs (Douglas and Strickland 1987). The fishers exhibit no harmful effects from these chemicals, which, except for DDT, must have been transported atmospherically. DDT use in Ontario ceased around 1970.

Incidence of parasites in fishers is lower than in many other mustelids (Hamilton and Cook 1955). Even in those studies of animals in which infestation has been common, individual fishers had few parasites (Coulter 1966). There have been no reports of fishers showing any signs of suffering from parasitism (Coulter 1966; deVos 1952; Douglas and Strickland 1987; Hamilton and Cook 1955; Powell 1977a).

Fourteen genera of nematodes, two genera of cestodes, two genera of trematodes, and a protozoan have been found in fishers (Table 7). In addition, three ectoparasites have been reported: one tick, one mite, and one flea.

Natural causes of fisher mortality are not well known. Fishers have been found to choke on food (Krohn, Arthur, and Paragi, in press) and to become debilitated by porcupine quills (Coulter 1966; deVos 1952; Hamilton and Cook 1955; see chapter 8). Mange or any of the parasites listed in Table 7 could adversely affect a fisher's health if the infestation were extremely advanced. Death could then result from the parasitism or the effects of the parasitism (such as susceptibility to disease, reduced hunting ability, and the animal's consequent starvation or predation). There is little evidence that healthy adult fishers are subject to predation. It is likely, however, that any predator would kill and eat a fisher that was unable to defend itself. A fisher in Maine was trapped on the ice and killed by coyotes (Krohn, Arthur, and Paragi, in press), and a fisher was killed by a dog in Ontario (Douglas and Strickland 1987). An adult

Table 7. Parasites and incidence of parasitism in fishers

Organism	Incidence (%)	Source
Nematodes		
Arthridephalus lotoris	11	Hamilton & Cook 1955
Baylisascaris devosi	5	deVos 1952
	32	Dick & Leonard 1979
Ascaris mustelarum	25	Meyer & Chitwood 1951
	-	Coulter 1966
Capillaria spp.	5	Coulter 1966
	-	Cheatum 1949
Capillaria mustelorum	35	Hamilton & Cook 1955
Capillaria plica and		Butterworth & Beverley-
C. *putorii*	-	Burton 1980, 1981
Crenosoma spp.	15	Coulter 1966
	3	Meyer & Chitwood 1951
Crenosoma petrowi	15	Craig & Borecky 1976
Dioctophyma renale[*]	-	Coulter 1966
	-	Douglas & Strickland 1987
Dracunculus spp.	-	Coulter 1966
Dracunculus insignis	13	Hamilton & Cook 1955
	-	Douglas & Strickland 1987
	-	Fyvie & Addison 1979
Molineus patens	5	Hamilton & Cook 1955
	1	Dick & Leonard 1979
Physaloptera spp.	5	deVos 1952
	6	Dick & Leonard 1979
Physaloptera maxillaris[*]	11	Hamilton & Cook 1955
Skrjabingylus spp.	12	Addison et al. 1988
Sobolevingulus spp.	2	Craig & Borecky 1976
Soboliphyme baturini	-	Erickson 1946
	-	Morgan 1942
Trichinella spiralis	1	Dick & Leonard 1979
	5	Dick et al. 1986
	-	Worley et al. 1974
Trilobostrongylus bioccai	-	Anderson 1963
	21	Craig & Borecky 1976
Uncinaria stenocephasa	2	Hamilton & Cook 1955
	-	Chitwood 1932
Cestodes		
Mesocestoides variabilis	7	Coulter 1966
	5	deVos 1952
	6	Hamilton & Cook 1955
	50	Meyer & Chitwood 1951
Taenia spp.	9	Coulter 1966
Taenia siberica	15	Dick & Leonard 1979
Trematodes		
Alaria spp.	6	Coulter 1966
Alaria mustelae	1	Dick & Leonard 1979
Metorchis conjunctus	1	Dick & Leonard 1979
Protozoa		
Isopara spp.[*]	-	deVos 1952

Ticks		
Ixodes cookei[*]	-	deVos 1952
Mites		
Sarcoptes scabei	-	O'Meara, Payne, & Witter 1960
	-	Coulter 1966
Fleas		
Oropsylla arctomys	-	Holland 1950

Note: – means that incidence was not reported.

* means that the identification was tentative at the time the source was published.

female fisher in northern California was killed by a large raptor, probably a golden eagle or great horned owl (Buck, Mullis, and Mossman 1983). Reintroduction of fishers to the Cabinet Mountains of Montana was hindered by predation (Roy 1991). Of thirty-two fishers from Wisconsin released in the Cabinet Mountains, at least nine were killed by other predators. All appeared to have been in good health. It is possible that the changes in habitat, topography, prey, and predators somehow made these fishers vulnerable to predation.

Past and Present Distribution and Population Fluctuations

Chapter 4

The genus *Martes* is Holarctic in distribution, but fishers are found only in North America. Their present range is reduced from their range before the settlement of the continent by Europeans (Gibilisco, in press; Graham and Graham, in press; Hagmeier 1956), but most of this reduction has occurred in the United States (Figure 28). The northern limit to the fisher's range during historical times has always been around 60° north latitude in the west and somewhat south of the southern tip of James Bay in the east, following the 15.5° C (60° F) isotherm. Habitat probably determined this northern limit. The tree line, and therefore the northern limit to habitat for fishers, is farther north west of Hudson Bay than east of it (Drew and Shagg 1965; Larsen 1965; Marr 1948). Once fishers ranged from what is now northern British Columbia into central California in the Pacific coastal mountains

74

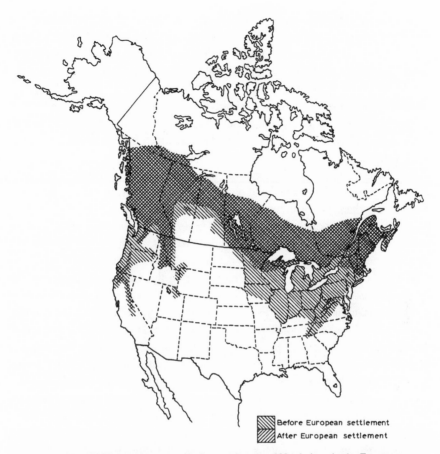

| | Before European settlement |
| | After European settlement |

Figure 28. Map of fisher species range before settlement of North America by Europeans, and at present. (Adapted by C. B. Powell; based on Banville 1980; Earle 1978; Gibilisco, in press; Graham and Graham, in press; Hagmeier 1956; Hall 1981; Petersen, Martin, and Pils 1977; and Powell 1977a.)

and south into Idaho, Montana, and probably Wyoming in the Rocky Mountains. In what is now the central United States, fishers may have ranged as far south as southern Illinois (Gibilisco, in press; Graham and Graham 1990, in press; Hagmeier 1956). And in the eastern part of the continent, fishers ranged as far south as what is now North Carolina and Tennessee in the Appalachian Mountains (Gibilisco, in press; Graham and Graham, in press; Hagmeier 1956). Pringle (1964) stated that they once ranged into Georgia, and Barkalow (1961) found remains of fishers in Alabama. It is possible, however, that the fisher remains found from southern Illinois to Alabama are artifacts created by the trading and travel patterns of Native Americans (Barkalow 1961; Graham and Graham 1990).

The fisher's former range is very similar to the combined distributions of northern hemlock-hardwood, western mountain, and boreal forests (forest ranges taken from Cronquist 1961), with some intriguing exceptions. In the Rocky Mountains of the United States, fishers never occupied extensive appropriate habitat from Wyoming south. In Idaho, Montana, Wyoming, Utah, and Colorado there are many isolated mountain ranges of various sizes with habitat for fishers. These mountain ranges are like islands, separated by variable and often long distances of arid grassland, through which fishers would have difficulty traveling. Gibilisco (in press) argued that patterns of local extinction and recolonization explain the pattern of American marten distribution in these mountain ranges. The same could be true for fishers. But, because fishers are much larger than American martens and therefore require large habitat patches to maintain viable populations, whatever fisher populations ever developed in these isolated mountain ranges have all gone extinct, leaving fisher populations only in areas with large, continuous northern and mountain forests.

This picture, however, is incomplete. During the Ice Ages, populations of American martens moved south, following the mountain forests as they moved south (Graham and Graham, in press). When the glaciers retreated, marten populations moved back north, but some remained in large patches of mountain forests found at high elevations in the Southwest. Today, American martens are found as far south as New Mexico (Gibilisco, in press). Were the fisher's range a product of historic vegetation patterns, fishers should be found in the extensive, high-elevation forests in Colorado; yet fishers have never been found further south than Wyoming or the Great Salt Lake (Graham and Graham, in press). This is probably a reflection of past competition with an extinct marten, the noble marten (*Martes nobilis*), closely related to the American marten but larger (Graham and Graham, in press). From the late Pleistocene, about 20,000 years ago, to the late Holocene, about 4,000 years ago, noble martens were found in western North America, and American martens were found across the continent. The fossil and subfossil record of the fisher is entirely confined to eastern North America until the late Holocene. Only when the noble marten range began to retreat to the Southwest did fishers begin to enter the Rocky Mountains of what is now the United States. By then, breaks in the mountains, and hence forests, in Utah and Wyoming may have prevented fishers from spreading south throughout the Rockies.

Because many mammal species exhibited gigantism during the Pleistocene, the noble marten may not actually have been a distinct species, but rather a large subspecies of the American marten (Youngman and Schueler 1991). Other subspecies of the American marten were also large in the Pleistocene but evolved smaller body sizes during the Holocene. The noble marten, however, appeared not to have become smaller (Anderson, in press; Graham and Graham, in press). Whether the noble marten was a distinct species or not is probably a moot point with respect to fishers. Noble martens were large, though not as large as fishers, and may have prevented fishers from colonizing mountain forest habitat in the central Rocky Mountains.

Population Decline

During the last part of the nineteenth century and the early part of the twentieth century, the number of fishers decreased strikingly, and fishers were exterminated over much of their former range in the United States (Brander and Books 1973; Coulter 1966; deVos 1951, 1952). The decline in population was significant in almost all areas populated by humans, and it was precipitous in some places. Fishers were nearly exterminated in the United States and in much of eastern Canada (Bensen 1959; Coulter 1966; deVos 1952; Dodds and Martell 1971; Dodge 1977; Hall 1942; Ingram 1973; Rand 1944; Schorger 1942; Weckwerth and Wright 1968).

There were two reasons for the decline in fisher populations: trapping and logging. Both are capable of reducing fisher populations today, and information available about the decline does not indicate if one may have been more important than the other in the past. In addition, trapping and logging are not independent because logging increases the access that trappers have to penetrate into forested regions.

Fishers are known by fur trappers as one of the easiest animals to trap (Young 1975), and prices paid for fisher pelts, especially the silky, glossy pelts of females, have always been high. Before the 1920s, there were no trapping regulations for fishers, and between 1900 and 1930 an excellent fisher pelt could bring up to $150 (Balser 1960; Hamilton and Cook 1955; Irvine, Magnus, and Bradle 1964; Petersen, Martin, and Pils 1977). Around 1920 one pelt went for $345 (Seton 1926). Except for prices in the 1970s and 1980s, the peak prices paid for fisher pelts came in 1920, when the average price was around $85 (Brander and Books 1973), providing trappers with strong incentive to trap fishers. Prices have never been stable, however, and have not been the same throughout the United States and Canada. Between 1916 and the early 1930s, average prices in New York, which were higher than those paid in California (Grinnell, Dixon, and Linsdale 1937), bounced from around $16 to $65, back down to $38, up to $50, and finally back down to around $20 (Balser 1960; Hamilton and Cook 1955). From 1930 to 1940, average prices paid for fisher pelts in Ontario ranged from around $40 to $53 each year, but some excellent pelts brought nearly $100 (Rand 1944). In 1940 the average price paid in Ontario for fisher pelts ($53) exceeded that paid for lynxes ($36), American martens ($30), beavers ($18), and silver foxes ($15) (Rand 1944). Fashions changed

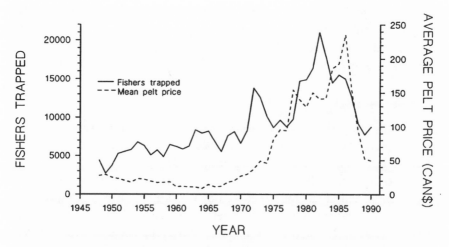

Figure 29. Numbers of fishers trapped and average prices paid to trappers for pelts in Canada from the 1948-49 through the 1991-92 trapping seasons. (Source: Anon. 1978, 1992.)

during the 1940s, however, and the demand for fisher fur dropped. Consequently, by 1951 fisher pelts brought only $20 to $25 and by the late 1950s and 1960s less than $15 (Balser 1960; Brander and Books 1973; Hamilton and Cook 1955).

The demand for fisher fur increased again during the late 1970s, and in 1979 the Hudson's Bay Company paid $410 for a pale-colored female fisher pelt. The average price paid to trappers increased through 1986, when it peaked at over $235, with the pelts of females averaging somewhat more than those of males (Anon. 1978, 1992). The total numbers of fishers trapped and the average pelt values in Canada from the 1948-49 through the 1990-91 trapping seasons are shown in Figure 29.

Fishers have seldom been considered to be common animals anywhere. Nonetheless, the changes in fisher populations were noticed. The decrease in fisher populations began earlier in the eastern than in the midwestern and western states, undoubtedly because of the longer history of European settlement in the East. New York's fisher populations had already begun to decrease by 1850 (Hamilton and Cook 1955), but the decrease in Wisconsin was not great before the first part of the twentieth century. In Wisconsin, 559 fishers were trapped during the 1917-18 trapping season; the following year, only 17 fishers; the next year, 5; and in the 1920-21 trapping season, only 3 (Scott 1939). (Schorger [1942] noted that the 559 figure may be inflated since otters were sometimes reported as fishers.) Wisconsin closed its fisher trapping season in 1921. There were scattered reports of fishers in Wisconsin for the following few years (Scott 1939), but by 1932 the fisher was believed to be extinct in Wisconsin (Hine 1975). A similar history is known for the fisher in Michigan. The last native fishers reported from Michigan were trapped during the 1931-32 trapping season in the Upper Peninsula (Schorger 1942), although a few still may have existed as late as 1936 (Manville 1948). Extremely small fisher populations remained in California, Oregon, and Washington (Aubry and Houston 1992; Schempf and White 1977; Yocum and McCollum 1973), but the last reliable reports of native fishers in Montana and Idaho came from no later than the 1920s (Dodge 1977; Weckwerth and Wright 1968).

Because of warnings from biologists, other states followed the example set by Wisconsin and closed their fisher trapping seasons. Minnesota closed its season in 1929, New Hampshire in 1934, Maine in 1935, New York and Wyoming in 1936, Oregon in 1937, and Montana sometime in the 1930s (Brander and Books 1973; Coulter 1966; Kelly 1977; Weckwerth and Wright 1968). Despite warnings as early as 1925, however, California delayed closing its fisher trapping season (Hall 1942). The number of fishers trapped in California dropped from 102 in 1920 to 34 during 1924 and did not rise above 20 after 1926 nor above 10 following 1933 (Hall 1942). By the time California finally closed its fisher season in 1946, no other states had open fisher-trapping seasons (Brander and Books 1973).

The decrease in the fisher population in Canada was more confusing than the decrease in the United States, but it was still obvious. Because of the large numbers of fishers trapped in Canada, the cyclic changes in fisher population sizes showed up in the numbers of fishers trapped (Figure 29). These cyclic changes confused some people attempting to analyze data on numbers of fishers trapped. Between 1920 and 1950, however, the number of fishers trapped, adjusted to the phases of the ten-year population cycle, declined by 75% in Ontario (deVos 1952; Rand 1944). Populations over all of Canada showed significant declines; the numbers of fishers trapped throughout the entire country declined by approximately 40% between 1920 and 1940 (deVos 1942; Rand 1944). Fishers were completely exterminated from Nova Scotia (Bensen 1959; Dodds and Martell 1971; Rand 1944). Because of the increase in pelt prices during the 1970s and 1980s, numbers of fishers trapped nearly doubled those of the 1940s (Anon. 1978; Figure 29).

During the same time that fishers were heavily trapped, their habitat was destroyed. By the mid-nineteenth century, the forested area of New Hampshire had been reduced to approximately 50% from 95% 200 years earlier (Silver 1957). A similar reduction in forested area occurred over much of the northeastern United States at about the same time (Brander and Books 1973; Hamilton and Cook 1955; Wood 1977). Forests were cleared by loggers and farmers and by frequent forest fires (Hamilton and Cook 1955; Silver 1957). Land cleared by logging often became farmland and did not return to forest. Land clearing in the Midwest occurred during the early twentieth century (Brander and Books 1973; Irvine, Bradle, and Magnus 1962; Irvine, Magnus, and Bradle 1964). "The forests of [Wisconsin and Upper Peninsula Michigan] were cut over by the early 1900's and much of the area was burned over during and after the logging era" (Irvine, Bradle, and Magnus 1962, 2). Because of the fisher's preference for extensive forests with continuous canopy, there is no question that logging and the associated fires had an adverse effect on fisher populations. The loss of habitat may have been more devastating than the overtrapping (Hamilton and Cook 1955).

Either trapping or habitat destruction by itself could have dramatically reduced fisher populations. Together, their effect was extreme. During the 1930s, remnant fisher populations in the United States could be found only on the Moosehead Plateau of Maine, in the White Mountains in New Hampshire, in the Adirondack Mountains in New York, in the "Big Bog" area of Minnesota, and in scattered regions in the Pacific coastal mountains (Brander and Books 1973; Coulter 1966; Ingram 1973; Schorger 1942). In eastern Canada, the only remnant population was on the Cumberland Plateau in New Brunswick (Coulter 1966).

Recovery and Reintroduction

Concurrent with the closure of trapping seasons during the 1930s, the logging boom came to an end, and abandoned farmland began to return to forest in the Northeast and Midwest in the United States and in eastern Canada. The return of forest allowed the remnant fisher populations in these areas to begin to recover (Balser and Longley 1966; Brander and Books 1973; Yocum and McCollum 1973). By 1949, wildlife managers in New York felt that the fisher population in that state had recovered enough to reopen a trapping season. Trapping seasons were reinitiated in Maine in 1955 after an experimental season in 1951 to collect data, in New Hampshire and West Virginia in 1969, in Massachusetts in 1972, in Vermont in 1974, in Minnesota and Nova Scotia in 1977, and in Wisconsin in 1985. State wildlife agencies are now better able to adjust trapping regulations to prevent population decline, but populations have nonetheless not remained stable. Maine limited the harvest in 1977, New Hampshire reclosed its season in 1977, New York closed its season for 1977, and Minnesota has adjusted its season to prevent overtrapping (Berg and Kuehn, in press).

Following the reduction in fisher populations, porcupine populations climbed to extremely high densities in much of the forested lands in the United States (Cook and Hamilton 1957; Earle 1978). Porcupines were blamed for much timber damage (Brander and Books 1973; Cook and Hamilton 1957; Earle 1978; Irvine 1960a, 1960b, 1961; Irvine, Bradle, and Magnus 1962; Irvine, Magnus, and Bradle 1964), though the damage was often exaggerated (Earle 1978). Earle (1978, 7) summarized the damage:

> The porcupine conflicts with human interests in its choice of winter foods. Consumption of the phloem disrupts the downward flow of sugars in a tree (Baldwin 1934). The resulting wound also provides an avenue for the entry of disease and insects (Frothingham 1915). Some species of trees respond to porcupine damage by impregnating the xylem beneath the surface of the scar with resin. An over-rolling of tissue from the perimeter of the scar is another method of responding to this damage, separately or in conjunction with xylem impregnation.

Many biologists have attempted to quantify economically the amount of damage that porcupines inflict on timber stands (Curtis 1944; Curtis and Wilson 1953; Krefting et al. 1962; Taylor 1935). This task is difficult because porcupines also beneficially prune trees (Curtis 1941). Damage does occur, however, in areas with very high porcupine populations. Krefting and co-workers (1962) reported that porcupines damaged 9.4% of the trees sampled in an area where porcupine population density had reached 81 porcupines per square kilometer in 1948-49. This is an exceptionally high porcupine population density, however, and the most common densities found during the 1940s and 1950s ranged from 8 to 22 porcupines per square kilometer (Brander 1973; Curtis 1944; Irvine 1960a).

During the 1950s, interest in reestablishing fisher populations in some of the fisher's former range began to increase. Concurrent declines in the porcupine populations were noted in those areas of Minnesota, Maine, and New York where the fisher populations were increasing (Balser 1960; Coulter 1966; Hamilton and Cook 1955). Cook and Hamilton (1957) suggested using fishers as a biological control for extremely high porcupine populations. They found during their study of fishers in the Adirondacks that high porcupine populations were never found in areas with fisher populations. Anecdotal evidence from trappers and loggers indicated that predation on porcupines by fishers was the reason for the low porcupine populations in areas with fisher populations (Cook and Hamilton 1957). Coulter (1966) warned, however, that there was no evidence that fishers could limit porcupine populations for long periods of time.

Nonetheless, during the late 1950s and 1960s, many states whose fisher populations had been eliminated or dramatically reduced reintroduced fishers. The purpose of these reintroductions was twofold: to reestablish a native mammal and to reduce high porcupine population densities, which were believed to be causing damage to the timber crop (Irvine, Bradle, and Magnus 1962; Irvine, Magnus, and Bradle 1964). The latter reason was given the most emphasis. Most introductions involved the cooperation of state wildlife officials from recipient and donor states, U.S. Forest Service officials, and, in some cases, wildlife officials in Canadian provinces. The first release of fishers actually took place in 1947-48 in Nova Scotia, where 12 fishers raised on fur farms were released (Bensen 1959; Dodds and Martell 1971). The release was successful, and there were scattered observations of fishers in the area during the 1950s and early 1960s. Between 1963 and 1966, Nova Scotia released 80 more fishers that had been caught wild in Maine. The fisher now appears to have been reestablished in Nova Scotia (Dodds and Martell 1971), and in 1977 the first limited fisher-trapping season since the 1947 reintroduction was allowed in the province (van Nostrand 1977).

With the apparent success of the reintroduction of fishers in Nova Scotia and the suggestion that the fisher could be used as a biological control for the porcupine, many reintroduction programs were initiated. Between 1956 and 1963, 122 fishers were moved within Ontario from the Algonquin region to northern Ontario and to Parry Sound (Berg 1982). Fishers were also moved from Bancroft Island to the Manitoulin and Bruce Peninsula areas of Ontario in 1979 through the early 1980s (Berg 1982). In Manitoba a reintroduction of 4 fishers to Riding Mountain National Park in 1972-73 apparently failed (Berg 1982). But a reintroduction of 17 fishers to the parklands of central Alberta in 1990 appears to have been successful (Gibilisco, in press; Proulx et al., in press). Proulx and co-workers showed that summer releases may be more likely to succeed than winter releases.

Eighteen fishers from the New York Adirondacks and 42 fishers from Minnesota were released in the Nicolet National Forest in Wisconsin between 1956 and 1963. Then, during 1966-67, 60 more fishers from Minnesota were released into Wisconsin's Chequamegon National Forest. Both releases were successful, and the fisher is now well established in northern Wisconsin (Irvine, Bradle, and Magnus 1962; Irvine, Magnus, and Bradle 1964; Johnson 1964; Olson 1966; Petersen, Martin, and Pils 1977; U.S. Forest Service, unpublished files; Wisconsin Department of Natural Resources, unpublished files). During the same period (1961 to 1963), 61 fishers from Minnesota were released in the Ottawa National Forest in the western end of Michigan's Upper Peninsula, just across the border from the Nicolet National Forest in Wisconsin (Irvine 1961, 1962; Irvine, Bradle, and Magnus 1962; Irvine, Magnus, and Bradle 1964; Olson 1966). The Michigan release has also been successful (Brander and Books 1973; Irvine and Brander 1971; Powell 1976, 1977a, 1977b; Michigan Department of Natural Resources, unpublished files; Thomasma, Drummer, and Peterson 1991; U.S. Forest Service, unpublished files). In 1968, 15 fishers were transferred from northeastern to northwestern Minnesota (Berg 1982).

Montana, Oregon, and Idaho all cooperated with British Columbia to obtain fishers for release during the late 1950s and early 1960s. Montana released 36 fishers in 1959 and 1960 (Morse 1961; Weckwerth and Wright 1968), Oregon released 24 in 1961 (Kebbe 1961; Morse 1961), and Idaho released 39 in

1962-63 (Dodge 1977; Morse 1961; Williams 1962). The Montana and Idaho releases appear to have been successful (Dodge 1977; Weckwerth and Wright 1968), and Montana established another release program in the Cabinet Mountains in 1988 (Roy 1991).

In 1969, West Virginia released 23 fishers from New Hampshire (Dodge 1977; Wood 1977). Unfortunately, due to a gross misunderstanding of fishers by citizens of that state, the 1971 West Virginia state legislature passed a law forbidding further releases of fishers into that state. Nonetheless, the fisher population has grown and is well established.

Fishers were probably never exterminated in Vermont. However, the population density was so low and emigration from established populations in nearby states so slow that wildlife officials decided to release 124 fishers from Maine between 1959 and 1967 (Dodge 1977; Wood 1977). The population in Vermont appeared to be well established by 1974 (Dodge 1977). A reintroduction of 25 fishers from northern to southern New Brunswick in 1966-68 apparently failed (Dilworth 1974), as did a transfer of 7 fishers from western to eastern Maine (Berg 1982).

New York never lost its fisher population, and the population seems to have expanded its range during the 1970s. In 1975, state hunters agreed to an increase in license fees to cover the expenses of reestablishing fishers in the Catskill Mountains. By 1979, 43 fishers had been transferred to the Catskills from the Adirondacks (Berg 1982; Kelsey 1977; Wood 1977).

Massachusetts and Connecticut have also reestablished fisher populations. The highest fisher densities are in north-central Massachusetts, probably due to fishers that emigrated from Maine and New Hampshire (Dodge 1977). By 1977 there were scattered sightings along the coast north of Boston (Wood 1977), an area that has never supported a high fisher population (Dodge 1977), and by 1991 there were sightings in southeastern Massachusetts (Gibilisco, in press). By 1992 fishers had spread down the Connecticut River corridor in Connecticut (Gibilisco, in press; Paul W. Rego, personal communication) and had been reintroduced to northwestern Connecticut. Fishers also traveled into Rhode Island (Dodge 1977).

Fishers have occasionally been sighted in a few other states. Since the 1960s, 2 fishers were trapped in Wyoming (Brown 1965; Dodge 1977), a fisher was trapped in far-northeastern North Dakota (Anon. 1977), and 2 fishers were trapped in South Dakota (Gibilisco, in press). Tracks were first seen in Maryland in 1974 and 1975, and a fisher was trapped in Maryland in 1977; these probably resulted from the West Virginia release (Cottrell 1978).

Thus, the range of the fisher in eastern North America has recovered much of the area lost during the first part of this century. The fisher is again living in areas from northern British Columbia to Idaho and Montana in the West, from northeastern Minnesota to Upper Michigan and northern Wisconsin in the Midwest, and in the Appalachian Mountains of New York and throughout most of the forested regions of the Northeast (Balser 1960; Banci 1989; Berg 1982; Bradle 1957; Coulter 1966; Earle 1978; Gibilisco, in press; Irvine, Bradle, and Magnus 1962; Irvine, Magnus, and Bradle 1964; Kebbe 1961; Kelly 1977; Kelsey 1977; Morse 1961; Penrod 1976; Petersen, Martin, and Pils 1977; Powell 1976, 1977a; Weckwerth and Wright 1968; Williams 1962; Wood 1977). Many states and provinces have trapping seasons for fishers, and regulations are adjusted in an attempt to maintain fisher populations that will not replicate earlier declines.

All is not necessarily well, however, with fishers. In the 1980s through 1991, trapping pressure on fishers in southcentral Maine appeared greater than the population's reproduction, and the population was probably declining (Arthur, Krohn, and Gilbert 1989a; Krohn, Arthur, and Paragi, in press). There are areas to which the fisher will never return unless there are major changes in the habitat. Such midwestern states as Illinois, Indiana, and Ohio may never again have forested areas extensive enough to support a fisher population. And in areas where there has been recent logging that fragments forests extensively, fisher populations have not recovered. There were only 88 sightings of fishers in Washington between 1955 and 1991, most of which were not supported with solid evidence, such as photographs, carcasses, or tracks (Aubry and Houston 1992). Research is being initiated to determine why fishers are so rare or extinct on the Olympic Peninsula in hopes of reestablishing a population there in the future (Keith B. Aubry and Douglas B. Houston, personal communication). Despite 3 reintroductions to Oregon, fishers are considered extirpated in the western part of the state (Harris et al. 1982). Fisher sightings were sparse following the release in 1961 and were mainly from areas near the release sites (Yocum and McCollum 1973). Ingram (1973) believed that the transplanted fishers barely supplemented the existing population. Although the fisher population in the far-northern counties of California appeared to be growing in the 1970s (Schempf and White 1977; Yocum and McCollum 1973), populations farther south in California were either low and stable or low and decreasing, depending on how far south they were (Schempf and White 1977). By 1991, biologists working for the California Department of Fish and Game projected that fishers would go extinct on the western slopes of the Sierra Nevada Mountains in the coming decades and might become extirpated throughout the Sierra Nevadas (Gibilisco, in press).

In 1990 a petition was sent to the U.S. Secretary of the Interior to have the fisher population in the Pacific Northwest listed as an endangered species (Central Sierra Audubon Society et al. 1990). The petition was denied because insufficient information was available on the past and present distribution, status, and ecological relationships of the fisher in this region (U.S. Fish and Wildlife Service 1991). This decision has placed these fishers in a catch-22: when populations are as low as they appear to be, how can one gain enough information about them? In short, the status of the fisher in the Pacific Northwest of the United States is disturbing and discouraging at best.

Population Densities

Fisher population densities vary with habitat and prey. Most of the first estimates of fisher population density were obtained from trapping records and from tracking fishers in the snow (deVos 1951, 1952; Grinnell, Dixon, and Linsdale 1937; Hamilton and Cook 1955; Quick 1953a; Rand 1944), which are at best only indexes of actual densities. DeVos (1952) interpreted fisher tracks to arrive at an estimate of 1 fisher per 2.6 square kilometers in his study area in Ontario. In contrast, Quick (1953a) estimated a density of approximately 1 fisher per 208 square kilometers from 20 fishers trapped along 1,335 kilometers of registered trap lines in British Columbia. Many other estimates have ranged from one extreme to the other (Coulter 1966).

From the first long-term study involving both extensive trapping returns and extensive snow tracking, Coulter (1966) arrived at estimated fisher densities ranging from 1 fisher per 2.6 square kilometers to 1 fisher per 11.7 square kilometers of suitable habitat in Maine. The higher density figure was found in an area from which fishers had never been extirpated, and Coulter doubted that such a high density could be sustained. Kelly (1977) used live-trapping and radiotelemetry to arrive at figures of 1 fisher per 8.9 to 9.2 square kilometers in the White Mountains of New Hampshire. These estimates adjusted to 1 fisher per 3.9 to 7.5 square kilometers of suitable habitat. Kelly also believed that such high densities could not be maintained, and he reported a decrease in the number of fishers in both New Hampshire and Maine between 1972 and 1977. From a study of fishers outfitted with transmitter collars, Arthur and co-workers (1989a) calculated a summer density of 1 fisher per 2.8 to 10.5 square kilometers and a winter density of 1 fisher per 8.3 to 20.0 square kilometers. These figures are the best available for the Northeast; they include seasonal changes in density caused by the spring birth pulse, and they give the ranges of densities possible, showing the uncertainty of the estimates.

Information on fisher densities outside the Northeast is limited. Densities in Washington and Oregon are too low to estimate. One density estimate from northern California in the late 1970s was 1 fisher per 3.2 square kilometers (Buck, Mullis, and Mossman 1983). Petersen and co-workers (1977), and I (Powell 1977a) all estimated fisher population densities in northern Wisconsin and Upper Peninsula Michigan to be at most 1 fisher per 12 or 13 square kilometers, and perhaps as low as 1 fisher per 19 square kilometers. These estimates were based on responses to questionnaires printed in magazines and sent to trappers, wardens, and county officials (Petersen, Martin, and Pils 1977); on state and federal records (Earle 1978; Petersen, Martin, and Pils 1977); and on findings from tracking and live-trapping (Johnson 1984; Powell 1977a).

The reasons for the variation in densities reported are many. It is difficult to estimate fisher population sizes because fishers do not behave according to the assumptions necessary to use most methods of estimating populations. In areas with reintroductions (Michigan and Wisconsin), low population densities may be related to a lack of time to build up large populations. Population fluctuations in the Northeast probably stem from two causes. Fisher populations are known to exhibit ten-year cycles in densities (Bulmer 1974, 1975; deVos 1952; Rand 1944) in response to ten-year cycles in snowshoe hare population densities (Bulmer 1974, 1975). However, trapping in New England has at times been intense even during recent times (Arthur, Krohn, and Gilbert 1989a; Krohn, Arthur, and Paragi, in press; Wood 1977; Young 1975), and overtrapping can reduce populations in local areas (Kelly 1977; Krohn, Arthur, and Paragi, in press).

That fisher populations do not remain stable is not surprising. Unharvested populations of all marten species exhibit marked fluctuations, sometimes in excess of an order of magnitude, in response to fluctuations in prey populations (Powell, in press a). The intrinsic rates of increase (commonly denoted as r in the ecological literature) for prey exceed those for fishers and other members of the genus *Martes*, all of which reproduce for the first time when age two or older and have small litter sizes (Mead, in press). This means that population responses of fishers always lag behind those of their prey, which, in turn, means that population sizes and mortality rates of fisher populations continually change. In the 1700s and 1800s fisher populations in Canada cycled, but the peaks and troughs of the cycles lagged about three years behind those of the snowshoe hare population. This time lag is expected for a population that declines because of juvenile or adult mortality rather than because of declines in reproduction (Bulmer 1974). A common goal of wildlife managers is to stabilize populations of fishers and other furbearers (Strickland, in press). Stable populations are easier to manage, but they cannot exhibit natural population dynamics or population structure. This, in turn, makes it more difficult to understand the mechanisms that cause natural population dynamics and that cause managed populations to fluctuate as well.

Because the age structure of a population (the proportion of individuals in each age class) is related to survivorship, the constantly changing survivorships in fisher populations lead to constantly changing age structures as well. In periods of high prey availability, juvenile fishers comprise a higher than average proportion of a population; when prey populations are low and fisher populations decline, cohorts of old fishers comprise higher than average proportions of the population (Douglas and Strickland 1987; Powell, in press a). Despite these changes, harvested populations of *Martes* species tend to be skewed more toward young animals on the average than unharvested populations (Powell, in press a). Average age structure for the heavily trapped fisher population in Ontario is heavily skewed toward young animals (Douglas and Strickland 1987).

Our understanding of age structure in fishers and other animals is hampered by biases in population biology and demography research, which have historically been oriented to understanding population stability (e.g., May 1973; Łomnicki 1978, 1988). Unstable age structure leads to variations in population responses to changes in prey populations. Because fishers do not reproduce until age two, populations skewed toward young animals may not be able to respond to increases in prey populations as rapidly as populations skewed toward old individuals. Thus, trapping may affect the abilities of fisher populations to respond to increasing prey populations (Powell, in press a). There is much yet to learn about unstable populations.

Sex Ratio

Sex ratios of unharvested fisher populations are not well known, and true sex ratios are difficult to determine. Live-trapping and kill-trapping results for all mustelines exhibit a significant bias toward trapping males (Buskirk and Lindstedt 1989; King 1975). Males have significantly larger home ranges than females. Home ranges of males and females overlap extensively, but the home ranges of individuals of the same sex do not. Therefore, populations should be biased toward females. But females tend to be harder to trap because they do not travel as far, leading to the male bias in trapping. I suspect that true sex ratios for natural fisher populations are close to 50:50. The trapping bias toward males might skew toward females those populations that are harvested for fur (Powell, in press a).

Chapter 5

Habitat

Fishers appear to prefer continuous forest over other habitats (Arthur, Krohn, and Gilbert 1989b; Clem 1977; Coulter 1966; deVos 1952; Johnson 1984; Jones and Garton, in press; Kelly 1977; Powell 1977a; Raine 1983; Thomasma, Drummer, and Peterson, in press). They have been found in extensive conifer forests (Cook and Hamilton 1957; Coulter 1966; Hamilton and Cook 1955; Kelly 1977) and in mixed conifer and hardwood forests (Clem 1977; Coulter 1966; Kelly 1977; Powell 1977a, 1978a) but have always been found in forested areas with continuous overhead cover.

The quality of a habitat for a species is ultimately a function of the fitness of the individuals that use that habitat (Fretwell 1972); fitness is a measure of an animal's genetic contribution to future generations. Thus, high-quality habitat is that which confers to its occupants the ability to contribute more offspring and more genes to future generations. Fitness is difficult to measure in most animals, especially mammals, and especially in solitary predators such as fishers. Thus, analyses of fisher habitat have bypassed the need to measure fitness or a correlate of fitness, such as survival and reproduction, and instead have assumed that relative time or distance spent in habitats is a measure of habitat preference, which, in turn, is a measure of fitness. This assumption may not always be true (Buskirk and Powell, in press).

There is no universally appropriate scale for analyzing habitat because the scale used must match the questions being asked. Rahel (1990) has shown that choosing the wrong scale can sometimes reverse conclusions. Habitat variables analyzed must be appropriate to the geographic scale of the study. Nothing is gained from knowing that the fishers I studied in Michigan used different forest types, as measured by dominant tree species, than fishers in northern California; the forests share no tree species. For such a comparison, habitat variables need to be quantified in terms of conifer versus hardwood, density of tree spacing, and so forth. For a field study site, habitat analyses can be done on different scales. Kelly (1977) found that the composition of the forests used by the fisher population in New Hampshire was different from the selections made by individual fishers for forest types within their home ranges. Finally, individual fishers may use different scales in choosing where to perform different behaviors. Where to establish a home range may be decided on a landscape scale; where to hunt may be decided on a scale of habitat patches; where to rest may be decided on a scale of both habitat patches and habitat characteristics within patches.

The habitats selected by animals are limited by the habitats available, but the physical structure of the forest appears more important than the species composition. One clear characteristic of all the habitats preferred by fishers is overhead cover, and fishers selectively use habitats with high canopy closure (80% to 100% closure) and avoid areas with low canopy closure (less than 50%; Kelly 1977). High canopy closure is characteristic of dense lowland forests, and these are often used disproportionately to their availability (Arthur, Krohn, and Gilbert 1989b; Coulter 1966; Kelly 1977; Powell 1977a, 1978a; Thomasma, Drummer, and Peterson, in press). Fishers also appear to use areas with low canopies selectively (Kelly 1977), but this behavior correlates with the availability of lowland habitat with dense canopy cover and low height (Kelly 1977). In Maine, the percentage of fisher tracks found in spruce-fir forest types is greater than the percentage of forest cover that is of the spruce-fir type (Arthur, Krohn, and Gilbert 1989b; Coulter 1966).

Fishers in the Northeast through the Upper Midwest in the United States and in the boreal forests of Canada show strong selection for dense lowland conifer forest types that are characterized by spruce, fir, white cedar, and some hardwoods. Wetland forest types also tend to be dense and have high canopy

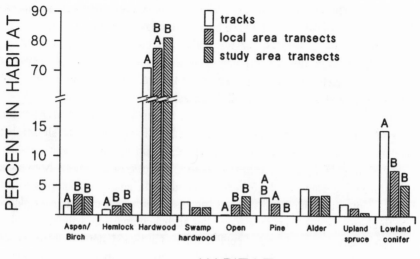

Figure 30. Percent of fisher tracks, of random transects in the vicinity of tracks (local area transects), and of random transects spread over the entire study area that were in nine habitat types. Within each habitat, bars with different letters designate significantly different proportions of tracks or transects in that habitat.

closure. In the West, riparian forests appear to be important for fishers (Buck, Mullis, and Mossman 1983, in press; Jones and Garton, in press).

While studying fishers in Michigan, I measured and mapped on forest-type maps 32 fisher tracks that covered nearly 90 kilometers (Powell, in press b). Distances that fishers traveled in different habitats, or forest types, were calculated as distances measured on maps times the ratio of map to track distances given in Table 9 (chapter 7). I measured the habitat available in two ways. First, using transects drawn on a map of my study area that showed forest types, I calculated the proportion along all transects that was in each habitat. Second, my study area was divided into 2.6 square kilometer quadrats (1 square mile). Using transects drawn on the quadrats in which tracks were found, I again calculated the proportion along all transects that was in each habitat. The first method provided the proportion of my study area in each habitat, whereas the second provided the proportion of forest in the vicinity of tracks that was in each habitat.

The mean proportions of tracks in each habitat and the proportions of habitat available measured in the two ways are shown in Figure 30. The two measures of habitat available were statistically significantly different only in the proportion of pine habitat, but were nearly significantly different for hardwood and lowland conifer types. This finding implies that the fishers preferred to hunt in areas that had more pine, more lowland conifer, and less hardwood forest types than found in the study area at large. The proportion of tracks in lowland conifer habitats was greater than and the proportions in aspen and birch, hemlock, and open habitats less than that available in the vicinity of tracks and in the entire study area. The proportion of tracks in hardwood habitat was less than that available in the whole study area but did not differ from that in the vicinity of tracks. The proportions of tracks in alder, upland spruce, and swamp hardwood stands did not differ from that available. This finding suggests that the fishers preferred to hunt in lowland conifer habitats.

When selecting for areas with overhead cover, fishers select against habitats with little overhead cover. Open hardwood forest types are frequently avoided (Figure 30; Arthur, Krohn, and Gilbert 1989b; Clem 1977; Kelly 1977), and, depending on the other available habitats, mixed hardwood-conifer forest types may be avoided (Buck, Mullis, and Mossman 1983, in press; Coulter 1966). Nonforested areas are always avoided (Figure 30; Arthur, Krohn, and Gilbert 1989b; Coulter 1966; Jones and Garton, in press; Kelly 1977; Powell 1977a, 1978a), though areas that have been subjected to clear-cutting are only avoided during the winter, because during the summer clear-cuts have dense cover from saplings that fishers apparently perceive as adequate overhead cover (Kelly 1977).

In contrast to all other studies, Johnson (1984) found that fishers selected for upland hardwood habitats and for edges between habitats. Johnson defined "edge" as areas within 65 meters of the boundary between two habitat types because this was the resolution of his radiotelemetric data. I believe that this definition, rather than the fishers he studied showing unique habitat characteristics, is what led to his results. Johnson's study area was about 50 kilometers south of mine. I often found from following fisher tracks that a fisher's behavior would change right at the interface between two habitat types, not even a few meters away let alone 65 meters away. If much of the lowland conifer habitat in Johnson's study area became subsumed within his "edge" habitat type, then his fishers may actually have selected for lowland conifer habitat without this being recorded.

Buskirk and I (in press) hypothesized that selection or avoidance of edges is primarily a function of the individual values of the habitats that form the edge. An edge between an open bog and dense lowland conifer habitat will likely be used by a fisher, albeit only from the conifer side, whereas an edge between an open bog and a recent clear-cut will not be used.

We must remember that the habitat requirements of fishers may not always coincide with the habitat variables we use to characterize habitats. Throughout the fisher's range, the dominant late-successional forest types are conifer types or include conifer types. In the Northeast and Upper Midwest, fishers recolonized and were successfully reintroduced into forests that are predominantly midsuccessional, second-growth mixed conifer and hardwood forests. These second-growth forests clearly meet the requirements to support viable fisher populations, but not all midsuccessional, second-growth forests can. In their study area in the Idaho Rocky Mountains, Jones and Garton (in press) found that fishers used predominantly old-growth forest of grand and subalpine fir. In the Pacific Northwest, fishers are associated with low- to mid-elevation forests dominated by late-successional, old-growth western hemlock and Douglas fir (Aubry and Houston 1992; Buck, Mullis, and Mossman 1983, in press). Most of the old-growth forests in the Pacific Northwest have been heavily logged, and fishers appear to find the second-growth forests unsuitable. The physical structure and prey found in late-successional forests are critically important to American martens. Buskirk and I (in press) hypothesized that for fishers, the physical structure and prey associations in the midsuccessional mixed conifer and hardwood forests of the Upper Midwest and Northeast in the United States are equivalent to the critical physical structure and prey associations found in the late-successional, old-growth western hemlock and Douglas fir forests in the Pacific Northwest. I suspect that the importance of this structure to fishers in many places is associated with how it affects snow depth, snow compaction, and other characteristics of snow.

Habitat preferences for fishers parallel those of preferred prey. Dense lowland forests in the Upper Midwest and Northeast are preferred by snowshoe hares, a major prey for fishers. In the Pacific Northwest, the range of the snowshoe hare coincides with the original distribution for late-successional Douglas fir. While looking for sign of fishers on the Olympic Peninsula, I found snowshoe hare sign most frequently in late-successional, old-growth Douglas fir stands and in stands of western hemlock and Douglas fir regenerating from logging or from fire (Powell 1991). Both the old-growth and the regenerating stands were similar in having much physical structure on and near the ground. In the old-growth stands the structure came from dead and down woody debris, whereas in the regenerating stands it came from low branches. Complex physical structure appeared important. I hypothesized that the wide spacing of the remaining patches of old-growth Douglas fir, with few appropriate patches of regenerating forest between, is what limits fishers on the Olympic Peninsula at present.

Although there have been some reports of fishers in bogs, on frozen lakes, and in burned-over forests (deVos 1952), fishers have an unexplained aversion to open areas (Figure 30; Arthur, Krohn, and Gilbert 1989b; Coulter 1966; Kelly 1977; Powell 1977a, 1978a; Quick 1953a). This aversion may be responsible for the strange character of local distributions in some states. It appears that the Penobscot River limited the distribution of the fisher population in

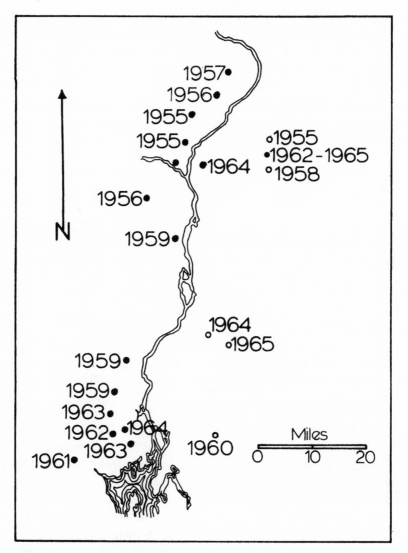

Figure 31. Distribution of fishers detected along the west and east shores of the Penobscot River, 1955 to 1965. The *solid circles* represent fishers trapped or collected, and the *open circles* represent track sightings only. Track sightings were not recorded for the west side of the river. By 1965, fishers had been trapped in twelve of the eighteen townships on the west side of the river but in only one of the fifteen townships on the east side. (Redrawn by C. B. Powell from M. W. Coulter 1966, by permission of the author.)

Maine (Figure 31) and delayed the geographic expansion of the population to the east side of the river by almost a decade (Coulter 1966). In Upper Michigan,

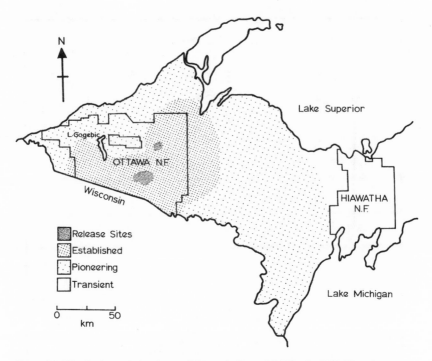

Figure 32. Distribution and abundance of fishers in Upper Michigan in 1977. Note the concave shape of the area of established population, which bends around Lake Gogebic and around the area of private lands in the middle of the national forest (this area is open farmland). (Redrawn by C. B. Powell from R. D. Earle 1978, by permission of the author.)

the 1977 distribution of the fisher population (Figure 32) had a concave shape that bent around a large area of open farmland and Lake Gogebic (Earle 1978).

The habitat preferences outlined earlier are largely found during all seasons for both male and female fishers, although female fishers may be less selective during summer (Arthur, Krohn, and Gilbert 1989b; Kelly 1977). Jones and Garton (in press), however, found that both male and female fishers were more selective for old-growth forests in summer than in winter in their Idaho study area. Some of the change in habitat preference is caused by avoidance of open habitats that exist in winter but not in summer. Open habitat vegetated with young deciduous trees and shrubs (typical of clear-cut areas) are used by fishers in summer but are truly open with no overhead cover in winter. Arthur and co-workers (1989b), Coulter (1966), deVos (1952), Kelly (1977), and Brander and I (Powell 1977a, 1978a; Powell and Brander 1977) all found that hunting fishers will use both open hardwood and dense conifer forest types, though foraging strategies appear to be different in different habitats (Clem 1977; Powell 1977a, 1978a, 1981; Powell and Brander 1977). Fishers hunting in open hardwood forests during the winter often alter their direction of travel in order to travel through small conifer stands (Coulter 1966; Powell 1977a). This reflects their preference for conifer forest types. It is not known whether the directional change is connected with the availability of prey in different forest types, preference for overhead cover, or some combination of these and other factors.

Kelly (1977) investigated the relationship between the type of forest selected by fishers and the availability of small mammals (shrews, mice, and squirrels). Using snap traps and pit traps in the major forest types in his study area, he trapped similar numbers of small mammals in each forest type during the autumns of 1974 and 1975. He found significant differences in the diversity of small mammals in the different forest types, however. Kelly measured diversity with the Shannon-Wiener information measure:

$$H_s = \sum_{i=1}^{S} p_i \cdot log p_i,$$

where H_s is a symbol of the diversity in a group of s species and p_i is the proportion or relative abundance scaled from 0 to 1 of the ith species. H_s increases as the number of species increases and as the relative abundance of each species approaches the average relative abundance of all species. Those habitats with the highest diversity of small mammals were those habitats with many small mammal species all of similar abundance. Habitats with high small mammal diversity—wetland and mixed conifer-hardwood forest types—were preferred by fishers in Kelly's study area. The hardwood forests in his study area had less-than-average small mammal species diversity and were avoided by fishers. The clear-cut forest type, however, had above-average small mammal diversity and was still avoided by fishers during the winter. Kelly believed that this avoidance was due to the lack of overhead cover in clear-cuts during the winter and the greater snow depth there that made small mammals less available.

Leonard (1980b) and Raine (1983) found that deep snow affected habitat use by fishers in Manitoba. The fishers they studied preferred ridges with coniferous forests. During midwinter, however, when the snow was deep and fluffy, movements of fishers were restricted. At these times fishers traveled less, and when they did, they traveled disproportionately often on snowshoe hare trails and their own trails. When they traveled in deep snow, fishers tended to leave body drags. Raine found that fishers would even travel on waterways, which they otherwise avoided, where the snow had been blown and packed by wind. One juvenile male fisher followed ski, snowshoe, and other trails almost exclusively during the month before dying, apparently of starvation (Raine 1979). Where snow is deep, fishers may forage for hares on packed, snowplow drifts along roads that bisect hare habitat (Johnson and Todd 1985). Arthur and coworkers (1989b) felt that snow affected fisher distribution and population density in Maine, and Aubry and Houston (1992) felt the same was true in Washington. In both places, fishers appeared confined to or had greater density in areas with low snow accumulation.

In the Pacific Northwest fishers were originally most common in low- to mid-elevation forests up to 2,440 meters (Aubry and Houston 1992; Grinnell, Dixon, and Linsdale 1937; Schempf and White 1977). The highest elevation recorded for an observation of a fisher in California was 3,475 meters (Schempf and White 1977). In the past forty years, most sitings of fishers on the Olympic Peninsula in Washington have been at elevations less than 1,000 meters, but sitings in the Cascade Mountains, where snow is less deep, have generally been between 1,800 and 2,200 meters. Kelly (1977) found fisher activity predominantly between 300 and 900 meters in New Hampshire. Activity in New Hampshire did not correlate with forest type as it did in California and Washington because of the less dramatic vegetational changes with altitude in New Hampshire. Fishers in New Hampshire significantly selected for elevations below 600 meters and against elevations above 600 meters. There was no correlation between the elevation selected and the season, but there was between the elevation selected and the sex of the fishers. The mean elevation selected by males was 505 meters, and that by females was 556 meters. Kelly also recorded a significant difference in the elevation selected for a male and a female occupying mostly overlapping home ranges. He hypothesized that the selection of elevation within overlapping home ranges may be a means of maintaining exclusive home ranges in mountainous areas, although he may only have documented mutual avoidance that happened to lead to elevation differences. Buck and co-workers (1983) felt that male fishers in the mountains of northern California restricted access of females to preferred habitat that lacked hardwoods.

All researchers who have studied rest sites used by fishers have found that fishers have stronger preferences for habitats in which to rest than in which to travel. Along the thirty-two tracks for which data are shown in Figure 30, fishers chose rest sites significantly more often in lowland conifer forests types than they used these types for hunting. Arthur and co-workers (1989b), Jones and Garton (in press), and Kelly (1977) found similar results. Many factors may affect a fisher's choice of a rest site. Proximity to prey and time since last meal may be important. Rest sites provide protection from inclement weather and are chosen differently in different seasons and probably under different weather conditions. During winter in Maine, fishers are most likely to rest in burrows, but during summer they are most likely to rest in witch's brooms, the clumps of wildly growing, densely packed branches found on spruce and balsam fir trees (Arthur, Krohn, and Gilbert 1989b).

Ultimately we must remember that fishers do not choose habitat on the basis of tree species or other habitat characteristics regularly categorized by humans. To fishers, physical characteristics of the environment that lead to high prey populations and successful foraging are what count. Thus, very different forest types may meet fishers' requirements in different places. I believe that the vegetative and structural components of the forest that lead to high prey populations are important as is the relationship between the structure of the forest and snow. Fishers will choose habitats with prey they can catch. Those habitats will meet the requirements of fisher prey and will be structured and have snow cover such that fishers can forage successfully without high foraging costs.

Habitat Suitability Index

Habitat Suitability Index models were developed by the U.S. Fish and Wildlife Service in order to quantify habitat quality for selected species. These indices all range from 0, representing unsuitable habitat, to 1, representing optimal habitat. The indices are assumed to have positive, linear relationships with the population sizes of the species that the habitat can support (U.S. Fish and Wildlife Service 1981). This assumption is seldom strictly true.

The Habitat Suitability Index model for the fisher was developed by Allen (1983) from the literature and from interviews with researchers and is meant to be applied to conifer forests, mixed conifer and hardwood forests, and forested wetlands throughout the range of the fisher. Allen assumed that prey availability and fisher foraging behavior determine use of habitats by fishers, that winter and early spring are the most restrictive seasons, and that dense old-growth forest stands provide the optimal winter cover for fishers and their prey. These assumptions are reasonable but must be accepted with caution. That fishers breed in late winter and early spring indicates that this may not be the most restrictive season, and healthy fisher populations are found in second-growth forests in eastern North America.

Allen (1983) developed four habitat variables that he felt contained the important information needed to evaluate fisher habitat: V_1, percent tree canopy closure; V_2, mean dbh (diameter at breast height) of overstory trees; V_3, tree canopy diversity; V_4, percent overstory in deciduous (hardwood) species. The relationships between these variables and the suitability of habitat having different values for these variables (I_1, I_2, I_3, and I_4) are shown in Figure 33. The model predicts increasing habitat suitability as tree canopy closure, tree size (dbh), and tree canopy diversity increase, and the model predicts that suitability decreases as the percent of the overstory in hardwoods increases beyond 50%. The final Habitat Suitability Index value is calculated as follows:

$$\text{HSI} = (I_1 \cdot I_2 \cdot I_3)^{\frac{1}{2}} \cdot I_4.$$

Thomasma and co-workers (1991) tested whether this model accurately rep-

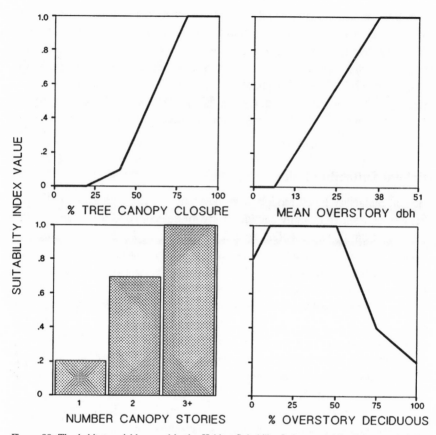

Figure 33. The habitat variables used in the Habitat Suitability Index model for fishers and their relationships to suitability of habitat having different values for these variables. (*Source*: Allen 1983.)

resented habitat suitability for fishers in Upper Peninsula Michigan. They hiked forty-nine 0.2-4.0-kilometer-long transects and calculated HSI values from values recorded for each V_i in an 18.3-meter diameter circle at 180-meter intervals and everywhere that a fisher track crossed the transects. They found that the distribution of HSI values from fisher tracks was significantly shifted toward high HSI values compared to the distribution of the available habitat HSI distribution (Figure 34). This result means that fishers used habitats with high HSI values more frequently than expected based on availability. A preference index calculated for habitat at various HSI values showed that fishers selected against habitat with HSI values less than 0.3 and selected strongly for habitat with HSI values greater than 0.8. Counterintuitively, fishers also selected against habitats with HSI values between 0.5 and 0.8. Thomasma and co-workers found

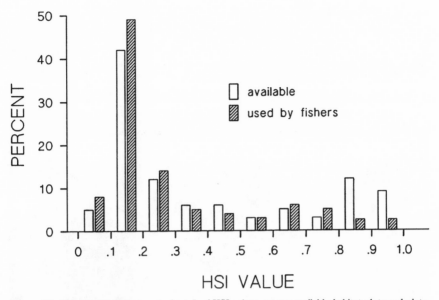

Figure 34. Distribution (as percent of total) of HSI values among available habitat plots and plots on fisher tracks. The Habitat Suitability Index model was developed such that habitats with HSI = 1 are supposed to represent optimal habitat and that habitats with HSI = 0 are unsuitable. HSI values are grouped by tenths from 0 to 1. The distribution of HSI values for fisher tracks is significantly shifted toward high HSI values compared to the distribution for available habitat. (Redrawn from Thomasma, Drummer, and Peterson 1991, with permission of the publisher.)

that in their study area, habitats with these values were largely pine plantations, a habitat that provided high HSI values yet offered little to fishers.

I used the Allen's Habitat Suitability Index for fishers as part of an evaluation of the Great Smoky Mountains National Park for a reintroduction of fishers (Powell 1990). For high-elevation habitats of spruce and fir and of mixed spruce-fir and northern hardwoods in the park, the mean HSI value was greater than that for the habitat with a viable fisher population studied by Thomasma and co-workers (1991). Great Smoky Mountains National Park is near to the southernmost extent of the historic distribution of fishers (chapter 4), and northern spruce-fir and associated northern hardwood habitats are not found farther south than the park. Present habitat in Great Smoky Mountains National Park appears suitable for fishers.

Chapter 6

Food Habits

The diet of any predator varies with the prey available to it. The availability of prey, however, depends on more than the abundance of prey (Charnov, Orians, and Hyatt 1976; Ewer 1973). Some prey are less easily found than others because of their coloration, hiding places, and other characteristics. Other prey are harder to kill once they are found because they can run fast or have other defenses. And, once the prey have become alerted to a predator, they are less easily caught by surprise. Prey are also more or less palatable to various predators; therefore, predators may prefer to kill one type of prey over another. Predators learn techniques to catch particular types of prey and so catch some types more often than their relative abundance (compared to other prey animals) would otherwise indicate. All of these factors (the abundance, catchability, and palatability of prey and the predator's experience) undoubtedly determine the diets of fishers in different parts of the species' range.

Characteristics of the Fisher's Diet

Fishers are generalized predators. They eat any animal they can catch and over-power, and they readily eat carrion. All the fishers in a population eat the same prey species, and there do not appear to be fishers that cannot kill particular prey species. Because fishers are solitary hunters, the size of the prey they can catch is determined by their own size. Mammals that hunt in groups or packs can kill prey much larger than they are. Large mammals, such as adult deer and moose, obviously are too large for a fisher to kill; a fisher weighs only a small percentage of the weight of such mammals. Therefore, fishers are limited to hunting animals of approximately their own size and smaller (Rosenzweig 1966)—prey that they can catch and handle without the help of other fishers. Fishers actively hunt only small- to medium-size animals.

All the predominant prey species that fishers hunt are herbivores. Herbi-vores are generally adapted to escaping predation by fleeing rather than fight-ing. So, when a fisher is able to overtake a prey animal, the fisher has only to overpower it and does not have to be particularly careful of the animal's fighting back. Other predators are only eaten by fishers as carrion, except, perhaps, the small weasels.

One species that is an obvious exception to the rule of fleeing herbivores is the porcupine. Porcupines are well armored with quills and do not depend on flight alone for escape from predators. Fishers use different techniques to kill porcupines than they use to kill other prey.

Early reports listed medium- to small-size rodents (such as mice and squirrels), hares and rabbits, birds (especially ruffed grouse), and porcupines as common food items for fishers (Coues 1877; Grinnell, Dixon, and Linsdale 1937; Hardy 1899; Quick 1953a; Schoonmaker 1938; Seton 1937). Recently, more specific data have supported the early reports (Table 8), and some diet studies with large samples have shown the great breadth of prey eaten by fishers. These data have been col-lected from fishers' gastrointestinal tracts (GI tracts, primarily those obtained from trappers) and feces (scats) collected along fisher tracks.

Coulter (1966) and Stevens (1968) collected both GI tracts and scats. Stevens's results are similar for both samples, but the results of Coulter's GI tract and scat analyses appear at first to be quite different. The relative amounts of nonscavenged prey (such as snowshoe hares, porcupines, mice, squirrels, and birds), however, are similar in both of Coulter's analyses. It ap-pears that a bias was introduced through the large number of scats retrieved from tracks located near deer and moose carcasses (Coulter 1966).

Stevens's (1968) GI tract analysis was the only one that found a high inci-dence of domestic animals. Chickens and cats were the most prevalent, and one or the other occurred in nearly a quarter of the tracts.

Table 8. Food habits of fishers reported as percentage occurrence of each prey type

Food Item	Calif.[a] stomach	Maine[b] GI	Maine[c] scat	Maine[d] scat	Maine[e] scat	Manit.[f] scat	Mich.[g] scat	Minn.[h] stomach male	Minn.[i] stomach female	N.H.[j] stomach	N.H.[k] scat	N.H.[l] GI	N.H.[m] GI	N.H.[n] GI	N.Y.[o] GI	N.Y.[p] GI	Ont.[q] GI	Ont.[r] GI male	Ont.[s] GI female
Snowshoe hare		28	9	18	15	84	31	19[z]	21[z]	5	17	3	10	9	13	12	44	21	12
Porcupine		26	9	21	9		20			3	-		3	4	8	6	35	32	20
White-tailed/black-tailed deer	25	24	50	7	3		20	22[z]	28[z]	7	11	2	7	17	18	19	22	3	8
Mice	37[z]	23	6	16[z]	3[z]	3[z]	20			24	36	50	20[z]	13[z]	23	20[z]	9	11	16
white-footed	25	7	2	3						14	16	17	15	4	7	5		6	12
red-backed		6		6		1				5	15	30	5	10	17	3	9		
meadow		5	4													9			
misc. & unident.	12	5	1			2	8	11[z]	8[z]	5						2[z]		5	5
Shrews/moles	12	24	6		3					12	8	2						8	8
short-tailed shrew		12								5	52	12	11	5	13	7[z]	7	5	4
masked shrew		2								1	50	2			13	2	4	3	4
misc. & unident.[t]	12	10								7	2	10				3[z]	4		
Squirrels	12	19	9	25[z]	22[z]	1	14			16	21	20	13[z]	4[z]	18	22[z]	4	3	3
red		10	1	3	3	1				7	11	12	6	2	17	20	2	2	1
flying		8	6	6	4					2	6	5			2		2	1	1
eastern chipmunk											4					1		1	2
gray and fox	12	1		16	15					8		2	7	2					
Muskrat[u]		-				1				4	1	7	3	9		5	2	15	16
Raccoon[u]		1	4							4	-	5				1		3	1
Beaver[u]		1	6									5	11	4		2	2		
Moose		2	17							17									
Misc. & unident. mammals[v]	100[z]	6	6	30[z]	10[z]	9[z]	14	13[z]	11[z]	25	-	7	30	21	2	45[z]	9		
Birds		24	8	13	6	8[z]				30	18	15			12	8[z]	11	23	22
blue & gray jays		7										2			5	-		16	8
ruffed grouse		2	2			7				12		2			5	3	4	9	14
misc. & unident.[w]		15	6			9[z]				19		19			2	5[z]	7		
Misc. & unident. vertebrates[x]	88[z]	2			3	3		35[z]	32[z]	4	3				2	3[z]	12	13	12

Table 8. Continued

Food Item	Calif.[a] stomach	Maine[b] GI	Maine[c] scat	Maine[d] scat	Maine[e] scat	Manit.[f] scat	Mich.[g] scat	Minn.[h] stomach male	Minn.[i] stomach female	N.H.[j] stomach	N.H.[k] scat	N.H.[l] GI	N.H.[m] GI	N.H.[n] GI	N.Y.[o] GI	N.Y.[p] GI	Ont.[q] GI	Ont.[r] GI male	Ont.[s] GI female
Arthropods	37[z]	3	4			2				5	4				3	3[z]	21		
Plant material[y]	100[z]	3	15	37	29	13[z]	6			33	24	12	32	18	32	61[z]			

Note: Each entry is the percentage of samples containing that prey type. The type of sample (stomachs, GI tracts, or scats) are listed under each state or province. Exception: The data for Minnesota are reported as the aggregate percentage of total prey weight that is of each prey type.

[a] Grenfell and Fasenfest 1979, 8 stomachs collected 1977-78.
[b] Coulter 1966, 243 GI tracts collected 1950-64.
[c] Coulter 1966, 127 scats collected 1950-64.
[d] Arthur, Krohn, and Gilbert 1989b, 69 scats collected 1984-87.
[e] Arthur, Krohn, and Gilbert 1989b, predominant food in each of 69 scats collected 1984-87.
[f] Raine 1987, 159 scats collected 1978-80.
[g] Powell 1977a, 35 scats collected 1974-76.
[h] Kuehn 1989, males sampled from 1,649 stomachs collected 1977-85.
[i] Kuehn 1989, females sampled from 1,649 stomachs collected 1977-85.
[j] Stevens 1968, 153 stomachs collected in 1968.
[k] Stevens 1968, 337 scats collected in 1968.
[l] Kelly 1977, 40 GI tracts collected 1973-74.
[m] Giuliano, Litvaitis, and Stevens 1989, 158 GI tracts collected 1965-67.
[n] Giuliano, Litvaitis, and Stevens 1989, 173 GI tracts collected 1987.
[o] Hamilton and Cook 1955, 60 GI tracts collected 1949-53.
[p] Brown and Will 1979, 332 GI tracts collected 1975-77.
[q] deVos 1952, 57 GI tracts collected 1939-51.
[r] Clem 1977, 117 male GI tracts collected 1973-74 in Algonquin region.
[s] Clem 1977, 153 female GI tracts collected 1973-74 in Algonquin region.
[t] Miscellaneous and unidentified mice: southern bog lemming, woodland jumping mouse, meadow jumping mouse, house mouse, western harvest mouse, unidentified.
[u] Includes bait.
[v] Miscellaneous and unidentified mammals (often bait): moles, cottontail rabbit, mink, red fox, American marten, weasels, otter, caribou, fisher, skunk, beaver, muskrat, woodchuck, domestic mammals, unidentified.
[w] Miscellaneous and unidentified birds: red-breasted nuthatch, thrushes, owls, black-capped chickadee, downy woodpecker, yellow-shafted flicker, sparrows, dark-eyed junco, red-winged blackbird, starling, crow, ducks, grouse eggs, domestic chicken, unidentified.
[x] Miscellaneous and unidentified vertebrates: snakes, toads, fish, unidentified.
[y] Plant material: apples, winterberries, mountain ash berries, blackberries, raspberries, strawberries, cherries, beechnuts, acorns, swamp holly berries, miscellaneous needles and leaves, mosses, club mosses, ferns, unidentified.
[z] Estimated from table or figure in source.

It is unfortunate that the only study of the food habits of West Coast fishers was limited to the analysis of eight GI tracts. Grenfell and Fasenfest (1979) found a high frequency of plant material, a large amount of which was mushrooms (false truffles). Black-tailed deer and mice were also common food items; deer and domestic cattle were probably taken as carrion.

Arthur and co-workers (1989b), Raine (1987), and I (Powell 1977a, 1978a) noted kills made by fishers while following tracks in the snow. We found porcupine, snowshoe hare, squirrel, mouse, and grouse kills as well as dead deer and small items that were scavenged. Arthur and co-workers (1989b) quantified the rate at which fishers intercepted tracks of prey and the rate at which tracks of prey were encountered along transects. Encounter rates for prey were the same along tracks and transects except for porcupines, which were encountered less often along tracks than along transects.

Noting the frequency of the occurrence of different foods (the percentages of the total number of GI tracts or scats that contain a given food type) is one of the most common methods of describing the diets of carnivores. This method is often used in conjunction with the total volume of each type of food found in the tracts or scats or in conjunction with minimum or maximum numbers of prey individuals estimated present in the samples. Even so, these methods are at best only indices of foods eaten and are not precise, quantitative measurements of the relative amounts of various foods eaten. These methods do give a qualitative measurement of the foods eaten in a particular place at a particular time.

GI tracts and scats contain those parts of animals that are most resistant to digestion. Therefore, those food items with a relatively large proportion of undigestible parts are overrepresented in tracts and scats. Small mammals and birds have more fur or feathers and bones than do large mammals because small mammals and birds have larger surface-to-volume ratios. In addition, small food items are eaten whole, whereas large food items are selectively eaten, reducing still further the amount of recognizable remains to be found in tracts and scats. Floyd and co-workers (1978) showed that in wolf scats the weights of the remains of small mammals are overrepresented and the number of individuals distinguishable is underrepresented compared to large food items. Similar results have been obtained for the remains of prey in red fox scats (Lockie 1959; Scott 1941) and domestic ferret scats (Zielinski 1981). A quantitative analysis of scat or GI tract contents and weight of prey has yet to be performed for fishers.

A list of the foods identified from fecal remains or GI tract contents gives little information about where foods were obtained, when they were obtained, or how they were obtained. Coulter (1966) gave the example of a hunter looking at Table 8 and concluding that fishers are major predators on white-tailed deer in Maine. The hunter's conclusions would be strengthened by the popular literature, which exaggerates the predatory habits of fishers. Data on the habits of fishers and familiarity with the tracks from which scats were collected led Arthur and co-workers (1989b), Coulter (1966), deVos (1952), Kelly (1977), and me (Powell 1977a) to conclude that the remains of such large food items as deer and moose in fishers' scats and GI tracts resulted solely from scavenging.

Almost all of the GI tracts collected for the studies listed in Table 8 were obtained from trappers during legal trapping seasons. Trap bait is commonly found in the GI tracts of such animals, and this increases the difficulty of distinguishing between kills initiated by fishers and items obtained as carrion. As Kelly (1977, 97) pointed out, however, "Trap-bait is a legitimate component of the fisher's diet during the trapping season." That fishers are easy to trap (Young 1975), that they readily take trap bait, and that they habitually scavenge on deer carcasses suggest that fishers have a predilection for consuming carrion. Kelly (1977, 97) continued:

> Before Europeans populated North America, ungulates were regularly cropped by carnivores capable of killing them and by normal winter mortality; thus carrion was probably more available on a regular basis than it has been in modern times. Man has reduced or eliminated most large carnivores and removes the yearly ungulate crop from the fisher's environment, leaving only incidental hunting losses and, because of management, minimal winter mortality. The fisher must therefore be more dependent on availability of prey species that it can kill than it once was; these prey species may be primarily on a seasonal basis. Unfortunately, seasonal abundance of carrion coincides with the trapping season, when material is most readily obtainable for food-habits analysis.

Trap bait and carrion may not be quite the problem that Kelly implied they are. First, because bait is a legitimate component of the fisher's diet during the trapping season, it must be acknowledged. It would be desirable to obtain an estimate of how much is carrion scavenged from other sources. The scat analyses listed in Table 8, though more limited in scope than most of the GI tract analyses, do not differ in a substantial qualitative manner from the GI tract analyses, except that Raine (1987) studied fishers that experienced an abundance of snowshoe hares. In addition, information from the kills and scavenges gathered along fisher tracks agrees qualitatively with the GI tract analyses (Arthur, Krohn, and Gilbert 1989b; Powell 1977a, 1978a; Raine 1987). All of the evidence suggests that fishers eat those medium- to small-size mammals and birds and the carrion that they can find.

Second, fishers have a source of carrion that Kelly (1977) did not mention: deer and other animals that are killed along highways. Highway deer kill is a source of carrion that is totally unrelated to the trapping season and has peaks at different times of the year than the peak of trap bait as a source of food. Bashore (1978) showed that the number of highway-killed deer has seasonal spring and autumn peaks all over North America. The spring peak is the higher peak and does not coincide with trapping seasons. Earle (1978) found that spring highway kill of porcupines was substantial enough to be used as an estimate of several population and demographic parameters. I suspect from the location of the deer carcasses I found during my study that most dead deer found by fishers in my study area were killed on the highway.

The Fisher's Prey

Snowshoe Hares

Remains of snowshoe hares (Figure 35) are the most common items found in fishers' GI tracts and scats. The species range of the snowshoe hare (Figure 36) is coincident with almost the entire fisher species range, and, therefore, the snowshoe hare should be expected to occur frequently in the diets of fishers. Trappers generally believe that the snowshoe hare is the fisher's most common food (deVos 1952; Hamilton and Cook 1955; Young 1975) and occasionally use hares for bait. Such use is illegal in some states because hares are game animals, and this use is not common enough to influence the incidence of hare remains in fisher scats and GI tracts to any significant degree.

The occurrence of snowshoe hare remains in fisher scats ranges from 7% to 84%, and there is a correlation between low incidence of snowshoe hare remains and high incidence of bird, deer, mouse, and squirrel remains (Table 8; Figure 37). Northern snowshoe hare populations have an approximate ten-year cycle in size over which densities can change by the thousandfold. Hare-plant interactions best explain the cycle (Bryant and Weiland 1985; Keith and Windberg 1978; Pease, Vowles, and Keith 1979; Vaughn and Keith 1981), but hare-predator interactions can exacerbate hare population lows (Keith et al. 1984). Fisher populations follow a cycle approximately three years behind the hare cycle. This is the expected time lag for a predator in which a shortage of prey has the greatest effect through increased juvenile and adult mortality and not through depressed reproduction (Bulmer 1975).

Kuehn showed (1989; Figure 37) that as a snowshoe hare population declines, snowshoe hares decrease in fishers' diets. He hypothesized before collecting his data that fisher health (indexed by fat content in carcasses) or reproduction (indexed by the percentage of females with corpora lutea in their ovaries) would decline as hares became scarce. This did not happen. Instead, fishers replaced snowshoe hares with other foods. Had hares remained important to fishers as the hare population declined, then the indices of health and reproduction would surely have declined. Such a decline might have been easier

Figure 35. A snowshoe hare in white winter pelage.

Figure 36. Map of the species range of the snowshoe hare. Note the broad overlap of this range with that of the fisher (shown in Figure 28). (Adapted by C. B. Powell from Bittner and Rongstad 1982 and Burt and Grossenheider 1964.)

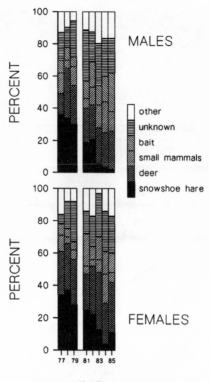

Figure 37. Mean aggregate percent of
weight of different fisher prey in the
stomachs of male and female fishers trapped
in Minnesota between 1977 and 1985.
(Redrawn from Kuehn 1989 with permission
of the publisher.)

to observe in incidence of placental scars or, better yet, in denning rates. The
low incidence of snowshoe hares in some fisher diets also simply reflects generally low hare populations in those study areas.

Hares use a variety of habitat types (Keith and Windberg 1978), but areas
with sparse cover appear to be poor hare habitat (Keith 1966). Hares tend to
concentrate in conifer and dense lowland vegetation during the winter and to
avoid open hardwood forests (Litvaitis, Sherburne, and Bissonette 1985). Fishers often hunt in those forests used by hares (chapter 5; Arthur, Krohn, and
Gilbert 1989b; Clem 1977; Coulter 1966; Kelly 1977; Powell 1977a, 1978a;
Powell and Brander 1977) and may direct their travel toward those forest areas
(chapters 7 and 9; Coulter 1966; Kelly 1977). Hares rest in well-protected hiding places such as under boughs, brush, and fallen logs. They generally remain

Figure 38. A porcupine leaving its winter den.

motionless until approached closely by a predator. Coulter (1966), however, felt that in areas frequented by fishers hares became wary and fled more quickly when they perceived danger.

Porcupines

The fisher-porcupine relationship is discussed in detail in chapter 8; therefore, this discussion will be brief.

Porcupines (Figure 38) have received by far the most attention of any of the fisher's prey. Both the popular literature and the early scientific literature emphasize fishers' abilities to kill porcupines. Porcupines are an important food for fishers in many places, and the frequency of their occurrence in diet samples is as high as 35% (Table 8). But porcupine remains are seldom as common as hare remains and are even completely absent from one diet sample; this is never the case with snowshoe hares.

The importance of porcupines as prey for fishers is reflected in the evolution of the unique hunting and killing behaviors used by fishers on porcupines (chapter 8). By evolving these behaviors, fishers have acquired a prey species for which they have almost no competition. The importance of this cannot be overlooked and should not be underemphasized. Fishers are adaptable, however, and do live in areas with no porcupines.

Figure 39. Deer carcass used extensively by a fisher. The fisher slept in the vicinity of this carcass for several days and is responsible for much or most of the packed snow, scattered hair, and scattered bones around the carcass.

White-tailed Deer

Remains of deer (Figure 39) were found in GI tracts and scats in all the studies listed in Table 8. Except in Kuehn's (1989) study, where deer remains were common, the total volume of deer remains was small in comparison to its incidence (Clem 1977; Coulter 1966; deVos 1952). Coulter (1966, 113) observed that fishers "returned to the remains of deer carcasses long after all edible parts were gone. They dug about the sites, carried tufts of hair and bones for short distances, and hunted intensively in the immediate areas." I made similar observations along tracks. Deer carrion was important for fishers in Upper Peninsula Michigan (Table 8), but that importance may have been inflated in the small number of scats I analyzed. Deer remains occurred almost exclusively in the scats of a few fishers that were tracked in the vicinity of deer carcasses (Powell 1977a). Coulter (1966) also felt that deer and moose might have been overestimated in his scat analysis because of the location of the fisher tracks around deer and moose carcasses. Some fishers may have deer hair in their digestive tracts and scats almost all winter and still have eaten few meals of venison.

Kuehn (1989), however, found that the amount of fat carried by fishers in

Minnesota increased when the number of deer harvested by hunters increased. Hunters leave viscera and other deer parts that fishers scavenge. Thus, Table 8 may not overemphasize the importance of deer and moose to fishers.

No recent research has been able to substantiate the secondhand reports of Hardy (1899, 1907) that fishers can kill healthy adult deer. Coulter (1966) devoted particular attention to fisher-deer relationships in order to clarify the falseness or reality of such reports. He questioned more than one hundred game wardens from the Maine Department of Inland Fisheries and Game and fourteen field biologists. None had ever observed a single instance of a deer having been killed by a fisher. Coulter also spent considerable time in deeryards during the periods of deepest snow. During these times, the deer were confined to deep, narrow paths in restricted areas. Fishers did hunt in these areas for other prey, but "they did not hunt deer" (Coulter 1966, 114).

There are anecdotal reports of sables killing musk deer, which weigh about ten times more than sables do (Bakeyev and Sinitsyn, in press), and of yellow-throated martens killing musk deer (Matjushkin 1974). McCord (1974) found deer remains in almost 80% of the bobcat scats he collected while studying the bobcat's predatory behavior in relation to its habitat. His data showed that the high incidence of deer remains in his bobcat scats was due to the bobcats' predation on deer and not from scavenging deer carrion. Marston (1942) reported similar results of bobcats preying on deer. It is likely that if fishers actively hunted deer, deer remains in fisher GI tracts and scats would be consistently more common and would be found in greater volumes than those reported.

Mice

As a group, the many species of mice appear in fishers' GI tracts and scats almost as frequently as snowshoe hares. White-footed mice, deer mice, red-backed voles, and meadow voles are the most common mice found in fishers' diets and are generally the most common mice in fisher habitat. Mice are probably not as important to fishers as their occurrence in the diet samples indicates. Because they are small, have a relatively large amount of fur and bones, and are eaten whole, mice are overrepresented in the GI tracts and scats of fishers.

Mice are often active on the surface of the snow during the winter, especially white-footed mice and red-backed voles (Coulter 1966; Powell 1977a, 1978a). Mouse tracks can frequently be seen on the snow's surface between mouse-size holes that descend to the surface of the ground. These holes are usually located around trees, shrubs, and sticks protruding above the surface of the snow. When the snow is deep, meadow voles and red-backed voles tend to use runways beneath the snow and in some areas may girdle many shrubs along their runways (Craighead and Craighead 1956). Fishers may catch mice on the snow's surface or dig into the snow after them during the winter. Meadow voles are probably less common in the fisher's diet than the other two species of mice because of their low relative abundance and because they are much less active on the surface of the snow than are white-footed and deer mice (Table 8).

Shrews

Shrews are found with unexpectedly high frequencies in the GI tracts and scats of fishers. In general, carnivores are reluctant to attack shrews (Jackson 1961). Lockie (1961) concluded that insectivores are distasteful to carnivores, and many mammalian predators are reluctant to eat shrews even after they have been killed (Lockie 1961; Lund 1962; Jackson 1961). Insectivores only appear consistently in most carnivores' diets when other small mammals are scarce (Lund 1962). Weasels, however, are known to eat shrews more frequently than most other carnivores (Aldous and Manweiler 1942; Glover 1942; Hamilton 1933).

Coulter (1966) found abundant signs of shrews under fallen trees, under accumulations of forest litter, and in ground cover. Such places are often inspected by fishers while they are hunting, and this may help to explain the high incidence of shrews in fishers' diets. Shrews are often active during periods of extreme cold (Getz 1961) and therefore may sometimes be relatively abundant locally. Thus, though shrews are probably overrepresented in fishers' GI tracts and scats because of their size, fishers (unlike other carnivores) apparently do catch and eat shrews whenever they can find them.

Squirrels

Squirrels are common mammals throughout the fisher's range but are fed upon less heavily than mice. Red squirrels and flying squirrels are found over more of the fisher's range and are therefore eaten more often than gray squirrels and fox squirrels. Because diet analyses have all been done on winter diets, chipmunks and other hibernating ground squirrels do not show up as frequently in Table 8 as they would were there more summer diet studies.

Red squirrels are common residents of northern coniferous forests and so are present in areas hunted heavily by fishers. Coulter (1966) felt that the difference in times of activity for fishers and red squirrels was the primary reason that squirrels were not eaten more often in Maine. Coulter also noted that red squirrels are not particularly vulnerable in trees. Jackson (1961, 174) stated that "natural enemies seldom capture a red squirrel."

Flying squirrels can be locally very abundant, but their nocturnal habits make population sizes difficult to estimate. Fishers capture flying squirrels on the ground (Powell, unpublished data) and perhaps in nest holes in trees (Coulter 1966).

Birds

Fishers often eat birds (Table 8). Jays and ruffed grouse, common winter birds in the fisher's range, are most commonly eaten. Jays are habitual scavengers, as are fishers, and it is likely that fishers capture some jays around deer carcasses and other carrion on which they are both scavenging. Grouse frequently rest beneath the snow and may be vulnerable to predation at these times. Brander and Books (1973) and Coulter (1966) could find no evidence, however, that fishers hunted for or ever captured grouse in their snow roosts.

Plant Materials

Vegetation of some sort has been found in all diet studies of fishers. Coues (1877) wrote that fishers are sometimes forced to eat beechnuts when other food is scarce. The popular press has repeated that fishers eat nuts but tends not to mention the scarcity of other foods as a reason for this behavior (Pringle 1973). Hamilton and Cook (1955) and then Coulter (1966) and Stevens (1968) substantiated Coues's (1877) report that fishers do eat beechnuts but showed that they were not an important part of their diet. Fishers in captivity generally refuse to eat any kind of fruit or nut (Davison 1975).

It is obvious from the wide variety of fruits listed in a footnote to Table 8 that fishers *will* eat a wide variety of fruits. Apples are often eaten by fishers in New England, where abandoned farms with orchards have regrown to forests that still include apple trees. Goszczynski (1976) and Lockie (1961) both found that European pine martens eat a great deal of fruit especially during the summer. There is no reason to believe that fishers would do otherwise, especially given that they will eat fruits during the winter and that fruits are more common during the summer than the winter. Other evidence, however, suggests that Coues's (1877) statement was correct: fruits and nuts are only eaten when other food is difficult to obtain.

Diet Analysis by Season and Age

Clem (1977), Coulter (1966), and Stevens (1968) analyzed fishers' diets by season. Coulter divided the GI tracts he examined into three groups by the season in which they were collected: autumn (85 tracts) was late September through November; early winter (99 tracts) was December and January; and late winter

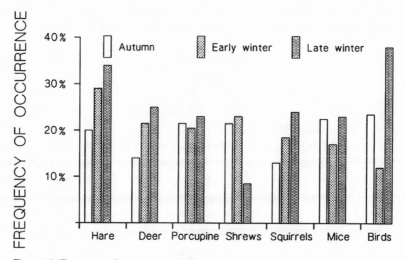

Figure 40. Frequency of occurrence of different prey types in the diet of fishers from Maine during different seasons. (From M. W. Coulter 1966, used by permission of the author.)

(48 tracts) was February through early April. Coulter felt that these periods are real and represent different hunting and prey conditions for fishers in Maine. Autumn is a period of low snow cover, bird migration, and the onset of hibernation for mammals that hibernate; autumn is probably the period when the greatest number of prey species is available to fishers. Early winter is characterized by deep, soft, fluffy snow and by the inactivity of winter mammals that do not hibernate; fishers experience a period of relative unavailability of prey. Late winter is characterized by firmly packed snow, shallow snow depth as the period ends, increased animal activity, and the return of migratory birds; these characteristics increase the availability of prey for fishers again. The frequency of occurrence of major food types in the fisher digestive tracts is shown in Figure 40. Coulter used a chi-square test on his raw data to test whether the proportions of each food types were the same for all periods. He found that the probability was between 0.05 and 0.10 that the proportions were the same, and he rejected the null hypothesis that season does not affect diet.

Coulter (1966) also found significant differences in the occurrence of some specific food types during the course of the winter. The change in the frequency of birds in fishers' diets (shown at the right in Figure 40) was significant at the 0.005 level. The decrease in the number of shrews in fishers' diets as the winter progressed was significant only at the 0.10 level. Considering the large number of prey types in the fisher's diet, however, a change in the frequency of a few items is to be expected from chance alone.

Clem (1977) had a slightly more extensive sample of GI tracts, but they were collected only from November through February. Clem was unable to detect any significant change in diet by month in his sample (the level of significance was 0.05), nor could he find any significant differences for any individual food types. Stevens (1968) found a significant increase in plant materials, especially fruits and nuts, during the summer.

Giuliano and co-workers (1989) investigated in New Hampshire whether fishers of different ages had different diets. They grouped the GI tracts they examined as having come from yearlings (less than one year old), juveniles (between one and two years old), or adult fishers, and they grouped foods as birds; fruits; and small, medium (squirrels), large (snowshoe hares, muskrats), and very large (porcupine, raccoon) mammals. The only age-specific difference they found was that juveniles ate more fruits. Because juveniles are learning to hunt, they may often go hungry (Raine 1979) and turn to apples and other fruits to ward off starvation.

Sexual Dimorphism and Diet

Clem (1977), Coulter (1966), Giuliano and co-workers (1989), Kelly (1977), Kuehn (1989), and Stevens (1968) were all unable to find any differences in diet between the sexes. This is of special interest because a difference in diet between the sexes has been hypothesized as one mechanism that might explain the substantial sexual dimorphism in the body size of fishers. The hypothesis predicts that substantial sexual dimorphism results in there being different diets for each sex and thus reduces competition for food. Douglas and Strickland (1987), Kelly (1977), and Kuehn (1989) did find significantly more male than female fishers with porcupine quills in their heads, chests, shoulders, and legs (probability < 0.01). Arthur and co-workers (1989) found similar results. In contrast, female fishers in one of Clem's study areas had more porcupine remains in their GI tracts than did males (probability < 0.01), and there was no difference in the number of quills in Stevens's small sample of males and females with quills. Whether these differences with respect to quills are caused by males attacking more porcupines, by females being more efficient or more careful, or females suffering greater mortality when attacking porcupines is not known.

No real, significant differences have been found between the diets of male and female fishers. Both male and female fishers are opportunistic predators that eat anything they can catch. Both sexes can kill porcupines, the largest living prey in their diets. It may be that a sexual difference in fishers' diets can be found only in the difference of the maximum size of porcupines that can be killed (see chapter 8). During the winter in northern North America, the next largest, active, potential prey species after the porcupine is the white-tailed deer, and it is known that fishers cannot kill healthy adult deer. Summer diet analyses may uncover a difference between the sexes in predation on mammals around the size of the beaver.

Most likely, biologically significant differences do not or seldom exist between the diets of male and female fishers. Anatomical analyses show that skulls of male and female fishers are less dimorphic in size than the rest of their skeletons and that teeth and jaws are less dimorphic yet (Holmes 1980, 1987; Holmes and Powell, in press; chapter 2). At most, diets may differ between sexes only occasionally. On those occasions, however, the differences might be important (Erlinge 1975; Wiens 1977).

Chapter 7

Hunting and Killing Behavior of Fishers Hunting Prey Other Than Porcupines

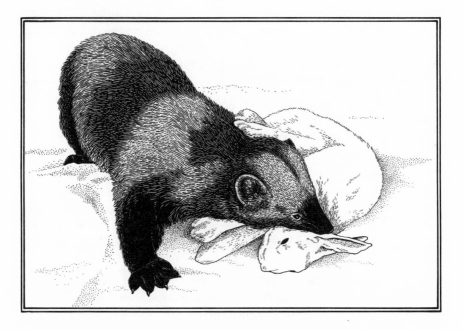

Fishers' foraging behavior has two distinct components, at least during the winter. One component is the search for patches of concentrated prey or patches of high prey vulnerability. The other is the search within those patches for prey to kill. Different prey animals are available to fishers in different habitats, and the use of the two components has been well correlated with habitat and prey by investigators who have followed fishers' tracks during the winter (Arthur, Krohn, and Gilbert 1989b; Clem 1977; Powell 1976, 1977a, 1977b, 1978a; Powell and Brander 1977; Raine 1987). The foraging component used by fishers to hunt within patches of concentrated prey is characterized by frequent changes in direction and zigzags. This hunting pattern is usually used in dense lowland coniferous forests where snowshoe hares are found in high densities, but it is also used in other habitats where prey are found in high densities. This hunting pattern is typical of the hunting patterns used by members of the subfamily Mustelinae and may have been used by primitive mustelids and by miacids. Between patches of dense prey, fishers travel nearly in straight lines, searching for and heading to new prey patches.

Hunting Behavior

Fishers use the zigzag foraging pattern typical of mustelines to hunt snowshoe hares, their most common prey, in areas of high snowshoe hare density. Fishers do not lie and wait to ambush hares, and they do not often chase hares for long distances. Rather, hunting consists of investigating places where hares are likely to be found (Arthur, Krohn, and Gilbert 1989b; Brander and Books 1973; Coulter 1966; Powell 1976, 1977a, 1978a; Powell and Brander 1977). Brander and Books (1973, 54) wrote that the fisher's "hunting pattern is a random investigation of brushy areas, windfalls, hollow trees and other places where hares and smaller mammals are likely to be found." In reality, this foraging pattern is hardly *random* in the strict sense of the word. *Random* is used because of the apparently unpredictable nature of fishers' track patterns. I prefer to use *zigzag foraging*. Coulter (1966, 117) stated: "In hare cover they dart beneath every low-hanging bough, fallen tree top, log or similar place where a hare might be sitting." Fishers' elongate shape facilitates this type of hunting and provides for them a pattern of hunting that leads to prey not available to other predators.

Fishers also run along hare runs (Powell 1977a, 1978a; Powell and Brander 1977; Raine 1987). Coulter (1966) believed that sometimes when a fisher enters an area with dense cover and high hare density, the hares scurry in all directions. The fisher then crisscrosses the area and intercepts fleeing hares by chance. No other studies of fishers, however, have found hare or fisher tracks that lead to this interpretation.

Hares are killed where they are found resting or, when they have perceived a fisher at the last minute and have been flushed from cover, after a short rushing attack (Powell 1978a). Hares may also be flushed from forms, or hiding places, when a fisher is some distance away. Coulter (1966) interpreted tracks in the snow to demonstrate that hares would sometimes be flushed from their forms when a fisher was as far away as 10 meters, even when the fisher was going in another direction. There are a few reports of fishers chasing hares for long distances (Hardy 1899, 1907; L. David Mech, personal communication), and Raine (1987) documented two chases that went farther than 1 kilometer. Such long chases appear to be rare.

The success rates of fishers hunting snowshoe hares are difficult to quantify because it is difficult to determine temporal relationships between fisher and hare tracks. Temporal relationships between tracks can only be determined when the tracks are on top of each other or when the tracks are made during a light snowfall. Even under these conditions, the temporal relationships between tracks are known only on a crude basis—either before or after. How often hares escape from fishers is usually impossible to calculate. Coulter (1966) believed that a fisher's success after a short rush attack was low. The quantified hunting success of other predators is often low (e.g., for wolves there is a 6% success rate for capturing perceived moose; Mech 1966, 1970). Therefore, fishers are expected to have low hunting success rates.

When fishers actively hunt prey other than snowshoe hares and porcupines, they use the zigzag method they use when foraging for hares. Coulter (1966) found that fishers in Maine actively hunted for mice. He followed tracks of fishers that investigated hollow logs and piles of forest litter. The fishers sometimes tore apart rotten stumps and scattered mouse nests and seed caches. From Coulter's findings, it is apparent that fishers investigate potential hiding places for mice the same way they investigate potential hiding places for hares. Raine (1987) reported similar behavior. During my field study, I followed one very confusing set of fisher tracks that led to a gray squirrel kill. The tracks could be interpreted to show that a fisher was hunting gray squirrels by using the zigzag method in an area of high gray squirrel activity. However, it was the breeding season, and the tracks crisscrossed, backtracked, and double-tracked much more than normal. In addition, there was evidence that the tracks may have been made by more than one fisher. Therefore, another interpretation of the tracks is that one fisher was trying to find another fisher during the breeding season and that one of the fishers happened to catch a squirrel.

Fishers are clearly not mouse, shrew, or squirrel specialists. Though mice, shrews, and squirrels are commonly found in diet studies (Table 8), as the discussion in the preceding chapter suggests, they may all be overrepresented in GI tracts and scats compared to their importance in fishers' diets. In addition, track patterns indicate that these prey are often taken fortuitously (Coulter 1966; Powell 1977a). In habitats where prey are found in low densities, fishers travel through the habitat in fairly straight lines with few changes of direction and zigzags. When fishers catch prey or find a carcass in such habitat, their subsequent foraging pattern does not change.

Fishers do not hunt in the best mouse-hunting habitats (Powell 1977a). Fishers rarely, if ever, hunt in the open habitats that are frequently used by foxes and coyotes to hunt mice. Wide, overgrown, unplowed logging roads and the right-of-way to a buried gas pipeline in my study area were frequently used by foxes and coyotes hunting mice. I once tracked a fox that killed four mice in less than 1 kilometer along a wide, overgrown logging road. In contrast, I tracked fishers for over 200 kilometers during my study and found only two small mammal kills. Both kills were found in forest habitat; the fishers made small zigzags from their lines of travel and dug down into the snow to get the mice. There is no evidence from track patterns that fishers catch mice with their paws with a pounce like the one used by foxes and coyotes to catch mice. Fishers avoid the habitats that provide the most successful mousing and do not use mousing techniques used by habitual mousers.

Despite stories of fishers chasing red squirrels in the trees (Grinnell, Dixon, and Linsdale 1937; Morse 1961; Seton 1937), there is no evidence that this takes place regularly (Brander and Books 1973; Coulter 1966). Fishers catch squirrels of any species in trees only when they happen to find the squirrels in holes large enough for a fisher to enter (Coulter 1966). On the ground, squirrels are caught only when a fisher happens upon one that is foraging (Coulter 1966; Powell 1977a) or when a fisher is able to dig one out from a shallow ground den after it has fled from the fisher (Coulter 1966).

The zigzag foraging method is also used by weasels (Powell 1977a, 1978a; Powell and Brander 1977). It is likely that this foraging behavior may also have been used by the miacids (Anderson 1970; Colbert 1969; Ewer 1973). Miacids had rather generalized limb structure and relatively long, slender bodies without long limbs. Their body structure was similar to that of present-day mustelines, though not so extreme in its slenderness. The most common prey for the miacids were probably small animals that could be captured on the ground. Because some miacids were probably good climbers, some prey may have been captured in the trees. It is likely, therefore, that miacids used foraging patterns much like those used by mustelines today.

I have quantified the foraging patterns of fishers and weasels in order to make a comparison (Powell 1978a). Five tracks of fishers hunting snowshoe hares in lowland coniferous forest were measured to determine the ratio of the actual distance traveled by the fisher to the distance along its general line of travel. The same was done for eighteen tracks of fishers traveling between patches of hare habitat in upland hardwood forest and for twenty tracks of weasels hunting mice. Along the tracks in upland hardwood forest, fishers searched for porcupine dens, which were only found in this habitat, and foraging behavior around the dens was measured. For all these tracks, the distances the animals actually traveled were measured by pacing along the track (for fisher) or by measuring the distance with a tape measure (for weasels). Then, the tracks were precisely mapped and the distances along the general line of travel were taken from the maps. Foraging distances around porcupine dens were measured from maps. The results are shown in Table 9. Total distance along the line of travel was 0.3 kilometers for the weasel tracks, 5.0 kilometers for the fishers

Table 9. Mean ratios (± standard deviation) of distance run (R) to distance along the direction of travel (T) for weasels and fishers foraging in Michigan

	$R/T \pm SD$	Range	Number of observations	Total Ts for all observations (km)
Fishers searching for patches of prey[a,b]	1.03 ± 0.03	1.00-1.11	18	10.4
Fishers searching in hare habitat[b]	1.55 ± 0.24	1.26-1.90	5	2.8
Fishers searching around porcupine dens	1.99 ± 0.50	1.39-2.60	4	0.5
Weasels[a]	1.48 ± 0.68	1.04-3.52	20	0.3

[a] Difference significant, $p < 0.01$, Student's t test.
[b] Difference significant, $p \ll 0.01$, Student's t test.

hunting hares, 10.4 kilometers for the fishers searching for hare habitat or porcupine dens, and approximately 0.5 kilometers for fishers investigating porcupine dens and feeding trees. Fishers hunting hares and weasels hunting mice change direction frequently and travel a considerable distance farther than the distance along their line of travel. The ratio of distance traveled to distance along the line of travel is about 1.5 for both animals, though the weasels had a much higher variance. Fishers investigating porcupine dens and feeding trees travel about twice as far as the distance along the line of travel.

Weasels not only zigzag on the surface of the ground or snow but also frequently change directions up and down. Sometimes weasels forage in low trees and shrubs, and during the winter weasels frequently forage beneath the snow (Klimov 1940; Kraft 1966; Nyholm 1959; Powell 1977a, 1978a; Seton 1929; Teplov 1948). American martens and European pine martens forage extensively under the snow for mice, especially red-backed voles (Buskirk 1984; Raine 1987). Although there are trappers' reports of fishers foraging under the snow for mice (deVos 1952), fishers are too large to forage extensively beneath the snow. They do occasionally forage in trees, however. Consequently, their foraging resembles that of weasels in this way, also. I believe that by frequently changing direction while foraging, weasels decrease their chances of being preyed upon by other predators (Powell 1977a, 1978a, 1978b, 1982a). Weasels are preyed upon by raptors (Craighead and Craighead 1956; Errington 1967; Mendall 1944; Selwyn 1966), martens (Weckwerth and Hawley 1962), foxes (Latham 1952), and cats (Gaughran 1950). An avian predator unable to predict a weasel's movements may be more likely to miss it when striking.

Predation on fishers is infrequent at most, and it is unlikely that fishers are under any selective pressure to adjust foraging patterns to reduce predation by predators other than humans. However, fishers and weasels have evolved from small, common ancestors (Anderson 1970) that probably had selective pres-

sures for predator avoidance similar to those of present-day weasels. Therefore, the selective pressure for zigzag foraging that reduces predation has been
secondarily lost by fishers.

Because prey are found at high densities only in localized patches of habitat,
a fisher (or any other predator) hunting in such a patch increases its chances of
finding and catching prey when it frequently changes direction. If the fisher foraged along a relatively straight line, inspecting only those likely hiding places for
prey that were found along that line, the fisher would soon find itself outside the
habitat patch with high prey density. By changing direction frequently, the fisher
is able to stay within the patch. In addition, the fisher should minimize in some
manner the frequency at which it recrosses its own tracks (Pyke, Pulliam, and
Charnov 1977): in areas already searched by the fisher, the prey animals would
be alert to the fisher's presence or they would have left. Thus, the foraging
pattern cannot be completely random (Pyke, Pulliam, and Charnov 1977).

Fishers should forage in a zigzag manner with frequent directional changes in
any habitat that has prey in high density. In general, hare habitat is the most
common habitat used by fishers in which this is the case and is thus the only
habitat in which fishers consistently forage by frequently changing direction and
zigzagging. When a fisher is traveling through habitat that is not hare habitat but
in which prey are found in high density, the fisher should forage in the zigzag
manner. Fishers do occasionally forage in this manner for mice and squirrels
(Arthur, Krohn, and Gilbert 1989b; Coulter 1966; Powell 1977a; Raine 1987).

At all other times, when a fisher perceives an isolated prey individual, the
fisher should attempt to catch it but not begin foraging in a zigzag manner. Remaining in the area would be of no advantage to the fisher because prey are in
low density. This has been found to be the case when fishers find single mice,
squirrels, and grouse (Coulter 1966; Powell 1977a).

Pyke (1978) analyzed the theoretically optimal directionality of foraging in a
habitat where prey are evenly distributed. He visualized the habitat in which an
animal foraged as a grid of points. Food was found only at the points, and the
foraging animal could move only from the point at which it was located to the
four adjacent points (forward, back, left, right). The probabilities of moving in
each of the four directions were chosen to be discrete approximations to the
truncated normal distribution with different variances; Pyke found support for
these choices in the literature. The probabilities of moving to the left and to the
right are assumed to be equal. Thus, the directionality of a foraging bout is simply the probability of moving forward minus the probability of moving backward
for that bout. This measure of directionality ranges from 1, when there is only
forward movement, to 0 when movement is random (forward and backward
probabilities are equal). Computer simulation was used to investigate how the
number of points visited in the grid during a foraging bout was affected by the

directionality of the bout, the size of the grid, the length of the bout, and the behavior of the animal at the edge of the habitat.

Pyke's (1978) analysis can be applied to fishers' foraging habits. In snowshoe hare habitat, fishers forage in large grids: each point on the grid is a potential hiding place for hares, and there are extremely large numbers of hares and hiding places in each patch of hare habitat. Foraging bouts are long because a fisher inspects a large number of hiding places during each hunting bout. And fishers run along the edges of a habitat patch (they do not always immediately move back into the interior of a patch when they reach its edge). With these aspects of foraging known, the optimal foraging directionality for a foraging bout is between 0.8 and 1.0.

Equivalent to Pyke's (1978) measure of directionality is the inverse of the ratio of actual distance traveled to distance along the line of travel given in Table 9. The inverse of the value for fishers in hare habitat is 0.64. Because of the large variance for the values in Table 9, this directionality measure for fishers is not significantly different from 0.8. However, since several other vertebrates have similar values for their measures of directionality (Pyke 1978), there may be a real difference between the directionality measure for the fisher and Pyke's theoretical optimum. Factors not considered by Pyke may affect fishers' foraging behavior. In Pyke's model, the predator remains in the prey patch because it comes back into the patch when it reaches the edge. Predators can also remain in patches by having different probabilities for turning right and left, which leads to circling (Curio 1976) and would reduce Pyke's measure of directionality. Another major factor not considered by Pyke is memory. Fishers do appear to remember certain aspects of their home ranges (Powell 1977a, 1978a; Powell and Brander 1977), and it is conceivable that they are familiar enough with the patches of hare habitat in their home ranges that they can forage in patterns that reduce the amount of reinvestigation of areas already searched. Such behavior would decrease the directionality measure by decreasing the probability of moving forward when an area already searched is approached.

Killing Behavior

Fishers kill small prey such as mice and shrews by applying the capture bite, by shaking them, or by eating them. Small prey are eaten whole, with little or no chewing, and they often show up in fishers' stomachs as identifiable, whole individuals (Kelly 1977). Prey as large as squirrels are killed with a bite to the back of the neck or head (Kelly 1977).

Prey the size of snowshoe hares and rabbits are also killed with a bite to the back of the neck or head (Figure 41; Coulter 1966; Powell 1977a, 1978a), but the fisher may use its feet to assist with the kill (Figure 42; Powell 1977a,

Figure 41. Adult male fisher killing a snowshoe hare with a bite to the back of the neck.

1978a). When a fisher attacks a hare, the fisher first attempts to secure a hold on the animal. The fisher bites any place available but tries to bite the back of the hare's neck or head. When this initial hold is not on the hare's neck or head, the fisher wraps itself around the hare and grasps it with all four feet. The fisher then releases its bite and finds the back of the hare's neck or head. Once the fisher has a firm hold on the hare's neck with its teeth, it releases the hold with its feet and waits for the hare to become immobilized. During this time, the fisher may repeatedly bite and loosen (but not release) its grip on the hare's neck and may relocate the bite a little without releasing its hold. Fishers sometimes shake hares after they are immobilized. Hares may be immobilized in an exceedingly short time; I recorded one killing time of 15 seconds when a fisher did not need to use the wraparound assist. However, hares are not always killed immediately by fishers. On three occasions I observed satiated captive fishers immobilize hares that later attempted to escape after about 15 minutes of apparent death. These hares had faulty equilibria and impaired running abilities and were killed immediately after the fisher noted their attempted escapes. It is doubtful that free-living fishers are often satiated enough not to eat a hare immediately after it is caught.

Figure 42. Female fisher using the wraparound assist to handle a snowshoe hare. (Drawing by C. B. Powell.)

Before beginning to eat a squirrel, rabbit, or hare, a fisher often licks the bloody eyes, nose, and mouth of the dead prey. A fisher does not commence eating a rabbit or hare at any particular body region and is just as likely to start at the head as at the rump. Rabbits, hares, and smaller prey are usually consumed in one meal. I found no evidence that fishers take hares into areas with dense cover to eat; some fishers ate hares in the open where the hares were caught. After eating, a fisher usually sleeps for several hours in a temporary den (Powell 1977a, 1978a, 1979a).

Fishers that are satiated still kill prey but cache those they cannot eat. Captive fishers cache food in their nest boxes (Powell 1977a, 1978a). Free-living fishers probably seldom encounter situations in which food items the size of a hare or smaller cannot be eaten. On those infrequent occasions, it is likely that a satiated fisher would cache a hare or similar food item in the temporary sleeping den in which it sleeps. Large items such as deer carcasses may be left after the fisher has finished eating, though the fisher usually sleeps in proximity to the carcass. I found a temporary sleeping den within 25 meters of every deer carcass used by fishers.

A neck bite is the most common killing technique used by species in the order Carnivora. Nevertheless, there is considerable variation and diversity in how the method is employed by species within the order. (See the review of carnivores' killing techniques in Ewer 1973.) As Ewer (1973, 225-26) pointed out:

It is impossible to believe that any carnivore could have evolved a dentition of the miacid types without some corresponding behavioral adaptations, the most obvious of which is not to attack at random but to direct the bite to the anterior region of the prey and aim at head or neck. This has the double advantage of giving a high probability of a quick kill and of making a retaliatory bite difficult. . . . One would not expect any very precise orientation of the bite in the early stages of evolution and the miacids probably increased the efficacy of a somewhat labile orientation in the two ways adopted by living viverrids—by iterant biting and snapping and by shaking.

The neck bite used by members of the Mustelinae, a bite directed to the back of the prey's head or neck, is a moderately developed neck bite. The bite is directed with fair precision, but a bite anywhere along the back of the head or neck usually suffices. The bite is a simple bite or a repeated bite and is not as developed as that of many felids. The wraparound assist, however, is an important evolutionary advance over primitive killing methods.

Weasels kill mice by using the same behavior fishers use to kill hares (Powell 1977a, 1978a). Weasels kill or immobilize mice with a neck bite (Allen 1938; Ewer 1973; Gillingham 1978; Glover 1943; Hamilton 1933; Llewellyn 1942; Powell 1977a, 1978a), and use the wraparound assist (Gillingham 1978; Heidt 1970; Miller 1931; Powell 1977a, 1978a). Weasels may curl on their sides or over the prey in their wraparound assist (Gillingham 1978) and may sometimes scrape at the prey with their hindpaws (Ewer 1973). The wraparound assist is not characteristic of canoids other than mustelids, probably because of the mustelids' body shapes. The wraparound assist is used by genets (*Genetta* spp. [Ewer 1973, Plate 9b]; genets are members of the Viverridae and thus are feloids), which are not dissimilar in shape to fishers. The wraparound is not used by mongooses (Ewer 1973), indicating that the behavior is not a direct correlate to body shape.

Movement by prey is an important stimulus for attack in fishers and other mustelines (Powell 1977a, 1978a). The fact that fishers sometimes lose interest in immobilized prey and allow them to recover indicates that movement may be a necessary stimulus for attack. Although hunger may affect a fisher's readiness and quickness of attack, hunger is not a necessary stimulus for attack because satiated fishers attack hares. Separating hunger from other stimuli for attack is important. Wild fishers seldom encounter conditions of overabundant food. Except when a fisher is camping next to a large carcass, its next meal is uncertain. Since hunger is not a necessary stimulus for attack, on those few occasions when several prey are encountered, a fisher can kill more prey than its immediate requirements demand and cache uneaten prey. Repeated killing and caching is one method of ensuring the future availability of food (Ewer 1973; Hall

1951; Kruuk 1972; Moors 1974, 1977). A satiated fisher attacks moving prey and thus acquires a future supply of food.

Repeated killing and caching explains the "henhouse syndrome." Many members of the weasel family, fishers included, have been known to raid henhouses and other poultry enclosures. Fishers have been known to raid duck pens on game farms. These raids are usually characterized by lots of feathers and by lots of poultry killed and left uneaten. So much poultry is left uneaten that members of the weasel family have gained a reputation for being ruthless, wanton, wasteful, bloodthirsty killers. But a henhouse is essentially a new, super-food-rich environment in which mustelids have not evolved and to which they are not adapted. When they are in new environments, animals act the same as they do in the environments to which they are adapted. So, in a henhouse mustelids kill as many chickens as possible, eat what is needed for satiation, and save the rest for later. Obviously, there are too many chickens to be carted off to sleeping sites, so a mustelid may take one or two, leave the rest, and return the next time it is hungry. The behavior is completely understandable, though it does not endear mustelids to farmers who have lost chickens. Fortunately for the fisher, its range does not overlap with much agricultural land, and chicken coops are seldom located close enough to forested land to be accessible to fishers.

Chapter 8

Fishers and Porcupines

The relationship between the fisher and the porcupine, first noted by early trappers and explorers, has long interested naturalists and everyone else who has heard of it. That any predator could habitually kill an animal so protected with quills is fascinating. Certainly, this aspect of fisher biology is the most widely known, though much of what people read and hear about the subject is more myth than reality. Reality, however, is just as interesting as myth in most cases, and the case of the fisher-porcupine relationship is no exception. The predator-prey relationship between fishers and porcupines and the evolution of this relationship do deserve an important place in any discussion of fishers.

The Porcupine

The Canadian porcupine (Figure 38) is the only porcupine native to North America. It is found over much of the United States and Canada in areas where

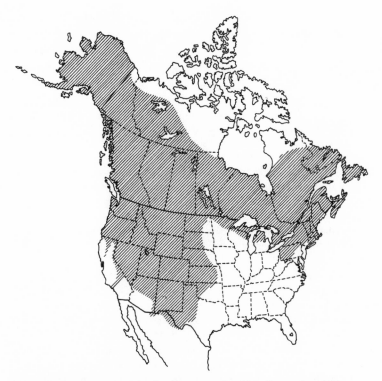

Figure 43. Species range of the Canadian porcupine. Note the overlap of this range with that of the fisher (shown in Figure 28). (Adapted by C. B. Powell, from Burt and Grossenheider 1964, Dodge 1982, and Taylor 1935.)

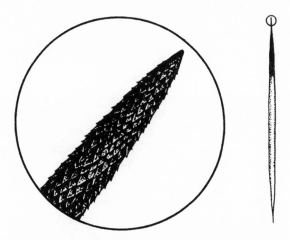

Figure 44. Porcupine quill with enlarged inset of tip showing barbs, which resemble sharp, overlapping scales. (Drawing by C. B. Powell.)

there are extensive forests (Figure 43). Roze (1989) has written an excellent book summarizing the biology of porcupines in the Northeast and discussing his research.

Porcupines are large rodents, weighing 4 to 8 kilograms or more. Taylor (1935, 32-33) described the porcupine well:

> The body of the porcupine is short, heavy, and obese in appearance. When at rest, the animal assumes almost the form of a sphere. The head, legs, and tail are never conspicuous. The neck is short and indistinguishable, the body appearing to swell out from the nose back to the middle, with no intervening constriction. The face is short, the muzzle blunt, the nostrils prominent. The whiskers are long and black. The eyes are small, usually somewhat protuberant and bearing a striking resemblance to shoe buttons. They are usually watery in daylight probably indicating their imperfect adaptation to strong light. . . . The ears are small, almost hidden by the surrounding hair. The upper incisors, yellowish in color, are usually visible when one catches sight of the lower part of the face.
>
> The legs are short, and conspicuously bowed. The claws are long and prominent, grooved beneath. The soles of the feet are naked and rough. They have been compared to those of a bear, and they are admirably suited to maintain contact with the bark of trees or surface of boulders. The feet are well adapted to either climbing, standing, or walking erect on a horizontal surface. . . . The forefeet are more mobile than the hind feet and especially adapted to grasping and holding. The tail is relatively short, thick and muscular, with a blunt and squarish appearance. It is a most important organ; on the side of a tree it is used as a prop. "The thickly set and rigid bristles covering its lower surface stick to the bark." When the porcupine walks along a branch, the tail is pressed down against the branch to help keep the animal's balance. When the porcupine sits up to eat with its hands, the tail serves as one "leg" of a tripod, the other two being the hind legs. The tail is also an effective weapon of defense.

Porcupines have never been known for the beauty of their pelts, but they have a unique beauty that is easy for the casual observer to overlook. The nose, muzzle, and face almost to the tiny, hidden, round ears are covered with fine, soft black-velvet fur. The muzzle is rounded, the lips are dark, and the eyes are black and liquid. All of these features give a porcupine a most beautiful face.

A porcupine's pelage is characterized by three types of hair: woolly underfur, long and coarse guard hairs, and the well-known quills. The woolly underfur acts as insulation but is not evenly distributed over the entire body (Clarke and Brander 1973). Quills (Figure 44) are found all over the porcupine's body, except its belly and face. The quills are usually creamy white with glossy dark brown tips and are longest and most prominent on a porcupine's rump and tail. The guard hairs are frequently all that can be seen on the upper back, sides, and neck, although there are a prodigious number of quills under the guard hairs. Quills are modified guard hairs filled with a spongy substance that makes them sturdy. There are numerous microscopic barbs at the end of each quill (Figure 44). These barbs are most accurately called scales and do not resemble the barb of a fishhook. They look more like the overlapping shingles on a roof. This arrangement of scales makes it easier for the quills to move into the body of a victim and more difficult for them to be pulled back out. The quills contain no poison or irritant and cannot be thrown. They are only lightly connected to the skin and pull loose easily when the points have entered another object. The rump of the porcupine is covered mostly by quills, and pelage in this area is sparse, allowing significant heat loss during the winter. Porcupines seem to reduce this heat loss by feeding in trees and by frequently using postures that reduce radiant heat loss (Clarke and Brander 1973).

Porcupines possess the chisel-like incisor teeth characteristic of rodents. They are opportunistic feeders and eat a wide variety of vegetation (Earle 1978; Roze 1989). During the summer, porcupines' diets vary greatly over North America: in some areas porcupines feed largely on the leaves of deciduous trees, and in other areas they feed on a wide variety of terrestrial and aquatic herbaceous vegetation (Brander 1973; Dodge 1967; Roze 1989). During the winter, the preferred foods of porcupines are the phloem of conifers and to a lesser extent the needles. Hemlocks and pines are generally favored (Brander 1973; Dodge 1967; Roze 1989; Taylor 1935), especially soft pines (white pine, limber pine, and others in the white pine group). In Upper Michigan, porcupines also eat the phloem of sugar maples, American elms, American basswoods, and yellow birches (Brander 1973). During the spring, herbaceous plants and grasses and the buds of several hardwoods are consumed (Earle 1978; Roze 1989).

Porcupines' daily activities change with the seasons (Roze 1989). Porcupines den in large hollow trees, hollow logs, and rockfalls during the winter (Figure 45). Dens are often used for many years in succession, and over the years porcupine excrement accumulates at the entrances of the dens. Porcupine excrement can be smelled from a considerable distance, at times even by humans (Powell 1977a, 1978a). Winter days are generally spent in dens, and winter nights are spent in nearby feeding trees (Brander 1973; Powell and Brander 1977; Roze 1989). A porcupine travels from its den to its feeding tree in the evening and back to the den in the morning but may, on occasion, spend the entire day in a feeding tree. During the summer, feeding is strongly diurnal (Brander 1973; Roze 1989). Most of the day is spent in feeding trees, but much of that time is spent sleeping and resting. On summer nights, porcupines travel to gathering sites, which are usually within 200 meters of their feeding trees. Many porcupines may gather at one site, and there is much interaction. Most activity takes place during the two or three hours before and after midnight.

Figure 45. Porcupine winter dens. *Top*, den in a large, hollow yellow birch; *middle*, den in a large, hollow log; and *bottom*, den in a rockfall.

Figure 46. Porcupine approximately one week old. Baby porcupines are fully quilled with short quills about 1 centimeter long. Baby-pelage guard hairs are longer than quills at this age giving the baby porcupine a fuzzy appearance.

Figure 47. Young porcupine using a crevice in a tree to protect its face.

Porcupines cease coming to gathering sites coincident with the mating season in September and October (Brander 1973; Roze 1989).

One and sometimes two offspring are born during the spring; parturition dates between March and June have been recorded (Roze 1989; Taylor 1935). The young are born fully quilled, and it takes about 30 minutes for the quills to dry. The underfur is more apparent in young porcupines, and underfur and guard hairs may cover almost all of a young porcupine's quills (Roze 1989; Taylor 1935), giving it a fuzzy appearance (Figure 46). Weight at birth is about 500 grams (Roze 1989; Taylor 1935). Taylor (1935) repeated an American Indian legend that claims that a mother porcupine drives her baby from her as soon as it is born and never nurses it. Although the legend is not completely true, it is true to the extent that baby porcupines are never totally dependent on mother's milk or are so only for an extremely short period. Almost from birth, porcupines eat nonabrasive solid food and may be completely weaned when they are very young. The actual period between birth and weaning may be very long, however, and there are records of porcupines having nursed into the autumn (Roze 1989; Taylor 1935). By autumn, though, young porcupines are quite capable of fending completely for themselves.

Porcupine quills are distributed to give the best protection against an attack from above or behind; they also protect a porcupine from being overturned. The quills are long and dense and are most apparent on the rump and tail of a porcupine, giving excellent protection from attacks oriented toward the back and from predators approaching from behind. The sides, back of the neck, and legs of porcupines are also well protected, providing protection from attacks to the back of the neck and from predators attempting to overturn them.

When porcupines walk on the ground between resting sites and feeding sites, they appear to choose routes that reduce exposure to predators, and when foraging on grasses and herbaceous vegetation on the ground, they do not venture far from the protection of trees. When attacked, a porcupine attempts to keep its back oriented toward the attacker. If the predator circles, the porcupine will circle with the predator, always keeping its back directed toward the predator. When possible, the porcupine tries to protect its face by facing a tree or similar object (Figure 47). The porcupine flips its rump and tail in a humping motion when the predator gets too close (Powell 1978a; Powell and Brander 1977; Roze 1989).

Fishers and Porcupines

There is evidence that porcupines and fishers have coexisted for many millennia. Both species are indigenous to North America and were part of the continental fauna by the Wisconsinan event of the Pleistocene, at least 10,000 years ago (Anderson 1970; Hibbard 1970). Ancient evidence of the interaction of porcupines and fishers is suggested by the comingling of their bones in caves used by archaic and woodland human cultures (900 B.C. to European settlement) in what is now Alabama and Missouri (Barkalow 1961; Parmalee 1971). Present ranges of the two species overlap extensively (Figures 28 and 43), and it can be assumed that their ranges overlapped extensively in the past.

Few predators kill porcupines. Wolves, coyotes, lynxes, bobcats, wolverines, and great horned owls occasionally kill porcupines, but none of these predators regularly preys on porcupines or affects porcupine populations (Earle 1978; Roze 1989). Brander and I discounted large felids as frequent porcupine predators (Powell and Brander 1977). Earle (1978), however, noted that they have dexterous front legs and paws and are capable of wounding a porcupine's face with a blow from the front paws. Mountain lions do prey on porcupines in some places, and porcupine remains are regularly found in their scats (Maser and Rohweder 1983). Mountain lions are rare in much of the porcupine's range, and Roze believed they were not capable of affecting porcupine population dynamics.

Of all predators known to kill porcupines, fishers are best adapted morphologically and behaviorally to be successful (Powell and Brander 1977), and porcupine remains are found more often and more consistently in the GI tracts and scats of fishers than in those of any other predators. Since porcupines spend approximately half of each day in the trees, canids are restricted to contacting porcupines when they are on the ground. Fishers are better adapted for arboreality and are more agile in trees than felids. Therefore, fishers are better adapted to taking advantage of encounters with porcupines in trees than are other predators (Powell and Brander 1977).

Both canid and felid predators are much taller than porcupines and, when they attack a porcupine, must make their major effort from above the porcupine. An attack made to the back of a porcupine's neck (a typical canid and felid killing technique [Ewer 1973]) encounters an area well protected by quills. Canids and felids do attempt biting attacks at porcupines' necks, and these attacks are known to be often unsuccessful (Figure 48).

Both the scientific and popular literature contain unsupported references to fishers overturning porcupines and attacking their bellies or attacking porcupines from under tree branches (Anthony 1928; Cahalane 1944, 1947; Coues 1877; Pringle 1964; Seton 1937; Schoonmaker 1938). Coulter (1966) was the first to report observations that showed that the popular belief was an exaggerated myth. Brander and I have been able to reconstruct fishers' porcupine kills from tracks and sign in the snow in Upper Peninsula Michigan (Powell and Brander 1977), and I have been able to reconstruct several more kills made by fishers both in the wild and in captivity and to observe one kill in captivity (Pow-

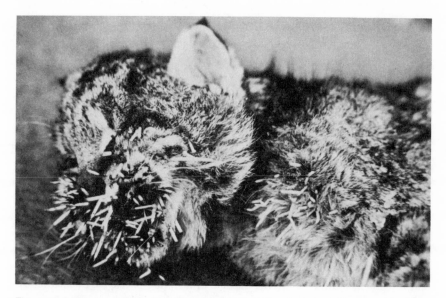

Figure 48. Bobcat found dead with its face full of quills. This animal also had numerous quills in its paws and shoulders. (Courtesy of the Wisconsin Department of Natural Resources.)

ell 1977a, 1978a). All direct observations show that fishers kill porcupines with repeated attacks on the face.

A fisher's attack behavior toward a porcupine involves a strategy that opens the porcupine's face to a bite. Repeated facial attacks have not been reported for other mustelids, but for long-tailed weasels (Allen 1938) and black-footed ferrets (Progulske 1969), "if prey is relatively large, a few preliminary bites delivered anywhere convenient may precede a definitive attack" (Ewer 1973, 177). I have observed the same behavior in European fitch ferrets attacking snowshoe hares. If ancestral fishers also displayed preliminary bites "anywhere convenient" when attacking large prey, such behavior could easily have evolved into repeated facial attacks on porcupines because the face is the only place convenient. The evolution of a successful and relatively safe technique for killing porcupines would have opened a new source of food to fishers, for which they had little competition (Powell 1977a, 1978a).

The concurrence of all recent reports that fishers kill porcupines by attacking their faces does not mean that this is the only method employed by fishers. It is possible that some or all fishers have other techniques for killing porcupines. Pringle and Mech (1961) cited a report from a trapper who believed that fishers turn porcupines over by holding on to the face the first time a good bite to the face is achieved. Though such speculations may have merit, all the present evidence still strongly indicates that making repeated facial attacks is the primary killing method.

Figure 49. Fisher circling a porcupine.

Figure 50. Fisher initiating a strike at a porcupine's face. Several wounds to the porcupine's face over the course of approximately 30 minutes are needed to kill the porcupine.

Pringle (1964) was the first to point out that a porcupine is not an easy source of food for a fisher. An attacked porcupine attempts to keep its back toward the fisher and, when possible, faces a tree, log, or rock to protect its face. An attacking fisher repeatedly circles the porcupine, attempting to bite its face (Figure 49). When it finds a chance, the fisher darts in (Figure 50), bites the porcupine's face, and darts back again before the porcupine has a chance to turn and strike the fisher with its tail. Repeated wounds to the face over a period of 30 minutes or more finally kill or bewilder the porcupine so that the fisher can turn it over and begin feeding on its ventral surface. Most attacks to the face are unsuccessful, and a fisher often has to check an attack after it is started because the porcupine is able to move quickly enough to protect itself. Coulter (1966) and I both observed attacking fishers receiving a few quills in the head and shoulder, but these appeared to cause little or no trouble. An attacking fisher is acutely aware of the porcupine's tail, which can embed quills deeply with movements so quick my eye could not follow them. A fisher I hand raised paid special attention to porcupines' tails when attacking.

A porcupine being attacked by a fisher attempts to escape. I observed a captive porcupine attempting to climb a fence post to escape an attacking fisher. The fisher climbed the fence and got above the porcupine. From this advantage, the fisher was able to attack the porcupine's face from above, forcing the porcupine back down to the ground. Evidence from kill sites suggests that wild fishers use this technique to keep porcupines from climbing trees and to force them back from the protection of trees.

Obviously fishers are uniquely adapted for killing porcupines. Fishers are built low to the ground, at the level of a porcupine's face, and can, therefore, attack a porcupine's face directly. They are large enough to inflict a substantial wound when they have a chance to bite a porcupine's face, and yet they are small enough to be quick and agile and dart in and out at a porcupine's face while avoiding the porcupine's tail. And fishers have arboreal adaptations that allow them to take advantage of trees and to reduce the protection afforded to porcupines by trees. No other predator possesses this array of characteristics, and so no other predator has the ability to attack and kill porcupines that a fisher has.

Figures 51 and 52 illustrate two sites where fishers killed porcupines. These kill sites are typical of those found by Brander and me in Michigan (Powell 1977a, 1978a; Powell and Brander 1977).

At the kill shown in Figure 51, fisher tracks led first to a hollow log, then to a porcupine den in a hollow log, and finally along a porcupine trail to a porcupine den in a tree snag. The packed snow covered with blood, urine, and quills at the base of the tree indicated the location of the actual kill site. Because the packed-down area did not reach the den hole, the fisher was somehow able to keep the porcupine away from its den. The location of the packed snow next to

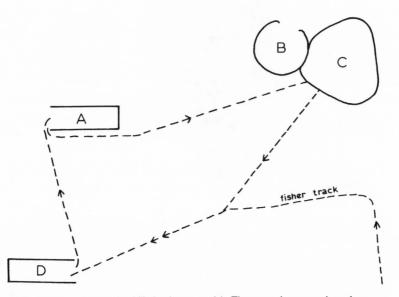

Figure 51. Map of porcupine kill site (not to scale). The porcupine was using a large hollow log (A) and a large, hollow snag (B) as dens. One well-used porcupine trail led from A to B, and a few additional trails led from B to nearby feeding trees. There was a packed-down area (C) at the base of the snag about 2 meters in diameter meeting the snag 90 degrees from the den hole. There were many claw scrapings around the lower 2 meters of the snag on the side where the kill took place. The entire area was littered with bark scrapings, quills, urine, and blood. Leading from the snag to another large hollow log (D) was a drag mark with fisher tracks. The fisher and the dead porcupine were both in the hollow log (D) when the kill site was found. A to B is approximately 20 meters, D to B is approximately 40 meters. (Drawing by C. B. Powell.)

the snag suggested that the porcupine tried to keep its face against the snag for protection. Scrapings on the tree and bark on the ground suggested that at least one animal climbed the snag. Tree climbing probably occurred in at least one of two situations: the fisher may have climbed the snag and come down headfirst toward the porcupine on the ground facing the tree trunk, or the porcupine may have climbed the tree, and the fisher may have climbed above and forced it back to the ground. The drag mark with the fisher tracks showed that the fisher dragged the porcupine to a hollow log some time after the kill.

The kill shown in Figure 52 was made at the base of the porcupine's feeding tree. The location of the packed snow suggested that the porcupine put its face into the scar on the tree trunk for protection. Blood, urine, and quills in the packed snow adjacent to the tree identified the kill site. Bark scrapings suggested the same possibilities for tree climbing as described for the kill in Figure 51. The carcass found in the smaller area of packed snow indicated that the fisher dragged the porcupine a few meters before or while eating it.

Figure 52. Photo of a site where a fisher killed a porcupine. The porcupine was killed at the base of an elm tree it had been using as a feeding tree. The area of packed snow was 1.5 meters in diameter and tangent to the tree at the site of a scar that formed an indentation. The packed snow was littered with bark scrapings, quills, urine, and blood. At the edge of the packed snow were two swish marks made by the fisher's tail. There were scattered tracks outside the packed area. The porcupine was found on its back in a smaller packed area about 3 meters from the tree. There were wounds on its face and a small hole in its chest cavity through which the heart, lungs, and part of one front leg had been eaten.

Fishers always begin eating porcupines somewhere on their ventral surfaces (Figure 53). Internal organs such as the heart, liver, and lungs are usually eaten first. Fishers minimize contact with quills while eating, skinning porcupines neatly and leaving only a few large bones, feet, intestines (sometimes), and skin with quills.

There are several ways that porcupines can reduce the danger of being attacked by fishers. Coulter (1966) gave a captive female fisher opportunities to kill four porcupines. She was able to kill three porcupines that weighed approximately 8 kilograms each but was unable to kill the largest of the four, which weighed approximately 11 kilograms. He argued that fishers may not be able to kill very large porcupines. Brander and I made the same conclusion from evidence in the field (Powell and Brander 1977). We found a kill site where the fisher was able to kill a small, young porcupine with little struggle. But the kill site for a porcupine that weighed 7.7 kilograms after being partially eaten (Fig-

Figure 53. Adult female fisher eating a porcupine she killed. The porcupine is on its back, and the fisher is eating through a hole in the chest cavity.

Figure 54. Porcupine in its den with its back facing outward and with its tail protruding slightly from the den entrance. A porcupine is safe from a fisher's attack when in a den such as this.

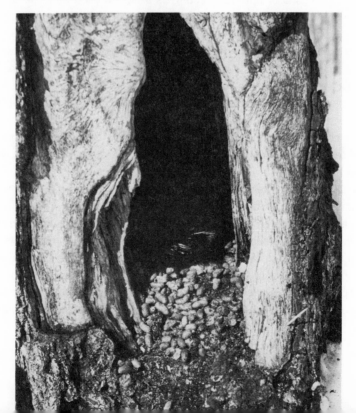

ure 52) showed signs of a great struggle (Powell and Brander 1977). If large porcupines were free from predation by fishers, one would expect that the porcupine populations in areas with established fisher populations should have larger proportions of very large porcupines than porcupine populations in areas without fisher populations. Earle (1978) found that this is not the case. The porcupine population in the Ottawa National Forest in Upper Michigan had a lighter average weight than the porcupine population in the Hiawatha National Forest, also in Upper Michigan, which lacked a fisher population. In addition, there was not an excess of very heavy porcupines in the Ottawa National Forest. Earle concluded that female fishers may not be able to kill very large porcupines but that large male fishers are probably able to kill any porcupine, given the proper environmental conditions. These conclusions agree with Coulter's (1966) observations. It is also possible that fisher predation on porcupines in the Ottawa National Forest is so effective that no porcupines are able to reach a size that is too large for a fisher to kill. The maximum known longevity for wild porcupines is approximately ten years (Brander 1971). Those porcupines just reaching a size too large for a fisher to kill at the time fishers were becoming reestablished in Upper Peninsula Michigan would have died by the time of Earle's (1978) study.

When a porcupine is able to find a tree, log, or rock pile with a properly shaped nook into which to face, a fisher is unable to make a successful attack (see Figure 47). Similarly, porcupines in dens are safe. When in its winter den, a porcupine faces in or upward directing its back and tail toward the den's entrance (Figure 54). I have observed fisher tracks that show that the fisher approached a porcupine's den in which there was a porcupine but left without making an attack. A den with only one entrance is completely safe from a fisher's attack (Powell and Brander 1977). Before the fisher's reintroduction to Upper Peninsula Michigan during the early 1960s, porcupines sometimes used dens in hollow logs with holes at both ends (R. B. Brander, personal communication). Since the reestablishment of fishers in the Upper Peninsula, the use of such dens has ceased where there are fishers. This may be because porcupines have learned that such dens are not safe from fishers' attacks and those that did not learn were killed.

Porcupines are also relatively safe from predation while they are in trees. On two occasions while I was working in the Ottawa National Forest, I followed fisher tracks that showed that the fishers had climbed trees in which there were porcupines but did not kill the porcupines. In both cases, the porcupines were facing out from the trunk of the tree when I came by several hours after the fisher (Figure 55). Out of twelve observations of porcupines in trees for which the direction the porcupine faced was noted, the porcupine faced away from the trunk in eleven (probability < 0.01, chi-square). If a porcupine were to face to-

Figure 55. Porcupine in a tree facing away from the trunk. When porcupines in trees face away from the trunk, they are safe from fishers' attacks.

ward the trunk, a fisher could either attack its face or force it backward until it fell from the tree, and then the fisher could make a normal attack on the ground (Powell 1977a, 1978a).

Fishers seeking porcupine dens in upland hardwood forests travel long distances with almost no changes in direction (Clem 1977; Powell 1977a, 1978a; Powell and Brander 1977). (See Figure 56 and Table 9.) I followed fisher tracks in Michigan that traveled up to 5 kilometers with little change in direction (Powell 1977a, 1978a). These long upland travels often passed within a meter of one or more porcupine dens. Sometimes a fisher abruptly changed direction before going directly to a porcupine's den, as though the fisher had smelled the den. Some porcupine dens were visited by fishers several winters in succession, even when the dens were not active during all winters. Therefore, fishers appear to use olfaction and memory in locating porcupine dens.

There were twenty-seven known porcupine dens in my Michigan study area that

Figure 56. Fisher track in porcupine habitat. Fishers travel long distances with little or no change of direction when in porcupine habitat.

were active during at least one of the three winters I was doing my fieldwork (Figure 57). Table 10 summarizes the numerical relationships among these dens and the tracks of fishers that visited them. To see whether fishers hunting porcupines had a tendency to inspect several porcupine dens before going back to hunting snowshoe hares, the right-hand column in Table 10 was compared to a Poisson distribution. The number of dens visited by a fisher was significantly different from a Poisson distribution (probability < 0.02), indicating that fishers visited several dens while foraging in porcupine habitat. This could be interpreted to mean that fishers specifically seek known porcupine dens and do not simply pass dens by chance on the way from one patch of hare habitat to another. However, several dens were close together (Figure 57), and if those dens were considered as one den (a fisher might be able to smell other nearby dens from one den in a cluster), then the number of dens visited by a fisher (Table 10, third column, in parentheses) is not different from a Poisson distribution. Consequently, the interpretation that fishers

Table 10. Numerical relationships between fisher tracks
and the porcupine dens they visited in Michigan

N	Number of dens visited by N tracks	Number of tracks visiting N dens[a]
0	3	13 (13)
1	14	7 (8)
2	4	3 (6)
3	2	4 (3)
4	4	3 (0)

[a] Numbers in parentheses are the number of dens if dens close
together are counted as a single den.

specifically seek to visit several porcupine dens should be taken with some caution. Nevertheless, I believe there is evidence that resident fishers know the locations of active porcupine dens within their home ranges and direct their foraging in porcupine habitat toward those dens.

In contrast to these data, Arthur and co-workers (1989b) did not note travel directed toward porcupine dens along 34 kilometers of fisher tracks in Maine. In fact, they found that fisher tracks intersected porcupine tracks (0.09 tracks/d/km) significantly less often than random transects intersected porcupine tracks (0.9 tracks/d/km). Nonetheless, porcupine kills were found along the tracks they followed, and porcupine quills and hair were common in fisher scats, indicating that the fishers they followed had some efficient method of finding porcupines that Arthur and co-workers could not discern.

Porcupine dens are discrete concentrations of prey located far apart in habitat that offers little else as prey for a fisher. Because of their odor, porcupine dens can be located from farther away by smell than by direct inspection. Locations of porcupine dens can be learned, and foraging can be directed toward them with little travel in other directions. Once a fisher has reached a porcupine den, however, it must locate the porcupine and learn if it is vulnerable to an attack. The fisher typically inspects the den, searches for other nearby dens or second openings, and searches along porcupine trails to feeding trees. This searching is similar to searching behavior in dense hare habitat and approximately doubles travel distance (Table 9). Thus, foraging by fishers for porcupines minimizes time spent in unproductive and unpreferred habitat while maximizing hunting efficiency.

Fishers and Quills

Every long-term study of fishers to date has found quills in at least some wild fishers but no sign that these quills caused infections or other complications. This fact and statements in the popular literature have led to the common pop-

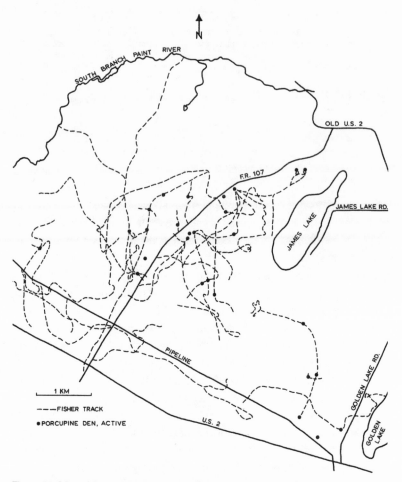

Figure 57. Map of fisher tracks in relation to known active porcupine dens in my study area in Upper Michigan. Several dens were visited by more than one track, and several tracks visited more than one den. (See Table 10.) (Drawing by C. B. Powell.)

ular belief that fishers are somehow different from other animals and are not affected by porcupine quills (Balser 1960; Bradle 1957; Cook and Hamilton 1957; Hamilton 1957; Hardy 1899, 1907; and others). There is no solid evidence to support these claims.

All mammals appear to react in the same manner to porcupine quills. Quills carry no poison or irritant and have no characteristics that should cause infection. Quick (1953b) looked at the incidence of quills in carcasses of mammals trapped in British Columbia and related this to the condition of the carcasses. Quills impaled in flesh appeared to have drifted about in the muscles and eventually became lodged against bones. Quick (1953b, 259) concluded that "ingested or injected quills are not necessarily lethal to mammals which prey upon porcupines." Coulter (1966) presented evidence showing that domestic dogs show no ill effects from quills that cannot be extracted. Therefore, there is nothing about quills that causes any animal harm other than the number of quills and the location of quills received during an encounter.

Roze (1989; Roze, Locke, and Vatakis 1990) showed that quills are covered with a thin layer of fatty acids, which have antibacterial action. This significantly reduces the probability of infection for an animal that has been quilled. Roze hypothesized that porcupines evolved antibiotic-coated quills to minimize infections from self-quilling that occurs during occasional, but regular, falls from trees.

Fishers, like other animals, can suffer ill effects from quills under certain conditions. Coulter (1966), deVos (1952), Hamilton and Cook (1955), Morse (1961), and Pringle (1964) all cited information gained from trappers indicating that porcupine quills can blind or kill fishers when many become embedded in a fisher's face. One of my captive fishers somehow embedded a quill from a dead porcupine deep in her chest and acquired a bad infection in the wound. Had I not removed the quill and administered an antibiotic, she might not have survived.

There is good evidence that fishers are unlikely to receive a large number of quills in an area such as the face or paws that would hinder their hunting or killing prey or their defending themselves. Any predator with a mouth full of quills will have trouble killing prey and eating carrion and will be subject to starvation before the quills work their way to harmless positions. A predator with quills in its paws will have trouble running. Similarly, a face full of quills prevents an animal from properly defending itself against an attack from another predator. These problems combined with food deprivation should predispose animals with large numbers of quills in strategic areas to starvation or mortality from predation by other predators. Because fishers have developed a technique for killing porcupines that minimizes the chances of receiving a large number of quills, fishers are less likely than other predators to suffer serious problems from porcupine quills.

Skip Whittler (personal communication) proposed that porcupines evolved antibiotic quills to train individual predators to avoid them and thus to minimize predation. If all predators, other than fishers, that attacked porcupines died from infections, those individuals would be replaced by other members of their species, probably naive, dispersing juveniles. These new predators would not know not to attack porcupines. By not causing infections, quills may increase the probability of maintaining resident predators who have learned to leave the resident porcupine alone.

Long-term Stability of Fisher and Porcupine Populations

The reported association between increasing fisher populations and decreasing porcupine populations was discussed briefly in chapter 4. Hamilton and Cook (1955, 29) wrote that "it seems probable that the increase of the fisher has had a part in the reduction of the once populous and destructive porcupine" in the Adirondack Mountains of New York. Using a Wisconsin county highway department's twelve-year record of porcupines killed on highways, Olson (1966, 22) concluded that "there is now good evidence that the fisher, restocked in the national forests of Wisconsin and Michigan, is becoming effective in controlling porcupines." Coulter (1966, 164) noted the decrease in the porcupine population in the Moosehead Plateau region in Maine concurrent with the increase in the fisher population during the 1950s, but he also found evidence that the high porcupine densities "were temporary and were associated with a population irruption." He (1966, 164) concluded that "there is no conclusive evidence to indicate that fishers will control porcupine populations over a long period."

In 1975, Brander and I (Powell and Brander 1977) were the first to present quantitative data documenting the impact of predation by fishers on a porcupine population. Our data covered the porcupine population in part of my fisher study area from 1962 through 1975. Figure 58 shows porcupine population census data, plus the data through 1979. We reported that the porcupine population in our original study area declined from 21 porcupines in 1962 to 5 porcupines in 1975; this constituted a 76% reduction during the first thirteen years after the fisher's reintroduction. The census for 1979 for the original study area showed 1 porcupine, indicating that the decline in the porcupine population had not ceased by that time. The census for a larger study area over a smaller number of years shows the same trends as those of our original study area. A partial search of the study area in 1990 revealed no porcupine sign at all.

Brander and I (Powell and Brander 1977) were unable to find any evidence that porcupine mortality factors other than the fisher (such as disease, predation by other predators, and human-related deaths) had increased during the thirteen years for which we had data. There was some evidence that other mortality factors had decreased. Therefore, we concluded (1977, 48) that "the fisher appears to be the sole causal agent for the decline in porcupine population that we have documented."

Fieldwork done by Earle (1978) provided further evidence that fishers are responsible for the decrease in the porcupine density in the Ottawa National Forest. Earle compared the population densities, sex ratios, and weight distributions of the porcupine populations in the Ottawa and Hiawatha national forests in Upper Peninsula Michigan. Although there were no differences in sex ratios and weight distributions for the two national forests, there was a significant dif-

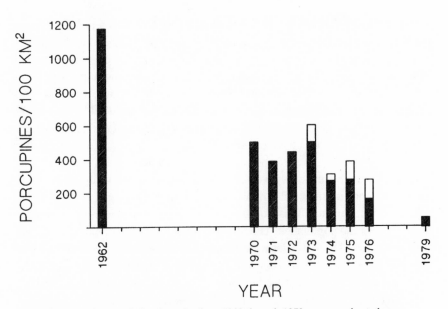

Figure 58. Porcupine population dynamics from 1962 through 1979 on a sample study area (1.79 square kilometers) in Upper Michigan, converted to porcupines per 100 square kilometers. Data are taken from Powell and Brander (1977, unpublished data) and Powell (1977a, 1980a). The hollow histograms for 1973 to 1976 are population dynamics on an enlarged census area (2.83 square kilometers) encompassing the original census area. Porcupine populations were the same in the original and enlarged census area in 1979.

ference in the population densities of porcupines in the forests. During a winter census of all porcupines in four study areas in each national forest, Earle found that the porcupine population density ranged from 2.3 to 4.6 porcupines per square kilometer in the Hiawatha National Forest but ranged from 0 to less than 1.0 porcupine per square kilometer in the Ottawa National Forest. The difference was highly significant (probability = 0.014, Mann-Whitney U test). Similarly, Earle found a significant difference in the number of road-killed porcupines found per kilometer of road driven during the springs of 1976 and 1977; road-killed porcupines were found over twice as frequently in the Hiawatha National Forest as in the Ottawa National Forest both years (probability = 0.0011 and probability = 0.0040 in 1976 and 1977, respectively, Mann-Whitney U test).

Earle (1978) felt that the only significant difference between his study areas in the two national forests was the presence of the established fisher population in the Ottawa National Forest. Two measures of forest composition (distributions of importance values for the major tree species and proportions of cover types along highways) showed that the two national forests did not differ significantly (probability < 0.016 and probability < 0.001, respectively, Kendall rank correlation test). Therefore, Earle concluded that differences in habitat were not responsible for the difference seen in the porcupine population densities.

Limited information indicates that the porcupine population in southcentral Maine is increasing (William B. Krohn, personal communication), perhaps in response to a fisher population decline (Krohn, Arthur, and Paragi, in press). This finding indicates that porcupine populations are not just reduced by fishers but are held at low numbers by fishers and not by some aspect of porcupine biology.

To date, no studies of fishers and porcupines have been carried on long enough to prove that the fisher can suppress porcupine populations over long periods of time. Such a study would have to cover at least twenty years, if not more. Evidence in the fossil and subfossil records of long-term coexistence of fishers and porcupines does not support a long-term stable relationship between fishers and porcupines. The fossil and subfossil record is not inconsistent with a scenario of repeated local extinctions and reestablishment of the species (Powell 1977a, 1980a). Therefore, Brander and I (Powell and Brander 1977) examined some factors that we believed would affect the long-term stability of the fisher and porcupine populations. The long-term coexistence of the two species indicates that they have had a period over which to coevolve with each other and to establish some pattern of stability. The existence of several alternative prey for the fisher should stabilize fisher and porcupine populations by allowing fishers to "switch" prey preferences as relative prey populations change (Murdoch and Oaten 1975). And in Michigan there was much unoccupied habitat into which the fisher population could expand. Consequently, Brander and I concluded that a long-term stable relationship between fishers and porcupines was expected.

Mathematical modeling and computer simulation of fisher-porcupine communities can give further insight into what the long-term population dynamics might be. To address this problem I developed from the literature five mathematical models that could be used to investigate population dynamics and long-term community stability in one-predator-one-prey and one-predator-three-prey model communities (Powell 1977a, 1980a). The model communities were based on the fisher community present in the Ottawa National Forest. Because the porcupine has only one major predator—the fisher—I developed one-predator-one-prey communities containing only fishers and porcupines. But, because fishers have other prey, I also developed one-predator-three-prey model communities containing fishers, porcupines, snowshoe hares, and deer carrion. Each model community had for each community member species a difference equation that provided the population size each year for that species, given the population sizes of that and other species during the preceding year, and values for several other parameters that represented different aspects of that species' biology. In all models, porcupine reproduction was assumed to resemble logistic growth; that is, porcupines had an environmental carrying capacity such that when their populations were below this carrying capacity, reproduction exceeded mortality and when above, mortality exceeded reproduction. Snowshoe hares were modeled in all models to have a ten-year population cycle, as they do in much of their range. Fisher-related prey mortality or removal and fisher reproduction and mortality were modeled in a wide variety of ways. In one model, prey losses were assumed to be proportional to the product of the predator and prey population sizes (Lotka-Volterra predator-prey model). In another model, prey losses were assumed to be proportional to the product of the predator and the square root of the prey population sizes (Gause [1934] predator-prey model). In the rest of the models, prey losses were modeled so as to be influenced by predator interferences, predator satiation, and maximum predation rates (Holling 1959; Ivlev 1961; Watt 1959). All of the models attempted to represent the biology of the community species accurately, but each model made slightly different assumptions about the species' biology and emphasized different aspects of the species' biology. Five models were investigated both for fishers with one prey and for fishers with three prey to see whether any of the assumptions made big differences in the results and to be able to draw conclusions from consistencies among all the models.

All of the models were explored for long-term stability of the community by using community matrices and computer simulations. A community matrix is a matrix whose elements represent quantified relationships among the species in the community. The magnitude and sign of an element are determined from the community model and represent the importance of the relationship and whether that relationship has positive or negative effects on the species involved. Computer simulations are simulations of the communities' population dynamics over many, many time intervals (in this case, years), assuming that the communities' member species are adequately represented by the mathematical equations put into the computer. The community matrices for all the models of the fisher community showed that the one-predator-one-prey fisher-porcupine community is stable and indicated that the one-predator-three-prey fisher-porcupine-hare-deer carrion community should be stable under real-life conditions. Computer simulations were run for the predicted long-term population dynamics of the model communities. Long-term community stability was defined as a fisher population that did not fall below 0.5 fishers per 100 square kilometers and a porcupine population that did not fall below 1.0 porcupines per 100 square kilometers in 100 years. Although there were quantitative differences between the models, all the models qualitatively predicted similar community population dynamics. In addition, I manipulated the values of the parameters in the models that represented different aspects of the species' biology. This work showed that the model communities remained stable over fairly large ranges of these parameter values. Consequently, I knew that errors in my original estimation of these parameter values would not greatly affect the conclusions I drew concerning the stability of the model communities.

My models of the fisher predator-prey community in Michigan indicated that neither fishers nor porcupines should become extinct or experience a population explosion, unless unpredictable events occur or major disturbances are created by humans. When species other than fishers and porcupines were included in the community, the possibility of extinction for either fishers or porcupines was smaller.

My models did not allow for unpredictable events that might affect fisher or porcupine populations. For example, when the porcupine population reaches a low level, as it did in 1979, an age structure skewed toward individuals with low reproductive potential (low reproductive value, v_x, in demographic models) could lead to further declines, even local extinction, even though fisher predation was low. Alternatively, the change in forest structure caused by logging and by Dutch elm disease killing the American elms could affect the development of future safe den trees for porcupines. Because such unpredictable events do commonly occur, the scenario of local extinction and recolonization is realistic.

Chapter 9

General Habits, Home Range, and Spacing Patterns

Fishers have been reported to be active predominantly during the day, the night, and both day and night (Coulter 1966; deVos 1952; Grinnell, Dixon, and Linsdale 1937; Hamilton and Cook 1955; Pittaway 1978). Sightings of fishers during the day have been the most common evidence of daytime activity. Nighttime activity has been deduced from the appearance of fresh tracks during the night and from observations at feeders. Coulter (1966) based his conclusion that fishers are predominantly active at night in part on observations of animals in captivity.

The fishers I monitored were active both day and night and had a small number of activity periods (one to three) that lasted for two to five hours during each period of monitoring. Figure 59 shows the periods of activity of three fishers during five periods of extensive and continuous radiotelemetric monitoring.

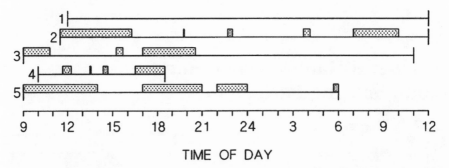

Figure 59. Fishers' activity patterns during five periods of extensive, continuous monitoring by radio. The broad blocks denote activity. Abscissa is time of day. Fishers were active both day and night and showed a small number of active periods that lasted for two to five hours each. The numbers preceding each bar are the same as the watch numbers in Table 13.

These activity patterns are similar to those found for short-tailed weasels in Sweden (Erlinge and Widen 1975).

Arthur and Krohn (1991), Johnson (1984), and Kelly (1977) identified a distinct activity pattern and different amounts of activity with changing seasons for fishers in Maine, Wisconsin, and New Hampshire. These fishers had peaks in activity around sunrise and sunset during all seasons and had the least activity during midday. All three studies found the least activity during midday, with several hours of low activity levels between 0800 and 1600 hours. The fishers I studied in Upper Peninsula Michigan during winter also were most active at sunrise and sunset but were least active during the middle of the night, when temperatures were often subzero (Figure 60). Arthur and Krohn found a distinct dip in mid-night activity for fishers in Maine in winter. My hand-raised fishers were active at all times of the day and night, but my captive wild fishers in general came out of their nest boxes only during the night. This activity pattern of captive fishers and general avoidance of humans by fishers has led me to question the conclusion made by Coulter (1966) and Pittaway (1978) that fishers may be predominantly nocturnal.

The fishers Kelly followed were much more active during all daylight hours during the summer than they were during the winter. During the summer the fishers were often active over 75% of the time, but during the winter they were seldom active more than 50% of the time. The fishers Johnson studied also were most active during summer (39% of locations found fishers active), least active during winter (18%), and intermediate during spring (27%) and fall (33%). In general, there was little difference in activity between the sexes, although the males Kelly monitored tended to be more active during the morning and the females more active during the evening peaks. These activity patterns are illustrated in Figure 61.

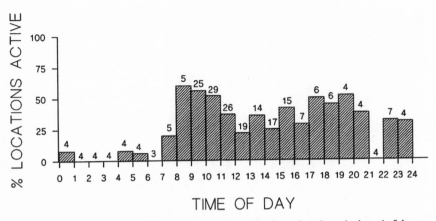

Figure 60. Percentage of 224 radiotelemetric location estimations that showed when six fishers were active. The locations are grouped in one-hour time blocks. The number above each bar is the sample size for that one-hour block.

Leonard (1980b) obtained good data on the times a female fisher was at or away from her natal den before her kits were weaned (Figure 62). This female tended to be away from the den during the daytime, some time between 1200 and 1800 hours, and to be in the natal den during the early morning hours, some time between 2400 and 0600 hours. During the early morning hours, the ambient temperature would be at its lowest, and the kits would presumably be in the greatest need of warmth from their mother.

Fishers may travel long distances during short periods of time. DeVos (1952) reported that a trapper followed a fisher approximately 97 kilometers during the course of three days. Hamilton and Cook (1955) reported that another trapper followed a fisher for 48 kilometers during two days and that one fisher was known to have traveled 10 to 11 kilometers in only a few hours. These long distances were undoubtedly caused partially by the fishers' being followed; less extensive daily travel is more common. Kelly (1977) and Johnson (1984) found that straight-line distances between radiotelemetric locations for a fisher on two consecutive days averaged between 1.5 and 3.0 kilometers. Though the fishers may have traveled considerably farther than these distances, and distances estimated from radiotelemetric location estimates often have considerable error (Zimmerman 1990), it is still unlikely that any of them traveled 35 kilometers in a day. Looking at averages for the entire year, Kelly found that there was a significant difference in activity by sex and by sex-age class. Adult males were the most mobile, and adult females were the least mobile. Subadults ($\leq$ 21 months old) of each sex were intermediate. Johnson (1984) found nearly the same pattern for the percentage of time active but did not find that adult females moved significantly less each day than did juvenile males and females. Kelly felt that

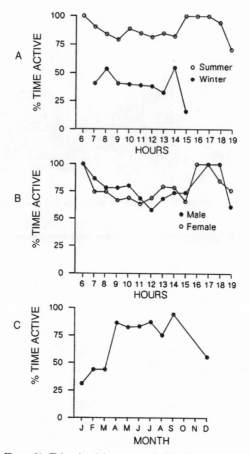

Figure 61. Fishers' activity patterns in New Hampshire, recorded by Kelly (1977). *A*, percentage of radiotelemetric locations that found fishers active, recorded by time of day and by summer or winter (summer is May through November; winter is December through April). Fishers were more active during daylight hours in the summer than in the winter. *B*, percentage of radiotelemetric locations that found fishers active, recorded by time of day and by sex. There was little difference in male and female activity patterns. *C*, percentage of radiotelemetric locations that found fishers active, recorded by month. (From G. M. Kelly 1977, used by permission of the author.)

sexual dimorphism in body size was largely responsible for the differences in movement. There is also a significant difference in mobility of fishers by month and a significant interaction of mobility with sex and season. Kelly found that distances covered were greater during the winter months (when the average

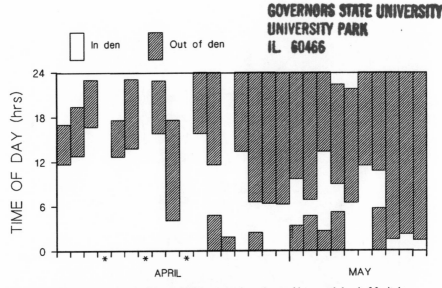

Figure 62. Times that a female fisher with kits spent in and out of her natal den in Manitoba. On days marked with an asterisk, the female did not leave the den because she was disturbed by an observer. (From R. D. Leonard 1980, used by permission of the author.)

distance between locations was greater than 1.5 kilometers) than during the summer months (when the average distance between locations was less than 1.5 kilometers). Also, males moved significantly greater distances during the summer than did the females, and females moved significantly greater distances during the winter than they did during the summer. Johnson found similar patterns. Kelly and Johnson concluded that both of these latter patterns resulted from a female fisher's restricted mobility during the summer when she has young. The females' restricted mobility probably also influences yearly mobility and may explain why subadult females are more mobile than adult females. Daily distances covered peak during May and then decline through the autumn months.

I tracked fishers to sleeping sites thirty-two times on thirty-three tracks; eighteen tracks included no sleeping sites (Powell 1977a). Counting the tracks with no sleeping sites as one active period and the tracks with sleeping sites as being divided into the appropriate number of active periods, I obtained a minimum estimate of the distance traveled per active period of 2.5 kilometers. Figure 59 shows that the fishers I followed tended to have a small number of active periods each day. Assuming two active periods each day and 2.5 kilometers traveled per active period yields a rough estimate of approximately 5 kilometers traveled per day. This estimate agrees closely with Kelly's (1977) and Johnson's (1984) minimum estimates from straight-line distances.

Although Kelly's (1977) and Johnson's (1984) movement data do not show any special movements during March and April, their home range size data do

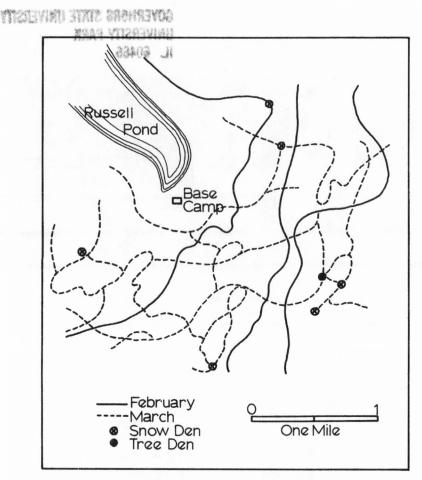

Figure 63. Comparison of travel patterns of fishers during three-day periods, February and March 1953. Note the circuitous track patterns for March compared to those for February. (From M. W. Coulter 1966, by permission of the author.)

show a seasonal peak during those two months. Coulter (1966) and deVos (1952) concluded that activity of fishers is at its peak during that period. Coulter found that fisher tracks in Maine during these two months frequently showed much circling and backtracking, which made the track patterns so confusing that he was unable to discern exact temporal movement patterns. I found similar track patterns in Michigan (Powell, unpublished data). The highly circuitous patterns prevalent at this time of year might explain why Kelly (1977) did not record increased movement: a fisher's activity may be very concentrated in small areas, where it moves many kilometers in total distance but only a few kilometers in straight-line distance. Such track patterns are shown in Figure 63.

I was able to discern one activity pattern in two radiotracked fishers during the autumn and early winter. Their activity appeared to be centered around lowland conifer forest habitats. Each fisher spent several consecutive days in an area of this habitat type, moving only about 0.5 kilometers in straight-line distance between radio locations on consecutive days. After several days in a particular patch of lowland conifer habitat, the fisher moved up to 5 kilometers through upland hardwood forest to another patch of lowland conifer forest in which it spent another several days. This pattern was repeated many times with only minor changes (the number of days spent in each lowland conifer habitat varied, the distance through upland hardwood to another lowland conifer patch varied, etc.).

DeVos (1951, 1952) noted from trappers' reports that fishers' movements appeared circuital. Depending on food and habitat, fishers visited a particular area at fairly regular intervals of time and appeared to make a circuit around their home ranges during these regular time intervals. Each circuit was from 65 to 160 kilometers long. Brander and I (Powell and Brander 1977) suspected that the fishers in our study area traveled circuits that brought them by porcupine dens at regular intervals, but we could not present any data to support that suspicion. Arthur and Krohn (1991) and Coulter (1966) did not mention such circuital movements for Maine fishers, although their data should have shown such patterns had they been present. Therefore, fishers in Maine probably do not travel in circuital patterns. Kelly's (1977) radiotelemetric data clearly show that fishers in New Hampshire do not travel in regular circuits. I now believe that when studying fishers that are not wearing transmitter collars, the methods used to find tracks lead to data that mislead researchers into believing that fishers travel in circuits.

Winter movements have been well documented by investigators who followed fisher tracks in the snow. DeVos (1952, 5-7) described one day's time spent in the field following a fisher track:

March 11th, 1949. The fresh tracks of a fisher, which crossed an old beaver house . . . in a creek, were followed. The animal covered about ⅓ mile running up a hill. After about ¼ of a mile a fox track was noticed to approach the fisher track and follow it for about 30 feet. The fisher crossed several snowshoe hare, red squirrel and grouse tracks, without changing its course. Before it travelled another ⅓ mile its trail ran into the track of a small fisher. The larger animal made a few jumps in the direction in which the other was going, but subsequently proceeded in the opposite direction. After following the track for another ⅕ mile, urine was found on a little head of snow along the trail. Farther on I came upon four beds made in the snow close to each other. In one of these several porcupine quills were found. The track subsequently turned in a southeasterly direction and crossed the creek close to where it was first picked up. The animal first crossed the creek about one and a half hours after I passed there. It walked about 300 yards in the open

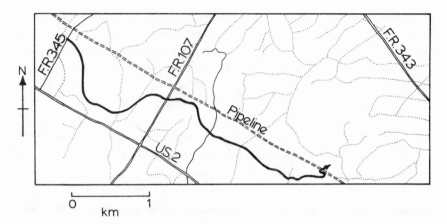

Figure 64. Map of fisher track described in the text. The dotted lines represent overgrown logging roads. (Drawn by C. B. Powell.)

part of the creek valley and then disappeared in a fringe of white cedar along the opposite shore. This shore was followed partly under the cover of the cedar and partly in the open. Track evidence indicated that snowshoe hares were common under the cedars. The fisher followed their tracks in several places, possibly in pursuit. At the mouth of the creek the tracking work was given up for the day. The fisher was noticed to walk on top of three logs during the entire tracking period.

DeVos was able to follow fisher tracks along lakeshores during the summer. The movement patterns he found did not appear to differ between the summer and the winter. DeVos (1952, 12) was able to conclude from his tracking that "although the travelling may appear to be more or less random, it becomes clear by following the tracks repeatedly that the animals have a detailed knowledge of the area covered. Short cuts across points in the lake and crossing of creeks are made at definite places, where frequently used trails can be seen. Occasionally an animal will back-track."

One of my more interesting days of fisher tracking went like the following (Powell, unpublished field journal). (The pipeline mentioned in the journal is a 25-meter-wide, cleared right-of-way for a buried gas pipeline that runs northwest-southeast). The track is mapped in Figure 64.

10 December 1974. I found a fisher track going south or southeast across [Forest Road] 345 ca. 100 m south of the pipeline. The tracks looked no older than night before last. The fisher was walking except for crossing 345. About 25 m east of 345 the fisher went up a hemlock and then jumped off. There was lots of red squirrel sign in this area. 25 m further east to northeast the tracks led into a large, fallen, hollow yellow birch and back out. Some 20 m more, the fisher dug about a 15 × 20 cm hole in the snow under a fallen tree. Another 10 m further easterly the fisher crossed a coyote track; the fisher went about

1 m beyond the track and then came back to sniff it (a spot in the snow looked like a nose print) and then took off easterly at a slightly faster pace.

The fisher reached an alder stand and headed south parallel to and ca. 10 m out of the alders in hemlocks. There was lots of squirrel sign here, too. The fisher suddenly turned 90° to the west, went some 5 m and appeared to have scavenged a grouse. There was very little blood and only a few breast feathers.

The fisher retraced its steps to the 90° turn and then continued south again for some 25 m. It turned into the alders (hare tracks all over) going southeast, turned south and came out of the south end of the alders not too far from where it had entered. Not too much further the fisher came to the north end of an open space with few standing trees. It went southeast through this area into a spruce bog with lots of hare sign.

Well into the bog the fisher ate part of a hare. There was very little blood so it seems as though the fisher found another old kill (scavenge) and finished off what was left. Skin may have been all that had been left.

The fisher continued southeast quite a ways through the bog to the southeast edge. In the bog near the edge it climbed on a big stump; I could not tell if it urinated. About 15 m further southeast it went into a large, hollow, fallen, very old white cedar. Then it headed out of the bog going southeast still.

The fisher went into an area with lots of [downed treetops from a logging operation]. Here it went over, around and through the tops, zigzagging a lot. After one good-sized zigzag it dug a small hole but I could not see anything [in the hole, e.g., blood, mouse fur, etc.]. After going fairly straight for about 50 m beyond the tops, the fisher made a sharp turn back west, dug in the snow and deposited a scat. The scat contained seeds resembling apple seeds and smelled only faintly of the characteristic fisher scat smell. It urinated on a mossy rock at the same spot. It left the spot going southeast again.

After another 100 m the fisher turned abruptly north-northeast. At one spot it looked as though the fisher stopped and snuzzled [sniffed] after a mouse. There were small mammal tracks around a seedling and the fisher seemed to have sniffed the area thoroughly and dug a very little bit. A little further northeast the fisher came close to and ran parallel with [Forest Road] 107 in a northeasterly direction for some 50 m. Then it turned and crossed 107 about 50 m south of the pipeline. The tracks crossing 107 were fresh since when I drove down 107 in the morning of 9/12/74, so I may have picked up a day on the fisher.

The fisher headed almost due east from 107 into a spruce-fir stand. The fisher got pretty close to the pipeline. Here it defecated again. The urine was maybe 5 cm from the scat—male? The fisher ran on through the spruce-fir stand and then south down the east side. Shortly after this it came to 3 trees (8-15 cm dbh) with a similarly sized tree fallen against them at a height of about 1.5 m. The fisher climbed one of the trees at least to the fallen one and then walked down the fallen one.

Continuing southeast and east, the fisher climbed up on several stumps, all ca. 1 m in diameter. Then it crossed a creek. There was hare sign in the creek bed and in the alders and squirrel sign on the east side of the creek.

The fisher ran some 25 m in a deer trail. Then it climbed onto more big stumps. Was it looking around? Was it looking for a specific stump? Some stumps were hollow, others not. Soon after this, the fisher caught a small mammal. The fisher was going east, then zigged back west-southwest. There was a little spot of blood and a small packed-down area. The fisher made a tail swish in the snow.

About 50 m further east the fisher crossed [Forest Road] 504 about 150 m south of the pipeline, heading southeast. It dug at another spot and then 10 m further defecated again—this time urine was about 7 cm from the scat—probably a male. Shortly after this last scat the fisher defecated a 4th time, this one filled with what appeared to be vegetable matter. 25 m further southeast the fisher dug a 5 × 7 cm hole. Another 25 m and the fisher turned northeast, ran through an alder stand and out going east-southeast. There were a lot of Collembola in the snow and the weather was getting warm (ca. 5° C). The fisher defecated for a 5th time and then pulled its first real trick of the day. Two sets of tracks came together from opposite directions and one set of double tracks left going north. I followed the double tracks. They headed north to northeast to about 20 m from the pipeline then turned back west parallel to the pipeline. They went right to the pipeline, even walked to the very edge, then went back further west and into a spruce-fir type. Finally the double track crossed the pipeline in a narrow spot with spruce-fir types on both sides.

I stopped tracking at this point. During six hours and fifteen minutes, I had tracked the fisher for approximately 8.5 kilometers.

Resting Sites

Fishers use a variety of resting sites. Most resting sites are temporary (Coulter 1966; deVos 1952; Powell 1977a), but some may be used more than once by the same fisher (deVos 1952). Hollow trees, logs, and stumps; nests of branches; squirrel and raptor nests; brush piles; rockfalls; holes in the ground; and even abandoned beaver lodges are commonly used as temporary resting sites during all times of the year (Arthur, Krohn, and Gilbert 1989b; Coulter 1966; deVos 1952; Grinnell, Dixon, and Linsdale 1937; Hamilton and Cook 1955; Powell 1977a, unpublished data; Pringle 1964). Arthur and co-workers (1989b) categorized resting sites as ground burrows, tree cavities, and tree nests. They found that tree nests were used most commonly all year, especially clumped growths of branches in balsam fir trees called "witches' brooms." Ground burrows were used most commonly in winter, and cavities in trees were used most commonly in spring and fall. These findings suggest that temperature affects resting site choice and that sites are chosen for warmth and insulation in winter and perhaps to prevent overheating in summer.

During the winter, fishers sometimes use snow dens (Coulter 1966; deVos 1952; Powell 1977a). Snow dens are burrows under the snow consisting of one or more tunnels leading 0.5 to 2.0 meters to a larger, hollowed space under the surface of the snow. Arthur and co-workers (1989b) found no use of snow dens, although they did find that fishers sometimes tunneled up to 1.5 meters through snow to get to a ground burrow. Thus, use of snow dens may be exaggerated in the literature. During three years of fieldwork, I found twenty-one winter resting sites where the tracks leading to the site and those leading away were obviously of different ages, showing that the fisher had definitely spent time at the site. All of these resting sites were temporary and used for not more than a day. Of these, six were hollow logs, five were believed to be snow dens, four were holes in the ground, two were in brushpiles, and one each was in a tree, in a snag, in a stump, and in a rockfall. I did excavate some snow dens but not all, thus some may have been ground burrows. In addition, I found twenty-three possible resting sites where I could not be certain that the fisher had actually rested because tracks could not be aged. Fishers may have investigated some of these sites but not rested in them. They included eleven possible snow dens, six holes in the ground, four hollow logs, one hole in a snag, and one in a stump. Coulter (1966), deVos (1952), and Raine (1981) found similar distributions of winter resting sites.

Fishers sometimes make a very direct approach to a temporary resting site; this indicates that the location of the site may be known to the fisher (deVos 1952; Powell, unpublished data). Resting sites are used for various lengths of time, depending on the availability of food, the weather, and the condition of the fisher (deVos 1952). Fishers often rest close to the carcass of a large food item for many days until the food supply dwindles. A fisher I monitored stayed by a deer carcass for over ten days. Some trappers believe that fishers even rest inside frozen carcasses (deVos 1952), but there is no supporting evidence for this claim from other sources. Fishers rest for shorter periods of time by smaller carcasses (porcupines). I once found a fisher that had pulled a porcupine carcass into the hollow log it was using for a resting site. Fishers may den for several days during a bad storm. DeVos (1952) believed that fishers entered the closest available resting site when a storm began.

DeVos (1952) interpreted his field results to suggest that fishers used a system of resting sites and that particular resting sites were used repeatedly by the same animal. He found that fishers used one resting site for several days and then switched to another. Arthur and co-workers (1989a), Coulter (1966), and I (Powell 1977a) were unable to find such a pattern in our field studies.

Resting sites used by American martens have been better studied. Besides using all the types of resting sites that fishers use, American martens often rest in red squirrel middens and in complexes of down and dead woody debris under the snow (Buskirk 1984; Buskirk et al. 1989; Hargis and McCullough 1984; Spencer 1987; Wilbert 1992; Wynne and Sherburne 1982). Protection from winter cold appears critical, and American martens use thermally insulated resting sites, especially subnivean sites (beneath the snow) in complexes of dead branches, logs, and roots, more in winter than in summer. In mild winter weather, American martens are more likely to rest in holes in trees. And in summer they, like fishers, will rest on top of branches. Sites are chosen for resting on at least two scales. Wilbert (1992) found that American martens in Wyoming chose to rest in particular habitats, apparently chosen by habitat characteristics, and then chose resting sites within those habitats using different characteristics.

Climbing and Swimming

All martens (members of the genus *Martes*) have clear adaptations for arboreality (Holmes 1980; Leach 1977a, 1977b; Sokolov and Sokolov 1971), but these adaptations may be partially due to their relatively unspecialized limb anatomy (Holmes 1980; Leach 1977a, 1977b). (See chapter 2.) Early reports about fishers often emphasized their arboreal habits. Fishers can and do climb high into trees to reach holes and possibly to reach prey (Coulter 1966; Grinnell, Dixon, and Linsdale 1937; Leonard 1980a; Powell 1977a). Lewis and Clark stated in their journal that the fisher is marvelously adept at climbing (Haley 1975, 40) and chases prey from tree to tree (deVos 1952, 16). E. T. Seton (1926, 472) quoted Bachman, who recorded the killing of an Ontario fisher: "A fisher was shot by a hunter named March, near Port Hope, who said it was up a tree, in close pursuit of a Pine Marten, which he also brought with it." Fishers in California have been observed to travel from tree to tree to avoid dogs and hunters, sometimes leaping great distances from the branches of one tree to the branches of the next (Grinnell, Dixon, and Linsdale 1937, 224-25):

> The fisher was near a fir, up which it soon climbed about fifty feet. . . . From there on for one-fourth mile we were treated to a rare spectacle. The fisher traveled through the tree tops nearly as fast as we could run. It leaped from a branch of one tree to a branch of another with the ease and assurance of a bird. It finally reached an extra large red fir with a heavy crown into which it ascended to within a dozen feet of the top.

Because of stories like these, to this day the popular literature describes fishers leaping through the treetops. The fisher has gained the reputation of being the fastest North American mammal and North America's most active arboreal mammal. For example, a photograph of a treed male fisher is shown in *Sleek & Savage* (Haley 1975, 53) and accompanied by this caption: "The fleet-footed fisher is the fastest tree-travelling animal." Morse (1961, 26) repeated the idea: "Fisher[s] are as much at home in the trees as on the ground; in fact, they have a reputation as the fastest tree-travelling animal, and will make long leaps from tree to tree in pursuit of prey."

Recent work, however, indicates that fishers may be less arboreal than the popular literature claims (Coulter 1966; deVos 1952; Holmes 1980; Powell 1977a, 1980b; Raine 1987). During the winter in Maine, "most of the fisher's activity is terrestrial, but the animals do climb trees readily and sometimes often. Arboreal activity [is] variable between animals and perhaps with individuals at different times" (Coulter 1966, 62). The same holds true for fishers in Michigan (Powell 1977a), and Raine (1987) never observed a fisher climbing a tree along 111 kilometers of tracks that he followed in Manitoba. There is no recent evidence that fishers regularly climb from tree to tree through the branches (Coulter 1966; Powell 1977a, 1980b; Pringle 1964), and anatomical analyses indicate that American martens (and presumably other martens, all of which are smaller than fisher) are more highly adapted for arboreal behavior than are fishers (Holmes 1980). It is probable that the fishers in the early reports traveled through the trees only as a method of fleeing pursuers (who were on the ground, could catch them on the ground, but could not climb trees). If this is the case, it is probable that fishers seldom travel in this manner even though they are able to do so.

Fishers regularly climb under and about brush piles and downed treetops while they are hunting, and they do often jump or climb up on large stumps, fallen logs, and leaning logs. It is common for a fisher to climb up a leaning log and jump to the ground from 1 to 2 meters.

It is likely that there is a sexual difference in the arboreal abilities of fishers (D. Leach, personal communication; Pittaway 1978; Powell 1977a). When fishers approach six months of age, the sexual dimorphism in body size has begun to develop, and males become less adept at climbing (Powell 1977a). On the few tracks I followed for which I knew the sex of the fisher, a male fisher climbed a tree once along six tracks, whereas females climbed trees on both of two tracks. Pittaway (1978, 488) observed a wild male fisher and a wild female fisher climbing the same tree: "The larger male climbed slowly and carefully and it was awkward on branches less than 6 cm in diameter. The smaller female climbed the same tree with much less difficulty and was a much more agile climber."

Fishers are not known for swimming, but there are scattered reports that fishers swim at times. DeVos (1952) recorded two observations of fisher tracks along a lakeshore that indicated that the fishers making the tracks had at least walked in the water. One of the tracks led directly from the water into the forest. Cahalane (1947), Hamilton (1943), and Seton (1926) all mentioned that fishers are known to swim in lakes and rivers. In a more recent study, some of the home ranges plotted by Kelly (1977) had a river flowing through them. The fishers crossed the river where it was narrow; however, where the river was wider farther downstream, it appeared to be a barrier the fishers could not cross. Coulter (1966) also observed that a river could act as a barrier to fishers' movements.

Sociality

The word solitary is subject to various interpretations. Animals are seldom completely out of contact with other members of their species, and, therefore, in the strict sense of the word they are never solitary. But, in general, solitary is applied to an animal that goes about its daily activities by itself and is not in physical proximity with one or more members of its species, except for reproduction. Under this generally accepted interpretation of the word, fishers are quite solitary (Arthur, Krohn, and Gilbert 1989a; Coulter 1966; deVos 1952; Powell 1977a; Quick 1953a). Occasionally, trappers have claimed that two or three adult fishers traveled together, but their reports are subject to question (deVos 1952; Quick 1953a). Outside the breeding season, a fisher may sometimes follow the trail of another fisher for short distances, and when an adult finds the tracks of a dispersing juvenile fisher, the adult is expected to follow the tracks for at least a short distance. Nonetheless, there is little evidence that fishers ever travel together (Coulter 1966; Powell 1977a; Quick 1953a; Raine 1983). During the winter their tracks are generally spaced out, and fishers appear to avoid proximity to other fishers (Arthur, Krohn, and Gilbert 1989a; Powell 1977a). Directed agonistic behavior has been observed between a captive adult female fisher and her young, among the young within captive litters five months old and older, and between two captive adult female fishers (Coulter 1966; Kelly 1977; Powell 1977a), and there is evidence of aggression between males (Arthur, Krohn, and Gilbert 1989a; Leonard 1986). These observations support the interpretation that fishers are solitary. Most fur farms have found it best to house fishers singly, but a few reports indicate that a single adult male and a single adult female have been housed in adjacent, connected pens for an extended period of time (Hall 1942; Hodgson 1937). Zoos have also been able to house two fishers of opposite sexes together for extended periods of time (Lincoln Park Zoo, Chicago Zoological Society, unpublished files; Bronx Zoo, New York Zoological Society, unpublished files), but this behavior may be an artifact of captivity.

The limited information available about other martens suggests that all are solitary (Powell, in press a). Wild American martens show social tolerance toward other American martens only during the breeding season, and American martens in the wild have been observed to show unsocial behavior toward other martens. When two martens meet, there may be growling from a distance, but the two individuals tend to avoid close approaches to each other (Hawley and Newby 1957). The close evolutionary relationships among *Martes* species supports the evidence that fishers are solitary.

Home Range and Territory

An animal's home range is the area over which it travels on its day-to-day activities and with which it is familiar (Burt 1943). Early estimates of fishers' home ranges from tracking data were substantially larger than those based on more recent data gathered by radiotelemetry. DeVos (1952) and Quick (1953a) reported that fishers' home ranges were approximately 12 to 30 kilometers in diameter and were approximately 100 to 800 square kilometers in area. These figures were obtained from following tracks of what appeared to be the same fisher for several days and from trappers' reports of distances fishers were followed. Using similar data-collecting techniques, Hamilton and Cook (1955) estimated that fishers' home ranges were approximately 25 square kilometers.

Home range size estimates documented using radiotelemetry, though far smaller than those calculated from tracking, are still variable (Table 11). This variation is due in part to different researchers' using slightly different methods and treating data differently, in part to most methods of quantifying home ranges being inadequate, and in part to true variation. Researchers will always use slightly different methods because methods must be adapted to each unique research situation. Researchers can use better methods to quantify home ranges, however. For decades, home ranges have been quantified by connecting the outermost location estimates to form convex polygons (Hayne 1949). Such complex polygons may include much area not actually used by animals and give no information about how animals use the area within their home ranges. In essence, using convex polygons to quantify home ranges uses only the 5% to 10% extreme data points (statisticians have shown that extrema tend to be very unreliable) while discarding the rest of the data that have taken so much effort to collect. Perhaps the only reason to use convex polygons is to compare present research with past research that used only convex polygons. Many researchers quantify home ranges now using the harmonic mean method, which assumes that animals use areas within their home ranges in a fashion that decreases from the center of activity in an inverse harmonic distribution. This method quantifies the home range outlines better than do convex polygons (Boulanger and White 1990; White and Garrott 1990) but still does a poor job of representing the internal structure of animal home ranges (Seaman 1993). Recently developed kernel methods quantify better than any other available method both the outlines of home ranges and the distributions of use within home ranges (Seaman 1993).

Table 11. Home range sizes (in km^2) estimated for fishers

Male	N	Female	N	Location	Method comments	Source
20 ± 12	3	4.2	1	California	Convex polygons adults with > 20 locations females all year males without breeding season	Buck, Mullis, & Mossman 1983
23 ± 12	4	6.8	2	California	Convex polygons adults + juveniles females all year males without breeding season	Buck, Mullis, & Mossman 1983
79 ± 35	6	32 ± 23	4	Idaho	90% harmonic mean adults + juveniles	Jones 1991
33 ± 25	7	19 ± 12	6	Maine	Convex polygon adults only May-December	Arthur, Krohn, & Gilbert 1989a
27 ± 24	7	16 ± 12	6	Maine	90% harmonic mean adults only May-December	Arthur, Krohn, & Gilbert 1989a
50 ± 40	7	31 ± 23	6	Maine	99% harmonic mean adults only May-December	Arthur, Krohn, & Gilbert 1989a
35	1	15	1	Michigan	Convex polygon adults only winter	Powell 1977a
19 ± 17	3	15 ± 3	2	New Hampshire	Convex polygon adults only all year	Kelly 1977
26 ± 17	3	15 ± 6	3	New Hampshire	Convex polygon subadults only all year	Kelly 1977
23 ± 16	6	15 ± 5	5	New Hampshire	Convex polygon adults + subadults all year	Kelly 1977
49 ± 37	2	8 ± 4	5	Wisconsin	Convex polygon adults with > 25 locations all year	Johnson 1984
39 ± 27	4	8 ± 4	7	Wisconsin	Convex polygon adults + juveniles all year	Johnson 1984
Mean 38		15				

Note: Figures given are means ± standard deviations. The overall mean was calculated using only one figure for each sex in each study.

Despite the limits of convex polygon and harmonic mean estimates of home ranges, their use has led to much knowledge about fishers' home ranges. In Table 11 I have calculated a mean home range area for each sex. Because methods were not consistent between studies, this figure can only be used for general comparisons; for this reason I do not give a measure of variation. The mean home range size for adult male fishers is 38 square kilometers (range 19-79) and that for females is 15 square kilometers (range 4-32). There are no apparent geographical patterns in home range sizes.

The home range sizes in Table 11 are larger than those of other members of the genus *Martes* (Powell, in press a), a finding which is expected from fishers' large sizes. Consistent with other martens, male fishers have home ranges far larger than those of females (Powell, in press a). The difference in size between male and female home ranges is greater than that expected from body size alone.

There are several possible explanations (not mutually exclusive) for the disproportionate sizes of male and female home ranges. First, males may have energy requirements greater than expected from body size and therefore need disproportionately larger home ranges. No field metabolic measurements have been made for fishers or for any other martens, but laboratory studies have found no unexpected sexual differences in metabolism and energy expenditure of fishers, American martens, or other mustelines (Buskirk, Harlow, and Forrest 1988; Casey and Casey 1979; Moors 1977; Powell 1979a, 1981; Worthen and Kilgore 1981). Second, the actual areas used by males and females may be proportional to body size, though areas within home range outlines are not. Home ranges of male and female fishers do overlap extensively. In other mustelines, however, males spend minimal time within the home ranges of females encompassed within their own home ranges (Erlinge 1977; Gerell 1970). No published data quantify the intensity of home range use by fishers. Third, males and females may space themselves to gain access to different resources: females may need access to food whereas males may need access to females. This has been shown to be the case for other mammals, including other mustelines (Erlinge and Sandell 1986; Ims 1987, 1988a, 1988b, 1990; Sandell 1986), and Sandell (1989a) has hypothesized this to be the case for solitary carnivores, such as fishers.

Kelly (1977) estimated twenty-four monthly home ranges, which were significantly smaller than mean yearly home ranges. Monthly home ranges showed no statistically significant patterns in size by month, season, or sex or age of fishers, probably because Kelly's sample sizes were too small to find significance when home ranges show so much variation in size. Nonetheless, monthly home ranges of females tended to be smaller than those of males, and the monthly home ranges appeared to show a cycle with two peaks. Monthly home ranges tended to be small in midwinter, to rise to a peak during April, May, and June, to decrease during the rest of the summer and early autumn, and to rise to a second peak during early winter. Kelly was unable to collect sufficient data to estimate sizes of monthly home ranges during March, October, and November. Because male fishers travel so widely during the breeding season, Arthur and co-workers (1989a) excluded estimated locations made between January and April when they calculated home range size estimates. Sizes of home ranges of males during the breeding season were clearly greater than the sizes reported by them and listed in Table 11. The monthly home range areas of two adult males monitored by Johnson (1984) were greatly enlarged during the breeding season (Table 11). Home range sizes of females do not increase during the breeding season (Arthur, Krohn, and Gilbert 1989a; Johnson 1984).

Despite fishers' solitary nature, fishers' home ranges appear to overlap extensively (Arthur, Krohn, and Gilbert 1989a; Coulter 1966; deVos 1952; Johnson 1984; Jones 1991; Kelly 1977; Powell 1977a). There is a distinct pattern to this overlap, however (Powell 1979b, in press a). Home ranges tend not to overlap between individuals of the same sex but tend to overlap extensively between the sexes (Figure 65; Arthur, Krohn, and Gilbert 1989a; Buck, Mullis, and Mossman 1983; Johnson 1984; Kelly 1977; Powell 1977a). I have called this intrasexual territoriality (Powell 1979b). An animal's territory is an area over which it has exclusive, or perhaps priority, use, and territories are established only when there is some resource, such as food, that is so limited in supply that there is not enough to share. Territories are defended against trespass, but the defense need not be with tooth and claw. Scent marks can be used to communicate territory ownership, and as long as scent marks are respected, overt aggression is averted.

Fishers undoubtedly communicate with other fishers by scent marking. During the winter, fishers sometimes walk over and apparently drag their bellies on small stumps or mounds of snow that protrude from the surface of the snow (Figure 66; Leonard 1986; Powell 1977a, unpublished data). They usually urinate on the stump or snow mound. Fishers also frequently walk along the tops of fallen logs or climb up on stumps. Sometimes, especially in late winter, fishers leave black, tarry marks. These resemble feces resulting from rich meals of much meat with little fur and bones but do not smell like feces. They may be small amounts of fecal matter with anal gland secretions. To date, no one has collected data on whether fishers react to marks left by other fishers. I did follow two sets of tracks, both of which walked over and showed signs of urinating on the same stump within the space of four days. I do not know whether the tracks were made by the same fisher or by two different fishers; in either case, this particular stump apparently was recognized. Fishers also urine mark at the entrances to resting sites and on large carcasses they are scavenging (Pittaway 1978, 1984; Powell, unpublished data). Pittaway (1984, 57) described a fisher urine marking on a deer carcass: "Marking was performed by the fisher crawl-

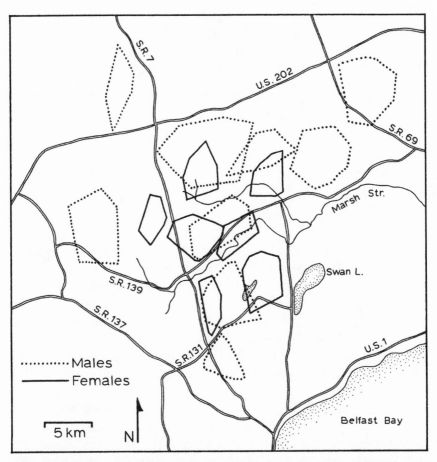

Figure 65. Home ranges of adult fishers radiotracked by Arthur and co-workers (1989b) from May through December 1985. Home ranges of members of the same sex have minimal overlap, though there may have been some resident fishers who were not outfitted with transmitter collars. Home ranges are plotted as convex polygons.

ing forward over the carcass with its hind legs spread, allowing the genital region to be pressed and dragged against the carcass."

Chemical communication is enhanced when animals mark prominent places (Ewer 1973). In winter, such marks may be noticeable by both olfaction and vision. If fishers leave scent marks from the glands on their hind paws, the marks will be smelled from a longer distance when placed on the tops of logs and stumps than when placed only on the forest floor. Scent marking behavior has been documented in other martens as well (Lockie 1964; Pulliainen 1982; Rozhnov 1991).

Figure 66. Small stump on which a fisher urinated. The fisher approached the stump from the right of the photo, apparently dragged its belly over the stump while urinating, and left going to the left.

All the studies in Table 11 reported little or no overlap of home ranges for adult fishers of the same sex but extensive home range overlap for fishers of opposite sex. Intrasexual territoriality has been found in all other martens (reviewed by Powell, in press a) and in most other mustelines (reviewed by Powell 1979b). Usually a female's home range overlaps with that of only one male, but a male's home range may overlap with those of one, two, or more females. Thus, two individuals compete for limiting resources within the area of territory overlap. Many territorial mammals have territories that overlap with no other member of the same species. Intrasexual territoriality may be possible in fishers because large sexual dimorphism allows the two competing individuals to have different diets. Research has consistently refuted this reason for fishers, other martens, and other mustelines (chapter 6; Clem 1977; Coulter 1966; Erlinge 1975; Holmes 1987; Holmes and Powell, in press; Kelly 1977; King 1989; Powell 1981; Tapper 1976, 1979; reviewed by Powell, in press a). I have proposed (Powell, in press a) that intrasexual territoriality is found in fishers and other martens because the most likely limiting resource, food, is very patchily distributed, allowing a trade not possible for species with intersexual territories. This, in turn, allows male spacing to be affected by female spacing as well as by the distribution of available prey.

Animals defend territories only when the benefits accrued are greater than the costs of defense (Brown 1969; Carpenter and MacMillen 1976; Hixon, Carpenter, and Paton 1983; Kodric-Brown and Brown 1978). It may be that by regularly checking all of the habitat patches in its territory, a fisher increases the probability of encountering prey while decreasing the probability that a trespassing fisher will encounter prey (Possingham 1989). I believe, however, that a main benefit of maintaining a territory comes not so much from not having other fishers kill prey within the territory but more from not having other fishers alert prey, making them wary. Individual fishers are seldom able to kill significant proportions of the prey populations within their territories, and their abilities to capture prey are limited not only by prey population sizes but also by the vulnerability of prey to capture. The vulnerability of prey varies in space and time. Prey populations are generally patchily distributed because prey habitats are patchily distributed. In addition, hunting affects the vulnerability of prey by affecting prey behavior. Behavior of captive bank voles and grey-sided voles changes when a short-tailed or least weasel enters a local habitat patch; the voles move less, are more alert, and shift to different patches if possible (Jedrzejewski and Jedrzejewski 1990; Ylönen 1989). The vulnerability of these captive voles was greatest before the weasel was perceived, decreased thereafter, and remained depressed for a day or more. This change in vulnerability is called resource depression, in contrast to resource depletion, which occurs when a resource is permanently removed (Charnov, Orians, and Hyatt 1976). Prey vulnerability is depressed when prey perceive a foraging fisher and then slowly returns to its previous level; prey populations are more often depressed by foraging fishers than they are depleted.

Territorial behavior is economical only at intermediate levels of productivity for the limiting resource, which is usually food (Carpenter and MacMillen 1976). At low levels there is too little resource to warrant establishing a home range, and at high levels there are enough resources that they can be shared. The limits for resource productivity (P) that permit territorial behavior in a patchy habitat can be modeled as

$$\frac{E + T}{a + b} < P < \frac{E}{a} \quad (1)$$

where E represents an animal's energy requirements per unit time, T is the cost of territorial behavior, a is the proportion of resource productivity P available to the animal that is not territorial, and b is the additional proportion of resource productivity P that becomes available through defending a territory (Carpenter and MacMillen 1976). When resource productivity exceeds E/a, the resource is so abundant that animals can share. When resource productivity is less than $(E + T)/(a + b)$, the resource is so scarce that animals are transient. This model predicts territorial behavior in nectarivorous birds (Carpenter and MacMillen 1976) and appears to predict territorial behavior in black bears (Powell 1986); similar models predict territorial behavior in other small vertebrates (e.g., Hixon, Carpenter, and Paton 1983). Therefore this model should apply to fishers (Powell, in press a).

A fisher that maintains an intrasexual territory shares each part of its territory with one other fisher (for simplicity, assume that each suitable habitat patch is included within the territories of one male and one female). This decreases b below what it would be for individual territories. This is the important effect to quantify for understanding when intrasexual territories are possible (Powell, in press a).

Once one fisher has foraged in a habitat patch, prey vulnerability (P in the model) in that patch is depressed, and there are fewer or no vulnerable prey. If a fisher maintains a home range with x patches (i.e., learns the necessary information to be familiar with x patches) and uses an average of y patches per day, then it uses the proportion y/x of its patches each day. If the fisher shares each section of its home range with z other fishers who use patches at random with respect to each other (i.e., do not know before entering a patch whether it has been depressed by another fisher), then the probability that a particular patch entered by a fisher has not been visited by another fisher in the previous 24 hours is

$$(1 - y/x)^z.$$

If each patch is depressed for a proportion d of a day (d = [hr depressed]/24), then the probability that a particular patch entered by the fisher has not been depressed by a recent visit from another fisher is

$$(1 - yd/x)^z.$$

This expression is also the expected proportion of patches visited per day that have not been depressed recently by another fisher and thus is the proportion of the vulnerable prey available in the fisher's home range when the home range is shared, which is a. Let $p = (1 - yd/x)$. Then

$$a = p^z. \tag{2}$$

If the fisher does not share its home range with any other fishers, then the proportion of vulnerable prey available to it can be set to 1 (i.e., $a + b = 1$). Therefore the conditions under which a fisher can maintain an individual territory can be specified by inserting equation (2) into equation (1):

$$b = 1 - p^z \tag{3}$$

and

$$E + T < P < \frac{E}{p^z}. \tag{4}$$

If the fisher is intrasexually territorial and shares each part of its home range with one other fisher, then

$$b = (1 - p)^z - (1 - p)$$

and

$$a + b = p. \tag{5}$$

The conditions under which a fisher can maintain an intrasexual territory can be specified by inserting equations (2) and (5) into equation (1):

$$\frac{E + T}{p} < P < \frac{E}{p^z}.\qquad(6)$$

This means that a fisher that maintains an intrasexual territory loses the proportion $1 - p = y \cdot d/x$ of the vulnerable prey to which it would have access were it to maintain an individual territory. If an intrasexually territorial fisher must visit on the average y' undepressed patches per day in order to catch sufficient prey to survive, then it must actually visit a total of y^* patches, where

$$y^* = y'/p.\qquad(7)$$

The ratio $(y^* - y')/y'$ is the relative cost to a fisher of allowing one other fisher to share its territory. $(y^* - y')/y'$ represents the proportional increase in number of prey habitat patches that must be visited to meet daily energy requirements, or it represents the increase in time or energy that is devoted to foraging and thus cannot be devoted to other activities, such as reproduction.

The habitat in my fisher study area in Upper Peninsula Michigan was distinctly patchy with two distinct habitat (patch) types: open, upland northern hardwood habitats with interspersed stands of hemlock and white pine with porcupines as prey; and dense, lowland habitats with snowshoe hares (Figure 67). The average density of porcupine dens in the central part of my study area was 1.23 dens/km^2. If 25 km^2 is taken as a representative home range size for a fisher (Table 11), then such a home range contained approximately 30 porcupine dens. In some parts of my study area, hare habitat was so extensive that it is inconceivable that an entire habitat patch could have hare vulnerability depressed at once by a single fisher. Some fishers' home ranges, however, encompassed patches of lowland hare habitat each of which was small enough that the fishers never traveled more than several hundred meters in each patch and rested no more than once in each patch. In these areas, the average density of hare habitat patches was 1.86 patches/km^2. If 25 km^2 is taken again as a representative home range size for a fisher, then such a fisher home range contained approximately 45 hare habitat patches.

Thus the fisher home ranges in my study area each contained approximately $30 + 45 = 75 = x$ habitat patches. Again assuming that fishers average two active periods per day and travel a minimum of 2.5 kilometers per active period, I calculated (Powell, in press a) that fishers visited a mean ($\pm$ SD) of 2 ± 2 porcupine dens and 4 ± 4 hare habitat patches each day for a total of

$$y^* = 6 \text{ patches visited per day.}$$

If we assume that a fisher is equally likely to enter each of the two patch types

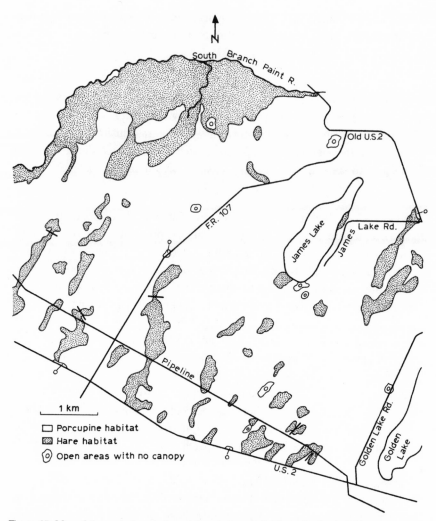

Figure 67. Map of the central part of my fisher study area in Upper Peninsula Michigan, showing snowshoe hare habitat (*shaded*), porcupine habitat (*not shaded*), and open habitats used by neither (marked with "o"). The area used to calculate the density of hare habitat patches was bounded by Golden Lake Road, U.S. 2, the linear, westernmost hare habitat patch and a line parallel to U.S. 2 intersecting the southern edge of James Lake. Lines subdividing hare habitat patches show where detailed forest type maps (U.S. Forest Service) showed separate patches. The pipeline subdivided all hare habitat patches that spanned it. (From Buskirk et al., eds., in press, used with permission of the publisher.)

per visit, then we can calculate y', the daily requirement for undepressed habitat patches, and $(y^* - y')/y'$, the cost of maintaining an intrasexual territory over maintaining an individual territory. $(y^* - y')/y'$ for different ds and different ys is shown in Figure 68. For fishers, which have many more habitat patches in

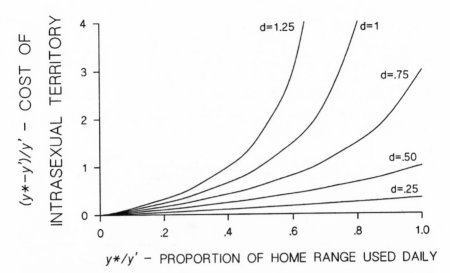

Figure 68. The cost of intrasexual territoriality caused by having another predator depress prey vulnerability within a predator's territory. The cost is greatest for a predator that forages through most of its territory daily and where foraging in a patch of prey depresses prey vulnerability for more than half a day. (From Buskirk et al., eds., in press, used with permission of the publisher.)

their home ranges than they visit in a day, the cost of sharing a territory with one other fisher is small (less than $[y^* - y']/y' = 0.1$, or 10%).

Figure 69 shows the relative predicted ranges of food availability or productivity for which a fisher benefits from maintaining an individual or an intrasexual territory. For fishers the range of food abundance or productivity for which intrasexual territoriality has the greatest benefit is large compared to that for individual territories.

From equations (1), (4), and (6) it is possible to predict how territorial behavior should change in fishers as prey populations, and hence prey availability and vulnerability, change. A given fisher population should exhibit intrasexual territoriality when conditions meet equation (6). As prey populations increase, fisher territories should decrease in size until further decreases eliminate critical patches of prey habitat. At this point the fishers should cease to maintain territories and should tolerate considerable home range overlap with members of both sexes. As prey populations decrease such that the left-hand inequality in equation (6) is no longer met, fisher spacing should change to individual territories. If prey populations decrease further such that the left-hand inequality in equation (4) is no longer met, the fishers should cease to maintain stable home ranges but become transient until prey populations again meet the conditions of the left-hand inequality in equation (4). Thus, from very low to very high prey

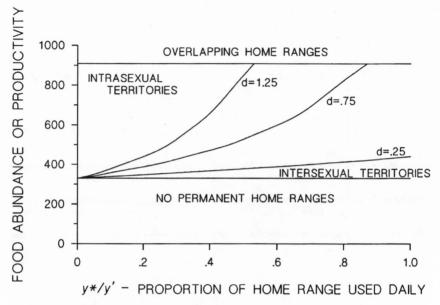

Figure 69. Predictions for territorial behavior in fishers, dependent on the proportion of habitat patches in a fisher's home range that are visited each day, the length of time that each visit depresses prey vulnerability, and the availability or productivity of prey in the home range. (From Buskirk et al., eds., in press, used with permission of the publisher.)

population densities, the following pattern of change in fisher spacing is predicted:

transient → individual territories, decreasing in size →
intrasexual territories, decreasing in size →
extensive home range overlap.

I believe that this may explain much of the variation in patterns of home range overlap that have been reported for other martens and some other mustelids. Too few studies have provided extensive data on fisher spacing patterns to test this prediction.

What is the benefit that outweighs the cost of sharing a territory with another fisher? There is no benefit to sharing a territory with a member of the same sex. I hypothesized (Powell, in press a) that the benefit of sharing a territory with a member of the opposite sex is increased reproductive success (fitness) due to familiarity with the resident member of the opposite sex. A simple probability model shows that a male with an intrasexual territory has a smaller probability of failing to reproduce than does a male with an intersexual territory (Powell, in press a). The model assumes that there is considerable territory trespass during the breeding season, as occurs with male fishers, but that territories are reestablished following the breeding season. I have been able to find no benefit for a female from sharing a territory with a male. Her access to males is unlikely to be affected by whether male territories are adjacent to or overlap with hers. Similarly, her energy expenditure to find a male will be unaffected because males come to her. Thus, I predicted that intrasexual territoriality found in fishers, other martens, other mustelines, and many other carnivores is imposed on females by males, who are larger than and dominant to females (Powell, in press a).

It must be remembered that territorial behavior is not a species-specific characteristic. When resource conditions, for example, prey population densities, change, spacing behavior is expected to change. In a gradient from low prey densities and productivity to high prey densities and productivity, fishers are expected to exhibit a gradient of spacing behaviors (Powell, in press a). At very low prey densities, fishers should not establish permanent home ranges but should be transient. At some threshold of prey availability, fishers should become resident and establish intersexual territories. At slightly higher prey availability, territories should become intrasexual. And finally, at very high prey availability, fishers should tolerate extensive home range overlap even among members of the same sex. In addition, we need to understand better how dispersing juveniles seek open territory spaces and how resident adults respond (Powell, in press a).

Chapter 10

Ecological Energetics
of the Fisher

Most discussions of the food requirements of free-living wild mammalian predators deal with food consumption capacities or consumption rates calculated
from observations of food intake (e.g., Burkholder 1959; Eaton 1974; Mech
1966, 1970, 1977a; Rudnai 1973; Schaller 1967). One cannot determine from
such studies alone how closely the measured rate of food consumption com-
pares with actual energy requirements or utilization. Mech (1977a) reported on
a wolf pack for which he could show that the wolves were eating less than they
required, but he needed extensive data on wolf blood to identify the deviant
blood parameters in undernourished wolves. He still could not determine how
much less than their requirements the wolves were eating.

There is information on the nutritional requirements of ranch minks and
foxes (summarized by Davison 1975), but there is very little information avail-

able on the nutritional or energetic requirements of wild predators. Litvaitis and Mautz (1976) and Golley and co-workers (1965) discussed the energy requirements of captive wild foxes and bobcats, respectively, but were unable to gain much insight into the requirements of free-living wild predators. Golley (1960), Moors (1974, 1977), and Sandell (1989b) assumed that the daily energy expenditure in the laboratory was the same as that in the field for least weasels and short-tailed weasels and then modeled energy budgets for free-living weasels. Direct measurement of the energy expenditure of free-living mammals has been limited largely to rodents and other small mammals (Koteja 1991; Nagy 1987; Weiner 1989), and data on carnivores is badly needed (Nagy 1987).

Energy Acquisition and Expenditure

Two studies have concentrated on the energetics of fishers. Davison and co-workers (Davison 1975; Davison et al. 1978) studied the efficiency of food utilization by fishers and the energy requirements of captive fishers. I studied the energy requirements of free-living fishers (Powell 1977a, 1979a, 1981). The information gained from these studies also provides insights about sexual dimorphism in the body size of fishers and about foraging choices.

Table 12 summarizes the energy available to fishers from different prey species. Davison and co-workers (Davison 1975; Davison et al. 1978) maintained four female fishers on four different diets to determine their gross energy intake, the digestibility of nutrients, the partitioning of dietary energy, the partitioning of dietary nitrogen, and the net maintenance energy requirements. Clements (1975) studied the digestive efficiency of fishers eating snowshoe hares, and I did research on fishers eating three different diets (Powell 1981). For Table 12, digestive efficiency was determined by subtracting the energy lost in feces and uneaten parts of prey from the total energy available from a member of a prey species. Metabolizable efficiency is determined by further subtracting the energetic cost of digestion and energy lost in urine.

The porcupine is the only major prey of fishers for which direct measurements of energy available are lacking. A fisher takes several days to eat a porcupine, and it is difficult to collect all of the uneaten material in feeding experiments. Therefore, I estimated the energy available to fishers from porcupines. From observations of more than twenty porcupines eaten by fishers, I determined that fishers usually eat only the meat, fat, internal organs, and very small bones of porcupines and leave the skin, quills, feet, leg bones, backbone, and skull. I dismembered five porcupines of known weight in a manner simulating the fisher's eating habits and estimated that fishers eat roughly 75% (a range of 72% to 79%) of the wet weight of a porcupine. That part of a porcupine that is eaten is roughly of the same composition as the deer used by Davison (1975).

Table 12. Digestive and metabolizable efficiencies of fishers eating different prey and the energy available from those prey

Prey species	Digestive efficiency	Metabolizable efficiency	Meal size	Digestible kcal/meal	Metabolizable kcal/meal	Source[a]
Snowshoe hare	83%[b]	-	1.25 kg	1440	-	Powell 1981
Snowshoe hare	83%	-	1.25 kg	1440	-	Clements 1975
Snowshoe hare	91%	77%	1.25 kg	1590	1350[c]	Davison 1975; Davison et al. 1978
Porcupine[d]	-	85%	4.35 kg	-	7050	Powell 1979a
Deer carrion	97%[e]	-	1.00 kg	1710	-	Powell 1981
Deer carrion	93%	86%	1.00 kg	1640	1520	Davison 1975; Davison et al. 1978
Red squirrel[f]	84%	-	380 g	520	-	Powell 1981
Squirrels[d]	-	75%	380 g	-	470	Powell 1979a
Small mammals[g]	81%	74%	25 g	33	30	Davison 1975; Davison et al. 1978
Coturnix quail	91%	87%	125 g	221	211	Davison 1975; Davison et al. 1978

[a] Source of measurement of digestive and metabolizable efficiency; digestive and metabolizable kcal/meal were calculated by Powell (1981).

[b] Values for percentage dry weight and kcal/g dry weight are averaged from Davison (1975), Davison et al. (1978), Golley et al. (1965), and Litvaitis and Mautz (1980).

[c] This value was incorrectly calculated by Powell (1979a); the correct value for a 1.25-kg hare is given here.

[d] Estimated.

[e] Values for percentage dry weight and kcal/g dry weight are averaged from Davison (1975), Davison et al. (1978), Golley et al. (1965), and Litvaitis and Mautz (1976, 1980).

[f] Values for percentage dry weight and kcal/g dry weight are averaged over hares and small mammals from Davison (1975), Davison et al. (1978), Golley et al. (1965), and Litvaitis and Mautz (1980).

[g] Included are *Microtus*, *Peromuscus*, and *Blarina*; digestible kcal per meal are calculated for *Microtus* and *Peromyscus* only.

Consequently, the values for the percentage of metabolizable energy, the kilocalories per dry gram, and the ratio of dry weight to wet weight were assumed to be the same for porcupines as they are for deer for the figures in Table 12. The weights for porcupines and hares listed in Table 12 are average weights for those species in the Ottawa National Forest, but they are representative of the weights of those species anywhere. The weights for squirrels and mice are approximate median weights taken from the literature.

The digestive and metabolizable efficiencies are both lower for mammalian prey with relatively large amounts of hair and bones (small mammals and squirrels) than for prey of which fishers eat mostly the meat and viscera (deer carrion and porcupines). The metabolizable energy available from prey items ranges from 30 kilocalories for a mouse to 7,050 kilocalories for a porcupine. Table 12 shows that there is some variation in the digestive efficiency values found for fishers eating snowshoe hares and deer carrion in different studies. The similarity of the values suggests that the trends shown in the table are correct. The variation in the values indicates that in addition to measurement error, there may be differences in the energy values from different populations or individuals of a given prey species and there may be differences in the digestive efficiency of fishers maintained under different captive conditions and when fed meals of different sizes.

Davison and co-workers (Davison 1975; Davison et al. 1978) did not know whether the information obtained for Coturnix quail is similar to that which would be obtained from other birds that are natural prey of fishers. Unfortunately, these quail were the only birds Davison could obtain in sufficient quantity to do the work. Quail and grouse are both in the order Galliformes but are very different in size, and captive quail are likely to have more fat than wild grouse.

High energy digestibility similar to that found for fishers has been reported for badgers (Jense 1968), bobcats (Golley et al. 1965), coyotes (Litvaitis and Mautz 1980), least weasels (Golley 1960; Moors 1974, 1977), minks (Roberts and Kirk 1964), and red foxes (Litvaitis and Mautz 1976).

Davison and co-workers estimated the daily maintenance energy requirements of captive fishers under laboratory conditions. They arrived at the figure of 172 kcal/$W^{.75}$/day (W = weight in kilograms). This is equivalent to 660 kilocalories for a 6-kilogram male fisher, 490 kilocalories for a 4-kilogram male fisher, and 290 kilocalories for a 2-kilogram female fisher.

To estimate the energy expenditures of free-living fishers, I developed a model for the daily energy expenditures of free-living solitary mammals (Powell 1977a, 1979a). The model can be applied to any mammal that does not spend much time in activities other than sleeping and running. From estimates of daily energy expenditures, daily food requirements can be calculated. The model was derived as follows.

The total energy expenditure (X) of an animal can be expressed as the sum of the energies expended in different activities and can be represented by a statement of the form:

$$X = \Sigma X_i,$$

where X_i is the energy expended in activity i and is a function of the time for which i occurs and the ambient temperature. Activities i must be exhaustive and mutually exclusive.

There are only three important nonreproductive activities for fishers: sleeping, running, and capturing prey. Fishers do not often climb trees, they remain solitary except for a brief mating period, and they hunt during a small number of periods each day that are separated by sleep. (See chapters 3, 7, 8, and 9.) Thus fishers spend almost all of their time sleeping or running on the ground while hunting, the energy expenditures of which are symbolized as X_1 and X_2, respectively. Prey capture is infrequent (Powell 1977a, 1978a), but when it occurs, energy is expended at a high rate. The energy expended during prey capture is symbolized as X_3.

The sleeping metabolic rate (X_1) of a healthy mammal in its thermoneutral zone is roughly the same as its basal metabolic rate (BMR). Kleiber (1975, empirical) and McMahon (1973, theoretical) have shown that (letting the BMR equal X_1/t_1)

$$\frac{X_1}{t_1} = k_1 W^{.75};$$

thus

$$X_1 = k_1 t_1 W^{.75}, \tag{1}$$

where k_1 is a constant, W is the weight of the mammal, and t_1 is the time spent sleeping. For mammals in general, Kleiber (1975) gave a value of 3 for k_1 (in kcal/kg$^{.75}$/hr).

Running metabolism (X_2) can be predicted from a mammal's weight. For a wide variety of mammals, Schmidt-Nielsen (1971), Taylor (1973), Taylor and co-workers (1970), Wunder (1975), and Yousef and co-workers (1973) showed that the metabolic rate increases in an approximate straight-line fashion with running speed. The relationship is:

$$\text{running metabolic rate} = k_2 W^{.75} + k_3 W^{.6} s,$$

where k_2 and k_3 are constants, $k_3 W^{.6}$ is the rate of increase of metabolic rate with running speed, and s is running speed. Heart rate also increases linearly with running speed in fishers, but individual variation is greater than for metabolic rate (Griffin and Gilbert 1992).

Because of this straight-line relationship, average running speed can be used to obtain average metabolic rate and energy expenditure during the time spent running (t_2). Average running metabolic rate is X_2/t_2, and the expression for energy expenditure becomes

$$X_2 = k_2 t_2 W^{.75} + k_3 W^{.6} s t_2.$$

Since the distance run (d) is equal to st_2,

$$X_2 = k_2 t_2 W^{.75} + k_3 d W^{.6}. \tag{2}$$

Running speed is not even needed. The energy expended can be calculated from the time spent running and the distance run.

The metabolic rate of a carnivore capturing prey (X_3) depends on the methods of capture, but for most carnivores (including fishers [Powell 1977a, 1978a]), energy is expended at a high rate, and a primary part of prey capture is running. A reasonable estimate of the metabolic rate during prey capture is the metabolic rate at maximum running speed. Thus

$$\frac{X_3}{t_3} = k_2 W^{.75} + k_3 W^{.6} s_m$$

and

$$X_3 = k_2 t_3 W^{.75} + k_3 s_m t_3 \, W^{.6}, \tag{3}$$

where t_3 is capture time and s_m is maximum running speed. Errors introduced by using this estimate are minimized by the infrequency of prey capture.

Adding equations (1), (2), and (3) yields a general equation for the energy expenditure of a fisher in its thermoneutral zone:

$$X = [k_1 t_1 + k_2(t_2 + t_3)]W^{.75} + k_3(d + s_m t_3)W^{.6}. \tag{4}$$

Equation (4) holds for ambient temperatures (T_a) above a mammal's lower critical temperature (T_c). When T_a is less than T_c, the metabolic rate of an inactive mammal is increased by the amount $mW^{1/2}(T_c - T_a)$, where the value of the constant m depends on the units used (Herreid and Kessel 1967). Sandell (1989b) calculated that even in winter, short-tailed weasels generate enough surplus heat while running to eliminate the energy costs of thermoregulation. Whether the same is true for fishers is not known.

I taught two fishers to run on a treadmill and determined the relationship between running speed and metabolic rate and the constants k_1, k_2, k_3, and s_m for fishers (Powell 1977a, 1979a). I also estimated T_c for fishers. The completed equation (4) for fishers is

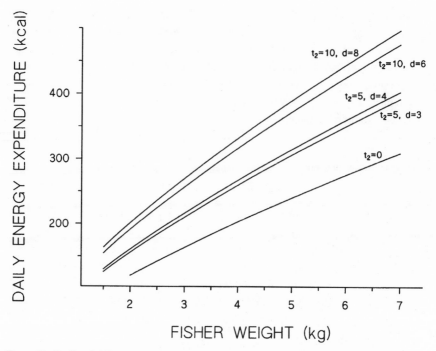

Figure 70. Predicted daily energy expenditure (in kilocalories) from equation (5) for fishers of different weights and different activity regimes that do not catch prey. Lines are labeled for fishers that were active 0%, 20%, and 40% of 24 hours and that traveled 0, 3, 4, 6, and 8 kilometers.

$$X = [3.0 \cdot t_1 + 5.4(t_2 + t_3)]W^{.75} + 3.3(d + 12.5 \cdot t_3)W^{.6}, \qquad (5)$$

where the units used are kilocalories, kilograms, and hours. Estimated T_cs were $-30°C$ and $-20°C$ for active male and female fishers, respectively, and $-80°C$ and $-40°C$ for male and female fishers curled up for sleeping.

Figure 70 shows the predicted daily energy expenditures of fishers of different weights and different activity schedules. The predicted daily energy expenditures range from about 130 kilocalories for a female fisher who sleeps all day to about 450 kilocalories for a large male fisher who is active 40% of the day and travels 8 kilometers.

Figure 71 shows the predicted energy expenditures from equation (3) for fishers of different weights that handle and kill a porcupine and a snowshoe hare. The more energy expended while capturing the prey, the more important that energy expenditure becomes compared to the energy obtained from the prey. Therefore, it is best to look at a high estimate of energy expenditure for handling prey in order to see whether handling energy expenditure is important and, when it is, how important it can potentially be. The maximum running

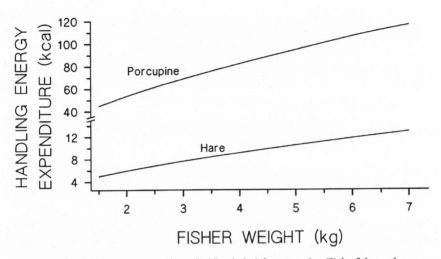

Figure 71. Predicted energy expenditure (in kilocalories) from equation (3) for fishers of different weights killing porcupines and snowshoe hares.

speed on the treadmill was used for s_m. A handling time of 45 minutes (1.5 times the handling times found by Coulter [1966]) was used to calculate porcupine-handling energy expenditure, and 5 minutes (far in excess of handling time observed during my study [Powell 1977a, 1978a]) was used to calculate the expenditure for hares. Prey-handling energy expenditures range from approximately 50 to 100 kilocalories for porcupines and 5 to 10 kilocalories for hares. It can be seen in both cases that the prey-handling energy expenditures are very small in relation to the energy acquired from the prey (Table 12) and that handling expenditures are also small compared to expected daily energy expenditures excluding prey handling (Figure 70).

Using radiotelemetric collars that told me whether a fisher was active or inactive, I estimated the energy expenditures of free-living fishers. On five occasions I maintained continuous radio contact with a fisher for periods of 8 to 26 hours and then measured how far the fisher had run while it had been monitored (Table 13). The estimated energy expended adjusted to 24 hours ranged from 206 kilocalories for a female fisher to 447 kilocalories for a male fisher.

There are two other sources of activity data that have been used to estimate the daily energy expenditures of fishers (Powell 1981). For fishers in New Hampshire, Kelly (1977) determined distances between radiotelemetric locations on two consecutive days (136 times for 31 fishers) and categorized distances traveled by sex and age of the fishers and by season. These data, inserted into equation (5) (Powell 1981), give estimates of daily energy expenditure that range from 191 kilocalories for females during the winter to 454 kilocalories for adult males during the entire year. The low value for females

Table 13. Fisher watches: activity, distance, and energy expended

Watch number	Fisher	Sex	Weight (kg)	Hours inactive (t_1)	Hours active (t_2)	Length of watch $(t_1 + t_2)^a$	Total distance run (km)	Total kcal expended	kcal expended per 24 hours
1	A	M	4.7	24.0	0	24.0	0	253	253
2	B	F	2.4	17.1	7.6	24.7	4.65	212	206
3	C	M	5.1	21.2	4.8	26.0	3.20	351	324
4	C	M	5.1	5.8	2.8	8.6	3.00	140	391
5	C	M	5.1	9.8	11.2	21.0	9.50	390	447

[a] Hours prey capture $(t_3) = 0$ for all watches.
Sources: Powell 1977a; Powell 1979a, used by permission of the publisher.

during the winter was due to their small average weight and the small amount of time they were active. The high value for adult males averaged over the whole year was due to a combination of their large size, long distances traveled, and a high level of activity.

Leonard (1980b) maintained continuous radiotelemetric contact with a female fisher for twenty-two days of the seven-week period during which she had kits in a natal den. He determined the time she spent at the den, the time she spent away from the den, and the general route of travel she followed while away from the den. When Leonard's data are inserted into equation (5), the estimated nonreproductive energy expenditures of this female ranged from 211 kilocalories (on a day when the kits were very small and the female stayed with them much of the day) to 337 kilocalories (on a day when the kits were growing quite fast and the female spent much time away from the den hunting [Powell 1981]).

From 123 kilometers of measured fisher tracks I calculated that the fishers had two active periods per day, traveled approximately 3 kilometers between sleeping sites, and averaged 0.8 kilometers per hour while hunting (Table 13; see chapter 5). These figures yield estimates ranging from 200 kilocalories to 480 kilocalories per day, depending on fisher weight.

Although Davison's estimates (Davison 1975; Davison et al. 1978) of daily maintenance energy requirements (290 kilocalories to 660 kilocalories per day) and the several estimates of daily energy expenditures of fishers in the field using equation (5) (130 kilocalories to 480 kilocalories per day) are broadly overlapping, the model estimates are consistently smaller than Davison's. There are two probable reasons for this discrepancy. First, free-living fishers spend a great deal of time sleeping, whereas captive-born fishers are very active (Davison 1975; Powell, personal observation). Also, as Table 13 shows, the average speed of a hunting fisher is very slow, but fishers pacing in cages usually move quickly (Powell, personal observation). Consequently, because Davison used captive fishers, his estimate may be biased to overestimate mainte-

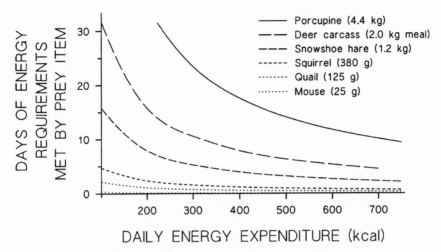

Figure 72. Days of a fisher's food requirements that are met by acquisition of an individual or amount of a given prey type at different daily energy expenditures.

nance energy requirements. Second, my model may underestimate the energy expenditures of free-living fishers. My model has many sources of error: several constants had to be determined, and each determination is subject to error; the constants were determined under laboratory conditions that did not always duplicate those in the field; and field measurements are always subject to error. Davison's estimates, however, are also subject to error for many of the same reasons. I believe all of these estimates together provide a good understanding of the fisher's daily energy expenditures. Equation (5) does not incorporate the cost of running in snow; the constants were calculated for fishers running on a solid surface. Deep, fluffy snow causes fishers to hunt in areas that would otherwise not be preferred for hunting, presumably due to the cost of running in deep snow (Raine 1983). How great this cost is has not been estimated, but it must be great enough to make the cost of foraging in deep snow greater than the expected gain from prey.

The frequencies at which fishers with different daily energy expenditures must catch prey, assuming none of the prey are shared with scavengers, are given in Figure 72. Scavengers can take a significant percentage of large prey items that cannot be eaten in one meal (porcupines, deer carrion). Davison (Davison 1975; Davison et al. 1978) and I (Powell 1977a, 1979a) have both measured and estimated fishers' actual food consumption. Under laboratory conditions, Davison measured a consumption of metabolizable energy ranging from 260 kilocalories per day to 450 kilocalories per day for the four female fishers on different diets. These estimates agree closely with the estimated maintenance energy found by Davison for these fishers: 440 kilocalories per day for each

Table 14. Energy available from each of the 14 kills and scavenges made along 123 kilometers of measured tracks in Michigan and average energy available per kill or scavenge

Kills and scavenges	Energy available (kcal)	Conservative estimate of energy available (kcal)
1 porcupine	7,050	3,500
1 snowshoe hare	1,350	1,350
2 squirrels	940	940
2 mice	60	60
7 small scavenges	210	0
½ deer carcass	8,000	4,000
Average kcal per kill or scavenge	1,258	704

Note: The third column is a conservative estimate of the energy a fisher is actually able to obtain from kills or scavenges since it shares large kills with other predators and scavengers. *Source*: Powell 1977a.

fisher weighing 3.5 kilograms. On a kcal/$W^{.75}$ basis, Davison's estimates are similar to the consumption of metabolizable energy of minks reported by Cowan and co-workers (1957) but less than that found by Farrell and Wood (1968).

Along 123 kilometers of fisher tracks, I found fourteen kills and scavenges (Powell 1977a, 1978a, 1979a). These and their estimated kilocalories available to fishers are shown in Table 14. The average number of kilocalories available from each kill-scavenge is approximately 1,250. This estimate adjusts to approximately 860 kilocalories acquired per day on the average, with the same assumptions about activity periods, distance between rests, and running speed made earlier on page 188. The average number of kilocalories expended between each kill-scavenge ranges from about 300 to about 700, depending on the fisher's weight. Thus, the estimated number of kilocalories expended between kill-scavenges is of the same order of magnitude as the number of kilocalories available from each kill-scavenge.

There are three likely explanations for the difference between the estimates of energy expenditure and consumption that do occur. First, the estimates of energy expenditure from my model may underestimate the amount of energy expended between kill-scavenges. Second, it is possible that the amount of energy acquired from kill-scavenges has been overestimated. Porcupines and deer carcasses are large and are often shared with scavengers, and many scavenges are scanty and probably of no energy value to a fisher (chapter 6). With these facts in mind, recalculating the average energy acquisition yields approximately 700 kilocalories per kill-scavenge; this estimate is shown in the far right-hand column of Table 14. The calculations listed in this column assume that a fisher shares half of the large food items such as deer carcasses and porcupines with scavengers, that hares, squirrels, and mice are eaten in one meal, and that small scavenges are of no energy value to a fisher. Seven hundred kilocalories per kill-scavenge (490 kilocalories acquired per day) is almost exactly the estimated energy expenditure between kill-scavenges.

The third possibility is that the fishers that made the tracks I followed actually acquired more food than they needed to replace the energy they expended. Under such conditions, fishers should gain weight and should not eat all of large food items. Of the eighteen fishers I handled during my study, all were in excellent health, and eleven were well padded with fat over the pelvis and ribs. It was impossible to determine whether fishers did not eat all food available from porcupines and deer carcasses. Fishers always left porcupine kills shortly after I found them, probably because I disturbed them. Nor was it possible to determine how much of the large food items were eaten by fishers; tracks of foxes, coyotes, bobcats, and weasels were seen around the large food items eaten by fishers. Further evidence that the fishers in my study area were able to obtain more than an adequate food supply comes from the sexual dimorphism in the body sizes of fishers in Michigan. Before we can explore this evidence, however, we must explore the energetics of reproduction because the two are interrelated.

Energy Expenditure and Reproduction

Richard Leonard and I (Powell and Leonard 1983) developed a model to estimate the energy expenditure of female fishers with kits, and we applied the model to a female fisher that Leonard followed radiotelemetrically in Manitoba. This female gave birth to a litter of four kits in a den in a quaking aspen tree in April 1977. Her kits remained in this den tree for about seven weeks, during which time continuous radiotelemetric contact was maintained during twenty-two days. We were able to calculate the distance the female traveled each time she left the den tree, the amounts of time she spent with the kits (time spent active or hunting), and the amounts of time she spent away from the den tree (time spent active or hunting) for each of those twenty-two days. From weights of this female known at two other times, we estimated that her weight during this period was 2.64 kilograms.

We believed that seven categories of energy expenditure might be important to a female fisher during lactation: (1) maintenance energy, (2) energy for running (hunting), (3) energy for capturing prey, (4) lactation energy, (5) copulation energy, (6) energy to climb the den tree, and (7) energy for thermoregulation. To estimate the maintenance, hunting, and prey-capturing categories of energy expenditure, we used equation (5).

Lactation energy (L) has been estimated for other mustelines by estimating the energy kits require for growth and maintenance (Moors 1974). Thus

$$L = \frac{\text{(litter size)} \cdot \text{(kit growth energy + kit maintence energy)}}{\text{(efficiency of lactation)} \cdot \text{(efficiency of milk assimilation)}}.$$

We used a litter size of four because our female fisher had litters of four for three years in a row. We estimated kit growth energy (11.2 kilocalories per day) from kit growth rates (6.8 grams per day, starting at 40 grams) recorded by Coulter (1966) and by me (Figure 27) and from energy content per unit weight of other mustelines (energy content per unit weight of fishers is not known). The efficiency of milk production was assumed to be 0.90 (Brody 1945), and the efficiency of lactation was assumed to be 0.95 (Moors 1974). Lactation energy (L) was estimated as

$$L = \frac{(4)(11.2 + 77[0.040 + (age) \cdot 0.0068]^{.75})}{(0.90)(0.95)}$$

$$= 52.4 + 360.2(0.040 + 0.0068 \cdot [age])^{.75},$$

where *age* is kit age.

Because fishers are awake during copulation but are generally inactive (in that they remain in the same place), we estimated copulation energy as running energy (equation [2]), with the distance traveled set equal to 0. Copulation occurs during a female fisher's active hours away from her den and occurs at a time when she would be hunting if she were not copulating. This means that on those days when our female copulated, the time spent copulating was part of the calculated time spent active. Therefore, copulation energy is estimated within equation (5) as part of the energy spent while hunting.

We estimated the energy expended to climb the den tree by determining the change in potential energy required to move an object the weight of a fisher up to the den entrance and then down to the den floor, plus the kinetic energy required to move a fisher that same distance horizontally. This energy expenditure turned out to be approximately 1 kilocalorie per day, with the assumption that the female left and returned to the den only once per day.

We estimated thermoregulation energy expenditure by using the equation presented earlier in this chapter. This energy expenditure turned out not to be a factor.

The estimated total energy expenditure of our female fisher with kits ranged from 342 kilocalories on a day when her kits were small and she spent 21 hours with them to 544 kilocalories on a day when the kits were large and she spent 23 hours hunting. A linear regression of the total energy expenditure (E) of our female versus the age of the kits is

$$E = 4.42(age) + 312.$$

The correlation coefficient (r) for this equation is 0.94.

The average daily energy expenditure for our female was 435 kilocalories; the average daily maintenance energy expenditure before parturition was 228 kilocalories. When the female moved the kits from the den in the quaking aspen, there were still a few weeks remaining before the kits were weaned. Therefore, we estimated that the total energy expenditure of our female fisher would increase to about 600 or 700 kilocalories per day before leveling off or decreasing. This is an approximate trebling of the female's calculated maintenance expenditure before parturition. A similar increase in energy expenditure was found for a female least weasel during lactation by East and Lockie (1964).

A male fisher weighing 5 kilograms expends approximately 300 to 400 kilocalories per day (equation [5], Figure 70). Thus the daily energy expenditure of the female fisher with kits exceeded that of a male fisher twice her size. By the end of lactation her daily energy expenditure was approximately twice that of a male twice her size. Kenagy (1987) measured energy expenditure of male and female golden-mantled ground squirrels during reproduction and found that they were approximately equal. Such figures for daily energy costs led Seaman (1993) to hypothesize that the expected lifetime cost of reproduction for males and females will be the same. Thus the small size of females allows increased energy to be directed toward offspring, and this increases reproductive output over what would be possible for a large female.

Energetics and Sexual Dimorphism in Body Size

Moors (1974) concluded from his work on the energetics of least weasels that sexual dimorphism in body size is maintained by conflicting selective pressures. There is selective pressure for weasels to be large because large weasels are able to exploit a wider range of prey sizes and thus have more potential prey. There is also selective pressure among weasels for small size because small weasels have lower daily energy requirements. One would assume that the size range of a species is determined by these factors and by competition for food with other predators of different sizes. In addition, male weasels are under selective pressure for large size to win encounters with other males for mates (sexual selection). Female weasels are under selective pressure for small size to reduce maintenance energy requirements during gestation, lactation, and weaning. Moors (1974) calculated that, compared to a normal-size female, a female least weasel the size of a male would have 25% higher maintenance energy requirements during reproduction. This requirement is approximately the equivalent of one additional mouse per day during the period of gestation through weaning, or approximately fifty mice for the entire period. This is a sizable increase in the amount of food required.

This argument for weasels applies equally well to fishers because of the many similarities between weasels and fishers. Fishers and weasels are both long and skinny and have high surface to volume ratios. Because of these characteristics, both species have high convective heat loss and high energy requirements (Brown and Lasiewski 1972; Powell 1977a, 1979a). And, as we have just seen, female fishers during lactation raise daily energy expenditure costs to be equal to or greater than the daily energy costs of males twice their size.

There are two correlates to Moors's (1974) hypothesis: during extended periods of abundant food, males should (1) show an increase in average body size (because size is no longer limited by nutrition and fishers can approach maximum size; this has been generally predicted by the cost-benefit analysis made by Schoener [1969]) and (2) show an increase in size variance (because males do not reach full size immediately). Females should not show such increases in size and variance in size because their maximum size is much smaller and more easily attained with limited food supplies.

The average weight of male fishers in Michigan did increase significantly during the fifteen years between their introduction to the area and my study (see Table 1 in chapter 1). Fishers in Michigan were released into an area with a food supply (porcupines) unexploited by other predators, and populations of that food supply were at high levels (Brander and Books 1973; Powell 1980a; Powell and Brander 1977). After their release, fishers exploited the porcupine population (Brander and Books 1973; Powell 1977a, 1978a; Powell and Brander 1977). The average weight of male fishers from Minnesota released in Michigan during the early 1960s was 4.0 kilograms. Since that time the weight of male fishers in Minnesota has remained stable. The average weight of males in Michigan in the 1970s was 5.0 kilograms. This weight is significantly higher than that of the introduced males. The difference in weights was not caused by a disproportionate number of juveniles in the released population (Irvine 1961, 1962). The average weight of females in Michigan was the same as that of the females released (Table 1, chapter 1). Porcupines have become less available (Figure 58, chapter 8), and I predict that the present weights of adult male fishers in Michigan are lighter than those I collected in the 1970s.

In addition, the variation in male weights is significantly greater than the variation in female weights. A measure of variation that can be used to compare distributions with different means is the ratio of the variance (σ^2, estimated as $s^2 = SD^2$) to the mean. The variance to mean ratio for weights of male fishers in Table 1 is 0.11 and that of female fishers is 0.04 ($p < 0.001$, Student's t-Test).

Thus, the patterns of sexual dimorphism seen in fishers support Moors's (1974) hypothesis that sexual dimorphism in body size in mustelids is maintained by energy considerations (Powell 1979b). Genetically constrained to a body size of 2 to 2.5 kilograms because of reproductive costs, female fishers did not grow larger when presented with an abundant food supply. Male fishers, however, did, because large size in males is favored by sexual selection. These patterns indicate that the fishers I studied in Michigan may actually have been able to acquire more food than was required to replace the energy expended in daily activities.

These patterns are also consistent with the lack of support for the niche partitioning hypothesis shown by anatomy (chapter 2) and diet (chapter 6). Energetics of reproduction and sexual selection appear to be the selective forces that led to the large sexual dimorphism in body size in fishers and in other mustelines as well. There is general lack of support for the niche partitioning hypothesis (Ralls and Harvey 1985; Holmes 1987; Holmes and Powell, in press) and support for energetics and sexual selection (Powell and King, in preparation).

Energetics and Foraging Behavior

I used my energy budget model (equation [5]) to investigate the foraging strategies of fishers in Upper Peninsula Michigan (Powell 1977a, 1979a). Many theoretical models of the foraging strategies of predators and parasites have been proposed (reviews in Charnov 1976; Krebs 1973; MacArthur 1972; Murdoch and Oaten 1975; Pyke, Pulliam, and Charnov 1977; Pyke 1984; Schoener 1971). Most involve the rate of energy intake for a predator choosing between food types or habitat patches and assume a goal of maximizing the rate of energy intake. This assumption is probably reasonable, because most predators have evolved under conditions of periodic food shortages when it would be advantageous to maximize the rate of food acquisition.

The models of optimal foraging strategies deal with gross energy gain, energy expenditure, and net energy gain from different food types. All of these categories have been estimated for fishers in the preceding sections of this chapter. Recent models also incorporate variation in these variables and incorporate random variation in probabilities of encountering prey (e.g., Nishimura 1991). Unfortunately, such variation has not been measured for most predators, including fishers.

If a predator does not have specific nutritional requirements supplied by only a limited number of prey items, then the predator's optimal choice of food depends on the rate of energy gain available from each of its prey types:

$$E_j = \frac{A_j - X_{sj} - X_{hj}}{t_{sj} - t_{hj}}, \tag{6}$$

where E_j is the net rate of energy gain from prey type j, A_j is the metabolizable energy available from a food item of prey type j, X_{sj} and X_{hj} are the energetic costs of searching for and handling a prey item of type j, and t_{sj} and t_{hj} are search and handling times for a prey item of type j.

Charnov (1976) presented a theorem for the inclusion of prey types in a predator's optimal diet. The theorem is derived from a multispecies version of the Holling disk equation (Holling 1959). The assumptions made for the theorem apply to fishers, except that all prey types may not be available to fishers at one time. For example, porcupine and snowshoe hare habitats were the two distinct major habitats in my study area in Upper Michigan; therefore, only one of these prey types is available to a given fisher at any time. When each habitat is treated separately, however, it follows from the theorem that fishers in Upper Peninsula Michigan should eat all prey types found in a particular habitat (listed in Table 8) under my study, as long as the search time for small mammals and squirrels is minimal. Dead deer, squirrels, and small mammals are found in both porcupine habitat and hare habitat and are eaten by fishers when they are encountered. Therefore, modeling fishers' foraging strategies in Upper Peninsula Michigan is reduced to modeling fishers foraging in porcupine habitat or hare habitat. Because the density of deer carcasses is very low and the energy returns from squirrels and small mammals are low, this strategy is equivalent to foraging for either porcupines or hares.

When a fisher in Upper Peninsula Michigan attempts to maximize its caloric intake, its decision to hunt for porcupines or hares is determined by whether E_p (for porcupines) or E_h (for hares) is larger. Reasonable estimates for all variables in equation (6), except t_{sj}, can be obtained from Table 12, Figures 70 and 71, fisher tracking data, and observations of captive fishers (Powell 1977a). Let $d = st_{sj}$ in X_{sj}.

A_p = 7,050 kcal (Table 12) A_h = 1,350 kcal (Table 12)

X_{hp} = 45 to 100 kcal (Figure 71) X_{hh} = 5 to 10 kcal (Figure 71)

$X_{sp} = (3.0)(0.8)W^{.6}t_{sp} + (5.4)W^{.75}t_{sp}$ $X_{sp} = (3.0)(0.8)W^{.6}t_{sh} + (5.4)W^{.75}t_{sh}$
       (equation [2])   (equation [2])

t_{hp} = 0.75 hours (Figure 71) t_{hh} = 0.083 hours (Figure 71)

A fisher should hunt porcupines when $E_p > E_h$. To two decimal places, this inequality reduces to the same criterion for fishers of any weight between 2 and 6 kilograms:

$$t_{sh} > 0.19 \cdot t_{sp} + 0.09.$$

Because

$$\frac{A_h}{A_p} = 0.19,$$

the above inequality can be expressed as

$$t_{sh} > (A_h/A_p)t_{sp} + 0.09.$$

A fisher should begin hunting porcupines only when the expected search time to find a hare is greater than the ratio A_h/A_p (which is about one-fifth) times the expected search time to find a porcupine plus 0.09 hours (about 5 minutes). For a fisher hunting porcupines or hares, the critical relationship between t_{sp} and t_{sh} is roughly the ratio of A_p to A_h, and the relationship between the E_js is roughly the relationship between the $(A_j t_{sj})$s. Even though the energy cost of handling a porcupine is much greater than that for a hare, the energy cost of handling a porcupine is only a small percentage of the metabolizable energy available from a porcupine. The difference between the X_{sj}s, X_{hj}s, and t_{hj}s for porcupines and hares reduces to an adjustment of 5 minutes in expected t_{sj}s. Fishers may shift between hunting porcupines and hares several times in a day, and yet the interval between kills is on the order of days. Therefore, the 5-minute adjustment in t_{sj}s can be ignored. A_j and t_{sj} are by far the most important components in E_j for fishers in Upper Peninsula Michigan. A fisher should hunt in porcupine habitat when the ratio of the energy acquired from each prey is greater than the ratio of expected search times:

$$A_p/A_h > t_{sp}/t_{sh}.$$

This inequality says that a fisher should hunt in hare habitat until t_{sh} becomes so high from resource depression (chapter 9) that the inequality becomes true. Then the fisher should leave the patch of hare habitat in which it is hunting and travel to the nearby porcupine dens. Once enough nearby dens have been checked and the porcupines have been found to be safe from fisher attack such that the inequality is no longer true, the fisher should begin hunting hares again in a new patch of hare habitat. Although I have no data that would allow me to check whether fishers change habitats for foraging when expected energy gains and search times predict they should, the behavior predicted by the model does agree qualitatively with fisher foraging behavior.

The addition of other prey found in Upper Michigan and eaten by fishers does not complicate the decision for a fisher. For other prey types, t_{sj} is so large and E_j is so small that none would be worth considering by itself if it had to be found in a separate habitat. But all the other prey types are found in both porcupine and hare habitats, and fishers do eat them. I have concluded that fishers take them when they are available but do not search for them specifically; thus the search time for them is zero.

In chapters 7 and 8, I pointed out that fishers have two components to foraging behavior, travel and zigzag hunting. Fishers use the zigzag component, typical musteline hunting behavior, for hunting hares and the travel component when moving between patches of hare habitat; fishers use predominantly the travel component when hunting porcupines. The actual distance a fisher travels between two points is approximately 1.5 times farther in hare habitat than in porcupine habitat (Table 9).

If fishers hunted in porcupine habitat the same way they hunt in hare habitat, the energy expenditure in porcupine habitat would increase by approximately 50%. Prey captured would be unchanged (or perhaps lowered because of longer distances traveled between porcupine dens), however, because the only major source of food for a fisher in porcupine habitat is porcupines, which are found only near porcupine dens. Thus, fishers appear to have made major energetic savings by using only the travel component in hunting porcupines and remembering porcupine den locations (Powell 1979a).

Models of optimum habitat use (Rosenzweig 1991) predict that animals should use habitats in accordance with an ideal free distribution (Fretwell and Lucas 1970). For fishers, this is equivalent to the proportion of time foraging in a given habitat type being the same as the proportion of energy gained from that habitat. Table 8 (chapter 6) indicates that the fishers I studied captured three hares for every two porcupines they captured. Table 12 shows that a porcupine provides a fisher approximately 3.75 times as much energy as a hare does. The ratio of the proportions of energy provided to fishers by porcupines and hares is approximately 3.3. If fishers forage in habitats optimally, the ratio of energy expended in porcupine and hare habitats should also be 3.3. This ratio equals equation (2) plus equation (3) for porcupines divided by equation (2) plus equation (3) for hares. We can estimate kill energy expenditure from Figure 71. If we solve this ratio for a 2-kilogram female fisher that travels 70 kilometers in porcupine habitat and 25 kilometers in hare habitat (chapter 5, Figure 72) and captures one porcupine and one hare (Table 14; for this table to agree with Table 8, I should have found 1½ hare kills), we are left with two unknowns: t_2 for porcupine habitat and for hare habitat. Because $t_2 = d/s$ and we know distances in both habitats, we are left not knowing running speed in the two habitats. The ratio is

$$\frac{(5.4)(70/s_p)(W^{.75}) + (3.3)(70)(W^{.6}) + 45}{(5.4)(25/s_h)(W^{.75}) + (3.3)(25)(W^{.6}) + 10},$$

where s_p and s_h are the speeds a fisher travels when hunting porcupines and hares. It is impossible for this ratio to equal 3.3. If fishers were to travel their average running speed in both habitats (0.8 km/h), the ratio would equal 2.8, meaning that fishers do not spend as much energy foraging for porcupines as they should. If fishers travel faster in porcupine habitat, as we know they do, the ratio decreases and equals 1.7 if fishers travel twice as fast in porcupine habitat as in hare habitat. This contradiction has three solutions, any of which might be true: (1) fishers do not use habitats optimally, (2) fishers do not actually get as much from porcupines as calculated from tables 8 and 12, or (3) the ideal free distribution model is wrong. Because fishers often share large food items with other scavengers, solution (2) can be checked by recalculating the ratios of energy gained from prey by assuming that a fisher only gains one-half of the energy available from a porcupine (Table 14). This yields a ratio of 1.6, which is in close agreement with the ratio of energy expended, 1.7, if fishers travel twice as fast in porcupine habitat as hare habitat. Before we accept the conclusion that fisher habitat selection optimizes energy gained and expended in those habitats, independent tests of solutions (1), (2), and (3) are needed.

Chapter 11

Conservation and the Fisher's Relationship to Humans

Evolution has molded fishers into predators keenly adapted to their environment. Fishers can survive the climate of northern North America, can travel long distances in short periods of time, and can hunt and capture a wide variety of prey animals, including porcupines. The selective forces that have molded the fisher in the past should keep the fisher adapted to the natural conditions in the forests of North America for millennia to come.

Yet, the fisher's future does not lie with evolution and the forces that have molded its evolutionary past. Today, direct and indirect interactions of fishers with humans are probably as important as any aspect of the fisher's biology, for humans have the capacity to affect every aspect of the fisher's environment.

Interactions with Humans

Our interest in fishers and our interactions with them fit into five general categories. First, since the time of its discovery, the fisher has been valued for its pelt. Fishers have always been considered furbearers and have always been subject to trapping and, to a lesser extent, fur farming. Second, humans have an important influence on fisher populations through forestry practices and other activities that result in the alteration of the fisher's habitat. Third, some hunters of small game fear that fishers have an adverse effect on populations of small game such as rabbits, hares, and grouse. Fourth, foresters have acquired and promoted an interest in the fisher as a tool for managing porcupine populations. And, fifth, the fisher is unique to North America and is an important member of the complex natural communities that comprise the continent's northern forests. Fisher populations are healthy when their forest communities are healthy, and thus fishers are directly related to the diversity of organisms found in North America's northern forests.

The fisher's reaction to humans in all of these interactions is usually one of avoidance. Even though mustelids as a group appear to be curious by nature, fishers seldom linger when they become aware of the immediate presence of a human.

Trapping

In the past, trapping was one of the two most important factors influencing fisher populations. Fishers are easily trapped, and the value of fisher pelts has created trapping pressure at times great enough to exterminate fishers completely from large geographic areas (chapter 4). Trapping still has an important impact on fisher populations. In some parts of the fisher's present range, trapping is a primary cause of death. In all parts of the fisher's present range where fishers are trapped, the interest in trapping requires management of fisher populations that guarantees the maintenance of healthy populations because fisher populations are sensitive to pressures from trapping. In addition to the clear evidence from past population declines, there is evidence from more recent changes in trapping regulations in New York and Ontario, evidence from changes in the fisher population in Maine, and theoretical evidence that small changes in mortality due to trapping can greatly affect fisher populations.

During the 1970s the fisher-trapping season in New York was in October (in part), November, and December. Annual returns remained approximately constant during the first half of the decade but increased by approximately 50% in 1976 (Parsons 1980), probably because the prices paid for pelts increased. The fisher season was closed for 1977, resulting in an estimated 70% decrease in the deaths of fishers from trapping (the 30% remaining was caused by the deaths of fishers captured in sets meant for other furbearers). In 1978, there was again an open fisher season, and the harvest went back to pre-1976 levels.

Population models indicate that the New York fisher population was seriously decreased after the 1976 trapping season, but the age structure of the fisher population, as indicated in the harvests, showed an immediate response to the season's closure in 1977. Good reproduction occurred during the closed season and an increased number of fishers survived to adulthood that year. Had a harvest similar to 1976 or even previous years been allowed in 1977, the fisher population would have dropped even lower. Closure of the season for one year allowed the population to regain its losses because the trapping season in New York was timed to harvest mostly juveniles, leaving adults for future reproduction (Parsons 1980; Douglas and Strickland 1987).

Before the 1975-76 fisher trapping season, fishers could be harvested in Ontario from 25 October through 28 February (Strickland and Douglas 1978). During the early 1970s, the fisher population in the Algonquin region was declining, and 6% to 8% of the adult females did not breed. Strickland and Douglas (1978; Douglas and Strickland 1987) found that during the first half of the trapping season (through December), roughly 80% of the male fishers trapped were juveniles (the young of the year) but that later in the season adult males were more commonly captured. They believed that the high mortality rate of adult males resulting from trapping was causing the reduced breeding rate (Douglas and Strickland 1987; Strickland and Douglas 1978) (see chapter 3). In 1975, the fisher season in the Algonquin region was shortened to end on 31 December; this change effectively reduced the trapping pressure on adult males. During succeeding years, the breeding rate of females increased to 98%, and the population began to increase (Douglas and Strickland 1987; Strickland and Douglas 1978). By 1978, the anticipated harvest was equal to that of the 1973-74 high. Therefore, a slight change in the length and timing of the trapping season resulting in a change in mortality rates for adult male fishers appears to have had a significant effect on the fisher population in the Algonquin region of Ontario. In addition, ending the trapping season on 31 December maximized pelt primeness in trapped fishers.

Working with the five one-predator-one-prey and one-predator-three-prey population models for the fisher community in Michigan (chapter 8), I found that a very small increase in mortality might reexterminate the fisher population. The increase in mortality that eliminated the fisher population from the model communities ranged from 3% to 98% of the equilibrium mortality rates for the models without trapping, depending on which model was used. All models were consistent in that none could tolerate an increase in mortality greater than about one to four fishers above natural levels per 100 square kilometers. Quantitative extrapolation of these results to fisher populations in areas other than Upper Michigan is not recommended because of the many differences in habitat, prey, and logging and trapping practices throughout the fisher's range. The qualitative results, however, reinforce the knowledge gained from past population declines: past fisher population declines were not a unique event and can be repeated; therefore all fisher trapping must be closely managed.

My models did not include differential trapping mortality for different fishers of different ages and sex. Krohn and co-workers (in press) found that adult female fishers in Maine during 1984-89 were significantly less vulnerable to trapping than were juveniles and adult males. Humans caused 94% of the fisher mortality they recorded, and 80% of the mortality was from trapping. Krohn and co-workers developed a model that included differential susceptibility to trapping for fishers of different ages and sex and found that annual fecundity needed to be approximately 1.5 offspring per adult female ($\geq$ 2 years old). Their estimate of actual fecundity was 1.3 offspring per adult female, which indicated a 2% per year population decline.

Management of fisher populations, either to stabilize populations to provide stable harvests (Strickland, in press) or to provide recreational harvests, appears more commonly to replace natural population cycles with fluctuations caused by periods of overtrapping followed by recovery when trapping eases or ceases. Kelly (1977), Wood (1977), and Young (1975) noted a decrease in fisher populations in New Hampshire during the mid-1970s and attributed the decrease to overtrapping. During the 1977-78 trapping season, New York, New Hampshire, and Maine were forced to limit or to close completely fisher trapping to allow populations to rebuild. The fisher population in Maine during the 1980s and early 1990s again appears to be declining due to heavy trapping pressure. Whether population fluctuations caused by trapping affect the social structure of fisher populations in the same manner as natural population cycles is not known.

Fishers are also easily trapped in sets for other furbearers (Coulter 1966; Douglas and Strickland 1987; Young 1975). Where fishers are scarce, the populations can be seriously affected by fox and bobcat trapping (Coulter 1966; Douglas and Strickland 1987). I released fishers accidently captured in coyote sets in Michigan. The number of fishers crippled by being caught in traps set for other species can be significant (Powell, unpublished data). In light of this problem, Wisconsin designated fisher wildlife management areas in the Nicolet and Chequamegon national forests (approximately 550 square kilometers and 1,000 square kilometers, respectively) where land sets for all furbearers were prohibited (Petersen, Martin, and Pils 1977).

Management of fisher populations can be very sophisticated if management agencies are conscientious and use and develop techniques that are tested for their effectiveness (Strickland, in press). In Ontario, the ratio of the number of juvenile fishers harvested to the number of adult females harvested in a given year can be used to project next year's relative population size and allowable harvest (Strickland, in press). The technique should be amenable to calculating an optimal harvest level set not only by the maximum number of pelts that can be harvested on a sustained basis but also by fisher population sizes that the general public wishes to maintain.

Pressure from the antitrapping movement, however, may reduce demand for wild fur products to a level unable to support an industry (Strickland, in press). This may not eliminate the need for trapping or the need for management knowledge gained from trapping. Forest management affects fisher habitat and creates the need for management of fisher populations in changing forests. All parties interested in fishers, interested in other animals with whom fishers share their forest habitat, and interested in the forests themselves must cooperate to maintain forests that support the diversity of species native to North America. This cooperation will require animal protection groups, trappers, other groups interested in using wildlife resources, wildlife management agencies, and forest management agencies to develop common, long-term goals. Increased research on fisher biology will contribute to such long-term goals.

Forest Management

Logging of forests has been the other major impact on fisher populations. As discussed in chapter 5, fishers prefer continuous or nearly continuous forests. Clear-cut logging has the greatest effect on forest landscape and thus on fishers' habitats and populations. Clear-cut logging involves removing all of the trees in an area and is sometimes followed by a controlled fire to burn the slash (branches and debris left after the logging is finished). Although the diversity of prey species may be little affected by clear-cutting second-growth forests, the composition of prey species is affected (Martell 1983). Extensive clear-cuts are avoided by fishers during the winter and selectively cut areas are not. The extensive clear-cutting done during the late 1800s and early 1900s, together with trapping, decimated fisher populations all over the continent. Fisher populations have not recovered in the Pacific Northwest, probably because of logging.

Clear-cutting is commonly practiced throughout the United States and Canada. Aspen and many types of early successional coniferous forests are most commonly clear-cut because these forests regenerate quickly from clear-cuts the same way they regenerate quickly from wind throw or fire. Such forests are found over most of the fisher's present range, and second-growth forests are the most common habitat of fishers in the eastern United States and Canada today. Fishers do use clear-cuts during the summer, when the cover formed by ground vegetation and young trees is dense, and do use young-growth forests, but the extent of clear-cutting in an area is important. For fishers, the problem is not clear-cuts per se, because fishers evolved in forests that experienced wind throw and fire, but the extent of clear-cut forests. Fishers must contend with the destruction of their habitat when clear-cut logging is more extensive than natural wind throw and fire. Small clear-cuts interspersed with large, connected, uncut areas may not seriously affect fisher populations. Large clear-cuts, however, can seriously limit the available foraging area for a fisher population during the winter and thus limit the population size.

The exact structure of forests that is important to fishers is just being learned. It is likely that forest type is not as important to fishers as the vegetational and structural aspects of the forest that lead to high prey populations and high prey vulnerability. This structure can be found in the second-growth forests of eastern North America but not in the Pacific Northwest. There, the structural complexity and the species and age diversity characteristics of the centuries-old old-growth forests appear necessary for healthy fisher populations. Bissonette and co-workers (1989) argued that landscape-level management is necessary for managing American martens. These generalizations hold for fishers as well.

Healthy forests with their natural diversity of plants and animals are important to more than fishers. A forest is more than trees, and forestry practices aimed at maximizing tree production while minimizing rotation times are of no more value to wildlife than is any other type of industrial farming. Forest management aimed at producing a diversity of trees, wildlife, and other forest products including recreation while maintaining natural communities will benefit fishers, other wildlife, and people. Sound forest management requires the cooperation of all groups interested in and responsible for all components of the forest. Research on forests and their plant and animal species is needed to understand best how forest communities function and how they can be managed to withstand the impacts of civilization.

Finally, if major changes occur in northern forests due to global warming (M. R. Heinselman, personal communication), this human impact on fisher habitat will be more profound than the worst effects of logging.

Effects of the Fisher's Predation on Other Animals

There is no evidence that predation by fishers has an important effect on any prey other than porcupines. Fisher populations have been found to cycle in response to snowshoe hare population cycles (Bulmer 1974, 1975), and the total effect of predation by all predators on snowshoe hares has been found to do little other than to speed up population declines (Keith and Windberg 1978). So, the fears of hunters that fisher populations may seriously affect the populations of game animals are unsubstantiated and partially refuted.

Fishers do kill prey to eat, however, and that must be considered in some management decisions. Reintroduction of fishers to the Great Smoky Mountains National Park has been proposed and is considered feasible (Powell 1990). Fishers do kill flying squirrels occasionally (Table 8), and the northern flying squirrel population in the southern Appalachian Mountains is on the federal list of endangered species in the United States. Fishers can only be reintroduced if they will have no impact on the endangered northern flying squirrel population.

Fishers and Porcupines

There is a growing body of evidence that fishers have long-term effects on porcupine populations (see chapter 8). Fishers can have short-term effects on porcupine populations (Coulter 1966; Hamilton and Cook 1955; Powell 1980a; Powell and Brander 1977). Declines in porcupine populations following increases in fisher populations have been reported in New York, Maine, and Wisconsin and have been documented in Michigan. A possible increase in porcupine populations in southeastern Maine following the recent decrease in fisher populations has also been noted. My work with model communities and computer simulations indicated that the short-term effects of a new fisher population on an extremely high porcupine population may be greater or at least more dramatic than the long-term effects (Powell, unpublished data). The modeling work also indicated that in the long run porcupine populations will be lower with fishers in the community than without them.

Thus, it appears that fishers may be used successfully as a forest management tool to limit extremely high porcupine populations. Porcupine populations may cycle in response to fisher and snowshoe hare populations and periodically reach population levels at which they may concern foresters. And porcupine populations may be locally extirpated during a population low. The success of fishers in reestablishing themselves in areas from which they have been eliminated and in which porcupine populations have reached high densities is also dependent on local logging and trapping practices. Even with an abundant food supply, fishers can be exterminated because of high trapping pressure. And both fishers and porcupines can be exterminated through extensive clear-cut logging practices.

The Fisher as a Part of Our Native Fauna

During recent years, there has been an increased awareness of the inherent value of natural communities of animals and plants that goes beyond the economic values individual animals and plants may have for humans. Brainerd and co-workers (Brainerd 1990; Brainerd et al., in press; Lindström 1989) concluded that European pine martens are important in old-growth forests and regenerating forests that have physical attributes of old growth; the martens are prey generalists but habitat specialists. As a large marten, fishers are important in a similar way to the forests of North America.

Within the forests that comprise fisher habitat, fishers interact with a diversity of other animals. Fishers are part of a suite of predator species, each of which survives by using in a slightly different way the food resources in the forests. Fishers do not hunt mice the way foxes and coyotes do but may be dominant to foxes in contests over carrion (Pittaway 1983). There is a beauty in the way that many organisms can live together and all survive as species for long periods of time. Fisher populations are healthy when their forest communities are healthy. Thus fishers fit into "this view of life" as part of the native fauna of North America.

There is also no doubt that the fisher itself, with its beautiful fur and graceful movements, is a creature of beauty. Seeing a wild fisher free in the woods is a thrill. For an increasing number of people, simply knowing that fishers can be found wild in an area is rewarding, even though they seldom see them.

Fishers in Captivity

Fishers have been maintained in captivity for extended periods of time (Hodgson 1937; Laberee 1941; Bronx Zoo, New York Zoological Society, unpublished files); however, this has never been an important aspect of the fisher's relationship with humans. Despite the value of their fur, fishers have never been raised extensively on fur farms (Hodgson 1937; Laberee 1941). The reason for this lies in the fisher's reproductive cycle, with the long-delayed implantation and consequent delay in knowing whether a female fisher has conceived. This delay, in turn, affects the decision whether a female's pelt can be harvested during a particular year. Both zoos and fur farms have had difficulty breeding fishers, though fur farms and the Minnesota Zoo have had some success (Hodgson 1937; Laberee 1941; Bronx Zoo, New York Zoological Society, unpublished files; Christopher A. Kline and Michael Don Carlos, Minnesota Zoological Society, unpublished files). Wild fishers make poor exhibit animals at zoos because they often hide from visitors all day. Some zoos have even had difficulty keeping fishers alive because of their susceptibility to many diseases in captivity (Brookfield Zoo, Chicago Zoological Society, unpublished files).

Because there are numerous healthy populations of wild fishers, there has been little pressure to develop dependable programs for maintaining and breeding fishers in captivity. This lack hampers research on fisher physiology and reproduction, including delayed implantation, and thus slows our gain in knowledge about fishers and hinders our abilities to manage wild populations.

The Value of the Fisher

The fisher is valued differently by different people. Foresters are interested in maintaining fisher populations in order to limit porcupine populations and thus limit any damage porcupines might do to timber crops. The influence of forest management on fisher populations will probably be taken into more consideration in the future now that it is known that fishers can limit porcupine populations to some degree. State game agencies are interested in maintaining fisher populations for trappers on a long-term and sustained-yield basis.

There are areas of conflict, however. Despite evidence to the contrary, some people still believe that fishers can have a detrimental effect on game animals. The conflict between these people and those who wish to maintain fisher populations can best be resolved through education.

Probably the greatest disagreement arises between those people who wish to protect individual animals totally, especially those of such aesthetic value as the fisher, and those people who wish to harvest animals from populations. Because this conflict is an emotional one, its resolution may be slow and difficult. The best resolution will come through cooperation between all parties to reach long-term maintenance of fisher populations, other wildlife populations, and the forests they share.

The Fisher's Future

The future of the fisher appears less controversial than do the futures of some other carnivores. Wolves, coyotes, and mountain lions frequently come into direct conflict with humans over livestock and big game (Cahill 1971; Fritts et al. 1992; Hendrickson, Robinson, and Mech 1975; Koford 1978; Mech 1970, 1977b; Robinson and Smith 1977; Weise et al. 1975). Yet red wolves have been reintroduced to the wild in North Carolina (Phillips and Parker 1988), and though hounded with controversy, timber wolves may be reintroduced into Yellowstone National Park. Although fishers are trapped, and thus are subject to the controversies concerning trapping for fur, fishers are not subject to the controversies met by large predators. In addition, recent activities of conservation and preservation groups have helped the fisher.

I do not wish to end by describing too rosy a picture. Cooperation has not yet developed between wildlife agencies, trappers, animal rights activists, forest management agencies and industries, and researchers to lead to proper understanding of fishers and other forest species and how they interact. This cooperation is badly needed; without it fishers, other animals, forests, and other habitats will be managed piecemeal and not within a landscape management scheme (Bissonnette et al. 1989). Across North America, animal populations must be managed. Because humans have altered the face of most of the continent, we cannot simply ignore animal populations and expect the populations to survive as they did before European settlement. Even a decision *not* to manage a species actively, for example, through trapping or through alteration of habitat for prey, is a management decision. Human impact on the living world is so pervasive that we must watch the lives of the other species with which we share this world. We must act to prevent our influence from leading to dangerous population declines or to the loss of functional communities of organisms. The species alive today evolved within living communities with great diversity. Loss of these communities and their diversity through the loss of individual species cannot be taken lightly. The future of the fisher may look good, but that future depends upon proper management. The future for the fisher is in our hands.

Appendix
Mammals, Birds, and Trees Mentioned in the Text and Tables

Mammals

armadillo
    Mulita   *Dasypus hybridus*
    nine-banded   *Dasypus novemcinctus*
badger
    American   *Taxidea taxus*
    Eurasian   *Meles meles*
    hog   *Arctonyx collaris*
    stink   genera *Mydaus, Suillotaxus*
bat
    equatorial fruit   *Eidolon helvum*
    Jamaican fruit   *Artibeus jamaicensis*
    lesser long-fingered   *Miniopterus fraterculus*
    Schreiber's long-fingered   *Miniopterus schreibersii*
bear
    Asiatic black   *Ursus thibetanus*
    black   *Ursus americanus*
    brown or grizzly   *Ursus arctos*
    polar   *Ursus maritimus*
    sloth   *Melurses ursinus*
    spectacled   *Tremarctos ornatus*
beaver   *Castor canadensis*
bobcat   *Lynx rufus*
caribou   *Rangifer tarandus*
cheetah   *Acinonyx jubatus*
chipmunks   *Eutamias* spp., *Tamias striatus*
coatimundi   *Nasua* spp.
coyote   *Canis latrans*
deer
    black-tailed   *Odocoileus hemionus*
    musk   *Moschus moschiferus*
    roe   *Capreolus capreolus*
    white-tailed   *Odocoileus virgianus*
euro   *Macropus robustus*

ferret	
black-footed	*Mustela nigripes*
fitch	*Mustela putorius*
fisher	*Martes pennanti*
fox, red	*Vulpes vulpes*
hare, snowshoe	*Lepus americanus*
lemming, southern bog	*Synaptomys cooperi*
lynx	*Lynx lynx*
marten	
American pine	*Martes americana*
beech, house, or stone	*Martes foina*
European pine	*Martes martes*
Japanese	*Martes melampus*
yellow-throated	*Martes flavigula*
mink	*Mustela vison*
moles	family Talpidae
Siberian	*Talpa altaica*
moose	*Alces alces*
mountain lion	*Felis concolor*
mouse or vole	
bank	*Clethrionomys glareolis*
grey-sided	*Clethrionomys rufocanus*
meadow	*Microtus pennsylvanicus*
meadow jumping	*Zapus hudsonicus*
red-backed	*Clethrionomys gapperi*
western harvest	*Reithrodontomys megalotus*
white-footed	*Peromyscus* spp.
woodland jumping	*Napeozapus insignis*
muskrat	*Ondatra zibethicus*
otter	
Canadian or river	*Lutra canadensis*
Eurasian	*Lutra lutra*
giant	*Pteronura brasiliensis*
sea	*Enhydra lutris*
polecat, European	*Mustela putorius*
porcupine	*Erethizon dorsatum*
rabbit, cottontail	*Sylvilagus* spp.
raccoon	*Procyon lotor*
ratel	*Mellivora capensis*
sable	*Martes zibellina*
seal	
Afro-Australian fur	*Arctocephalus pusillus*
bearded	*Erignathus barbatus*
California sea lion	*Zalophus californianus*
crabeater	*Lobodon carcinaphagus*
gray	*Halichoerus grypus*
harbor	*Phoca vitulina*
harp	*Phoca groenlandica*
hooded	*Cystophora cristata*
largha	*Phoca largha*
northern fur	*Callorhinus ursinus*
ringed	*Phoca hispida*
South American fur	*Arctocephalus australia*

southern elephant	*Mirounga leonina*
southern sea lion	*Otaria byronia*
Steller sea lion	*Eumetopias jubatus*
Weddell	*Leptonychotes weddelli*
shrew	
masked	*Sorex cinereus*
short-tailed	*Blarina brevicauda*
skunk	
striped	*Mephitis mephitis*
western spotted	*Spilogale gracilis*
others	genera *Conepatus*, *Mephitis*, *Spilogale*
squirrel	
douglas	*Tamiasciurus douglasii*
eastern gray	*Sciurus carolinensis*
flying	*Glaucomys* spp.
fox	*Sciurus niger*
golden-mantled ground	*Spermophilus lateralis*
red	*Tamiasciurus hudsonicus*
western gray	*Sciurus griseus*
tayra	*Tayra barbara*
walrus	*Odobenus rosmarus*
weasel	
least	*Mustela nivalis*
long-tailed	*Mustela frenata*
short-tailed	*Mustela erminea*
wolf	*Canis lupus*
wolverine	*Gulo gulo*
woodchuck	*Marmota monax*

Birds

blackbird, red-winged	*Agelaius phoeniceus*
chickadee, black-capped	*Parus atricapillus*
crow	*Corvus brachyrhynchos*
ducks	family Anatidae
eagle, golden	*Aquila chrysaetos*
flicker, yellow-shafted	*Colaptes auratus*
grouse, ruffed	*Bonasa umbellus*
jay	
blue	*Cyanocitta cristata*
gray	*Perisoreus canadensis*
junco, dark-eyed	*Junco hyemalis*
nuthatch, red-breasted	*Sitta canadensis*
owls	order Strigiformes
great horned	*Bubo virginianus*
quail, Coturnix	*Coturnix coturnix*
sparrows	family Fringillidae
starling	*Sturnus vulgaris*
thrushes	family Turdidae
woodpecker, downy	*Dendrocopos pubescens*

Trees

alder	*Alnus* spp.
aspen	
bigtooth	*Populus grandidentata*
quaking	*Populus tremuloides*
basswood, American	*Tilia americana*
birch	
white	*Betula papyrifera*
yellow	*Betula alleghanienses*
cedar, eastern white	*Thuja occidentalis*
elm, American	*Ulmus americana*
fir, balsam	*Abies balsamia*
hemlock, eastern	*Tsuga canadensis*
maple	
red	*Acer rebrum*
sugar	*Acer sacharinum*
oak, red	*Quercus rubra*
pine	
jack	*Pinus banksiana*
limber	*Pinus flexilis*
red	*Pinus resinosa*
white	*Pinus strobus*
poplar, balsam	*Populus balsamifera*
spruce	
black	*Picea mariana*
white	*Picea glauca*
tamarack	*Larix laricina*

References

Addison, E. M., M. A. Strickland, A. B. Stephenson, and J. Hoeve. 1988. Cranial lesions possibly associated with Skrabingylus (Nematoda: Metastrongyloidea) infections in martens, fishers and otters. *Can. J. Zool.* 66:2155-59.

Aldous, S. E., and J. Manweiler. 1942. The winter food habits of the short-tailed weasel in northern Minnesota. *J. Mammal.* 23:250-55.

Allen, A. W. 1983. Habitat suitability index models: Fisher. U.S. Fish and Wildlife Service, FWS/OBS-82/10.45.

Allen, D. L. 1938. Notes on the killing technique of the New York weasel. *J. Mammal.* 19:225-29.

Anderson, E. 1970. Quaternary evolution of the genus *Martes* (Carnivora, Mustelidae). *Acta Zool. Fenn.* No. 130.

———. In press. Evolution, prehistoric distribution and systematics of *Martes*. In S. W. Buskirk et al. (eds.).

Anderson, R. C. 1963. Further studies of the taxonomy of Metastrongyles (Nematoda: Metastrongyloidea) of Mustelidae in Ontario. *Can. J. Zool.* 41:801-9.

Anonymous. 1977. North Dakota fisher. *North Dakota Outdoors* 39(8):20.

Anonymous. 1978. Fur production. Statistics Canada, Agric. Div., Livestock & Animal Production Sec. Ottawa, Ontario.

Anonymous. 1992. Fur production. Statistics Canada, Agric. Div., Livestock & Animal Production Sec. Ottawa, Ontario.

Anthony, H. E. 1928. *Field Book of North American Mammals*. G. P. Putnam's Sons, New York.

Archibald, H. L. 1977. Is the 10-year wildlife cycle induced by a lunar cycle? *Wildl. Soc. Bull.* 5:126-29.

Arthur, S. M. 1987. Ecology of fishers in south-central Maine. Ph.D. thesis, University of Maine at Orono.

———. 1988. An evaluation of techniques for capturing and radiocollaring fishers. *Wildl. Soc. Bull.* 16:417-21.

Arthur, S. M., R. A. Cross, T. F. Paragi, and W. B. Krohn. 1992. Precision and utility of cementum annuli for determining ages of fishers. *Wildl. Soc. Bull.* 20:402-5.

Arthur, S. M., and W. B. Krohn. 1991. Activity patterns, movements, and reproductive ecology of fishers in southcentral Maine. *J. Mammal.* 72:379-85.

Arthur, S. M., W. B. Krohn, and J. R. Gilbert. 1989a. Home range characteristics of adult fishers. *J. Wildl. Mgt.* 53:674-79.

———. 1989b. Habitat use and diet of fishers. *J. Wildl. Mgt.* 53:680-88.

Aubry, K. B., and D. B. Houston. 1992. Distribution and status of the fisher (*Martes pennanti*) in Washington. *Northwestern Naturalist* 73:69-79.

Audubon, J. J., and J. Bachman. 1845-48. *The Viviparous Quadrupeds of North America*. 3 vols. Published by J. J. Audubon, New York.

Audy, M. C. 1976. Influence du photoperiodisme sue la physiologie testiculair de la Fouine (*Martes foina* Erx.). *C. R. Acad. Sci.* (Paris) 283:805-8.

Bakeyev, N. N., and A. A. Sinitsyn. In press. Sable (*Martes zibellina*) in the Commonwealth of Independent States. In S. W. Buskirk et al. (eds.).

Baldwin, H. I. 1934. Some physiological effects of girdling northern hardwoods. *Bull. Torrey Bot. Club* 61:249-57.

Balser, D. S. 1960. The comeback of the furbearers. *Conservation Volunteer,* Minn. Div. Game & Fish 23(134):57-59.

Balser, D. S., and W. H. Longley. 1966. Increase of fishers in Minnesota. *J. Mammal.* 47:342-47.

Banci, V. 1989. A fisher management strategy for British Columbia. Brit. Col. Min. Env., Wildlife Branch, Wildlife Bull. No. B-63.

Banville, D. 1980. Pages 133-35 in C. W. Douglas and M. A. Strickland (eds.), Trans. 1979 Fisher Conf. Ontario Min. Nat. Res. Unpublished report.

Barkalow, F. S. 1961. The porcupine and fisher in Alabama archeological sites. *J. Mammal.* 42:544-45.

Bashore, T. L. 1978. Highway deer mortalities: A non-random occurrence. Page 79 in M. H. Smith (chairman), Abstr. Tech. Papers, 58th Ann. Meeting Amer. Soc. Mammal. Publ. by the local committee, University of Georgia, Athens.

Belant, J. L. 1991. Immobilization of fishers (*Martes pennanti*) with ketamine hydrochloride and xylozine hydrochloride. *J. Wildl. Diseases* 27:328-330.

Bensen, D. A. 1959. The fisher in Nova Scotia. *J. Mammal.* 40:451.

Berg, W. E. 1982. Reintroduction of fisher, pine marten and river otter. Pages 159-74 in G. C. Sanderson (ed.), *Midwest Furbearer Management.* Kansas chapter, The Wildlife Society.

Berg, W. E., and D. W. Kuehn. In press. Return of two natives: Fisher and marten demographics and range in a changing Minnesota landscape. In S. W. Buskirk et al. (eds.).

Bernatskii, V. G., E. G. Snytko, and H. G. Nosova. 1976. Natural and induced ovulation in the sable (*Martes zibellina* L.). *Dokl. Akad.* (USSR) 230:1238-39. Translated by Consultants Bureau, N. Y.

Bissonette, J. A., R. J. Fredrickson, and B. J. Tucker. 1989. American marten: A case for land-scape-level management. *Trans. N. Am. Wildl. and Nat. Res. Conference* 54:89-101.

Bittner, S. L., and O. J. Rongstad. 1982. Snowshoe hares and allies. Pages 146-63 in J. A. Chapman and G. A. Feldhamer (eds.), *Wild Mammals of North America.* The Johns Hopkins University Press, Baltimore.

Blanchard, H. 1964. Weight of a large fisher. *J. Mammal.* 45:487-88.

Boise, C. M. 1975. Skull measurements as criteria for aging fishers. *N.Y. Fish & Game J.* 22:32-37.

Boulanger, J. G., and G. C. White. 1990. A comparison of home-range estimators using Monte Carlo simulation. *J. Wildl. Mgt.* 54:310-15.

Bradle, B. J. 1957. The fisher returns to Wisconsin. *Wisconsin Conserv. Bull.* 22(11):9-11.

Brainerd, S. M. 1990. The pine marten (*Martes martes*) and forest fragmentation: A review and general hypothesis. *Proc. of the Congress Internat. Union Game Biologists* 19:1-17.

Brainerd, S. M., J. O. Helldin, E. Lindström, and J. Rolstad. In press. Pine marten (*Martes martes*) in "old forest" in boreal Eurasia. In S. W. Buskirk et al. (eds.).

Brander, R. B. 1971. Longevity of wild porcupines. *J. Mammal.* 52:835.

———. 1973. Life history notes on the porcupine in a hardwood-hemlock forest in Upper Michigan. *Michigan Academician* 5(4):425-33.

Brander, R. B., and D. J. Books. 1973. Return of the fisher. *Natur. Hist.* 82(1):52-57.

Brinck, C., S. Erlinge, and M. Sandell. 1983. Anal sac secretion in mustelids: A comparison. *J. Chem. Ecol.* 9:727-45.

Brody, S. 1945. *Bioenergetics and Growth.* Reinhold, New York.

Brown, J. H., and R. C. Lasiewski. 1972. Metabolism of weasels: The cost of being long and thin. *Ecology* 53:939-43.

Brown, J. L. 1969. Territorial behavior and population regulation in birds: A review and re-evaluation. *Wilson Bull.* 81:293-329.

Brown, L. N. 1965. The fisher, *Martes pennanti*, in Sheridan County (Wyoming). *S. West Natur.* 10:143.

Brown, M. K., and G. Will. 1979. Food habits of the fisher in northern New York. *N.Y. Fish and Game J.* 26:87-92.

Bryant, J. P., and G. D. Weiland. 1985. Interactions of snowshoe hare and feltleaf willow in Alaska. *Ecology* 66:1564-73.

Buck, S., C. Mullis, and A. Mossman. 1978. Annual report: Corral Bottom-Hayfork Bally fisher study, 1 October 1977-1 October 1978. Unpublished report, Forest Service, U.S.D.A. and Humboldt State University, Arcata, California.

———. 1979. A radio telemetry study of fishers in northwestern California. *Cal.-Nev. Wildl. Trans.* 1979:166-72.

———. 1983. Final report: Corral Bottom-Hayfork Bally fisher study. Unpublished report, Forest Service, U.S.D.A. and Humboldt State University, Arcata, California.

———. In press. Fisher habitat utilization in adjoining heavily harvested and lightly harvested forest. In S. W. Buskirk et al. (eds.).

Buffon, G. L., and J. M. D'Aubenton. 1765. *Historie Naturelle*. Vol. 13. Imprimerie Royale, Paris.

Bulmer, M. G. 1974. A statistical analysis of the 10-year cycle in Canada. *J. Anim. Ecol.* 43:701-18.

———. 1975. Phase relations in the ten-year cycle. *J. Anim. Ecol.* 44:609-22.

Burkholder, B. L. 1959. Movements and behavior of a wolf pack in Alaska. *J. Wildl. Mgt.* 23:1-11.

Burt, W. H. 1943. Territoriality and home range concepts as applied to mammals. *J. Mammal.* 43:346-52.

Burt, W. H., and R. P. Grossenheider. 1964. *A Field Guide to the Mammals*. Houghton Mifflin, Boston.

Buskirk, S. W. 1984. The ecology of marten in southcentral Alaska. Ph.D. dissertation, University of Alaska, Fairbanks.

Buskirk, S. W., S. C. Forrest, M. G. Raphael, and H. J. Harlow. 1989. Winter resting site ecology of marten in the central Rocky Mountains. *J. Wildl. Mgt.* 53:191-96.

Buskirk, S. W., A. Harestad, M. G. Raphael, and R. A. Powell (eds.). In press. *Biology and Conservation of Martens, Sables and Fishers*. Cornell University Press, Ithaca, N.Y.

Buskirk, S. W., H. J. Harlow, and S. C. Forrest. 1988. Temperature regulation in the American marten (*Martes americana*). *Natl. Geogr. Res.* 4:208-18.

Buskirk, S. W., and S. L. Lindstedt. 1989. Sex biases in trapped samples of Mustelidae. *J. Mammal.* 70:88-97.

Buskirk, S. W., and R. A. Powell. In press. Habitat ecology of fishers and American martens. In S. W. Buskirk et al. (eds.).

Butterworth, E. W., and M. Beverly-Burton. 1980. The taxonomy of *Capillaria* spp. (Nematoda: Trichuroidea) in carnivorous mammals from Ontario, Canada. *Systematic Parasitology* 1:211-36.

———. 1981. Observations on the prevalence and intensity of *Capillaria* spp. (Nematoda: Trichuroidea) in wild Carnivorea from Ontario, Canada. *Proc. Helminthol. Soc. Wash.* 48:24-37.

Cahalane, V. H. 1944. *Meeting the Mammals*. Macmillan, New York.

———. 1947. *Mammals of North America*. Macmillan, New York.

Cahill, J. L. 1971. Puma. *Sierra Club Bull.* 56:18-22.

Carpenter, F. L., and R. E. MacMillen. 1976. Threshold model of feeding territoriality and test with a Hawaiian honeycreeper. *Science* 194:634-42.

Casey, T. M., and K. K. Casey. 1979. Thermoregulation of arctic weasels. *Physiol. Zool.* 52:153-64.

Central Sierra Audubon Society, Greater Ecosystem Alliance, Klamath Forest Alliance et al. 1990. Petition for a rule to list the fisher as endangered.

Charnov, E. L. 1976. Optimal foraging: Attack strategy of a mantid. *Amer. Natur.* 110:141-51.

Charnov, E. L., G. H. Orians, and K. Hyatt. 1976. Ecological implications of resource depression. *Amer. Natur.* 110:247-59.

Cheatum, E. L. 1949. Research in wildlife pathology and physiology. *Pittman-Robertson Quarterly* 9:521.

Chitwood, B. G. 1932. Occurrence of *Uncinaria stenocephala* from the fisher. *J. Parasit.* 18:307.

Clark, T. W., and T. M. Campbell. n.d. Population organization and regulatory mechanisms of pine marten in Grand Teton National Park, Wyoming. Unpubl. ms.

Clarke, S. H., and R. B. Brander. 1973. Radiometric determination of porcupine surface temperature under two conditions of overhead cover. *Physiol. Zool.* 46:230-37.

Clem, M. K. 1977. Food habits, weight changes and habitat selection of fisher during winter. M.S. thesis, University of Guelph, Ontario.

Clements, B. 1975. A report on subproject 2 of a proposal for an integrated study of wildlife resources of northeastern Minnesota. Unpubl. report, North Central Forest Experiment Station, Forest Service, U.S.D.A., St. Paul.

Colbert, E. H. 1969. *Evolution of the Vertebrates.* 2d ed. John Wiley & Sons, New York.

Cook, D. E., and W. J. Hamilton, Jr. 1957. The forest, the fisher, and the porcupine. *J. Forest.* 55:719-22.

Cottrell, W. 1978. The fisher (*Martes pennanti*) in Maryland. *J. Mammal.* 59:886.

Coues, E. 1877. Fur-bearing mammals: A monograph of North American Mustelidae. U.S.D.I. Misc. Publ. No. 8.

Coulter, M. W. 1966. Ecology and management of fishers in Maine. Ph.D. thesis, St. Univ. Coll. Forest., Syracuse University, Syracuse, N.Y.

Cowan, I. M., A. J. Wood, and W. D. Kitts. 1957. Feed requirements of deer, beaver, bear, and mink for growth and maintenance. *Trans. North Amer. Wildl. Conf.* 22:179-88.

Craig, R. E., and R. A. Borecky. 1976. Metastrongyles (Nematoda: Metastrongyloidea) of fisher (*Martes pennanti*) from Ontario. *Can. J. Zool.* 54:806-7.

Craighead, J. J., and F. C. Craighead. 1956. *Hawks, Owls and Wildlife.* Stackpole, Harrisburg and Wildlife Management Institute, Washington, D.C.

Cronquist, A. 1961. *Introductory Botany.* Harper & Row, New York.

Crowe, D. M. 1975. Aspects of aging, growth, and reproduction of bobcats from Wyoming. *J. Mammal.* 56:177-98.

Crowe, D. M., and M. A. Strickland. 1975. Dental annulation in the American badger. *J. Mammal.* 56:269-72.

Crowley, S. K., W. B. Krohn, and T. F. Paragi. 1990. A comparison of fisher reproductive estimates. *Trans. NE Sec. Wildl. Soc.* 47:36-42.

Crump, D. R. 1980a. Theitanes and dithiolanes from the anal gland of the stoat (*Mustela erminea*). *J. Chem. Ecol.* 6:341-47.

―――. 1980b. Anal gland secretion of the ferret (*Mustela putorius* forma furo). *J. Chem. Ecol.* 6:837-44.

Curio, E. 1976. *The Ethology of Predation.* Springer-Verlag, Berlin.

Curtis, J. D. 1941. The silvicultural significance of the porcupine. *J. Forest.* 39:583-94.

―――. Appraisal of porcupine damage. *J. Wildl. Mgt.* 8:88-91.

Curtis, J. D., and A. K. Wilson. 1953. Porcupine feeding on ponderosa pine in central Idaho. *J. Forest.* 51:339-41.

Dagg, A. I., D. Leach, and G. Sumner-Smith. 1975. Fusion of the distal femoral epiphyses in male and female marten and fisher. *Can. J. Zool.* 53:1514-18.

Daniel, J. C., Jr. 1970. Dormant embryos in mammals. *Biosci.* 20:411-15.

Davis, D. D. 1949. The shoulder architecture of bears and other carnivores. *Fieldiana Zool.* 31:285-305.

Davison, R. P. 1975. The efficiency of food utilization and energy requirements of captive fishers. M.S. thesis, University of New Hampshire. Concord.

Davison, R. P., W. W. Mautz, H. H. Hayes, and J. B. Holter. 1978. The efficiency of food utilization and energy requirements of captive female fishers. *J. Wildl. Mgt.* 42:811-21.

deVos, A. 1951. Recent findings in fisher and marten ecology and management. *Trans. North Amer. Wildl. Conf.* 16:498-507.

―――. 1952. Ecology and management of fisher and marten in Ontario. Tech. Bull. Ontario Dept. Lands and Forests.

Dick, L. A., and R. D. Leonard. 1979. Helminth parasites of fisher *Martes pennanti* (Erxleben) from Manitoba, Canada. *J. Wildl. Diseases* 15:409-12.

Dick, T. A., B. Kingscote, M. A. Strickland, and C. W. Douglas. 1986. Sylvatic trichinosis in Ontario, Canada. *J. Wildl. Diseases* 15:409-12.

Dilworth, T. G. 1974. Status and distribution of fisher and marten in New Brunswick. *Can. Field-Natur.* 88:495-98.

Dix, L. M., and M. A. Strickland. 1986. Sex and age-class determination for fisher using radiographs of canine teeth: A critique. *J. Wildl. Mgt.* 50:275-76.

Dodds, D. G., and A. M. Martell. 1971. The recent status of the fisher, *Martes pennanti* (Erxleben), in Nova Scotia. *Can. Field-Natur.* 85:62-65.

Dodge, W. E. 1967. The biology and life history of the porcupine (*Erethizon dorsatum*) in western Massachusetts. Ph.D. thesis, University of Massachusetts, Amherst.

_____. 1977. Status of the fisher (*Martes pennanti*) in the conterminous United States. Unpubl. report submitted to U.S.D.I.

_____. 1982. Porcupine. Pages 355-66 in J. A. Chapman and G. A. Feldhamer (eds.), *Wild Mammals of North America*. The Johns Hopkins University Press., Baltimore.

Douglas, C. W., and M. A. Strickland. 1977. Age class distribution and reproductive biology in the management of fisher, *Martes pennanti*. Ecology Coll., University of Western Ontario. Unpubl. ms.

_____. 1987. Fisher. In M. Novak, J. A. Baker, M. E. Obbard, and B. Malloch (eds.), Wild Furbearer Management and Conservation in North America. Ontario Ministry of Natural Resources, Toronto.

Douglas, W. O. 1943. Fisher farming has arrived. *Amer. Fur Breeder* 16:18,20.

Drew, J. V., and R. E. Shagg. 1965. Landscape relationships of soils and vegetation in the forest-tundra ecotone, Upper Firth River Valley, Alaska-Canada. *Ecol. Monogr.* 35:285-306.

Eadie, W. R., and W. J. Hamilton, Jr. 1958. Reproduction of the fisher in New York. *N.Y. Fish & Game J.* 5:77-83.

Ealey, E. H. M. 1963. The ecological significance of delayed implantation in a population of the hill kangaroo (*Macropus robustus*). Pages 33-48 in A. C. Enders (ed.), *Delayed Implantation*. University of Chicago Press, Chicago.

Earle, R. D. 1978. The fisher-porcupine relationship in Upper Michigan. M.S. thesis, Michigan Tech. University, Houghton.

East, K., and J. D. Lockie. 1964. Observations on a family of weasels (*Mustela nivalis*) bred in captivity. *Proc. Zool. Soc. Lond.* 143:359-63.

_____. 1965. Further observations on weasels (*Mustela nivalis*) and stoats (*Mustela erminea*) born in captivity. *J. Zool. Soc. Lond.* 147:234-38.

Eaton, R. L. 1974. *The Cheetah: The Biology, Ecology, and Behavior of an Endangered Species*. Van Nostrand Reinhold, New York.

Enders, R. K., and A. C. Enders. 1963. Morphology of the female reproductive tract during delayed implantation in the mink. Pages 129-40 in A. C. Enders (ed.), *Delayed Implantation*. University of Chicago Press, Chicago.

Enders, R. K., and O. P. Pearson. 1943. The blastocyst of the fisher. *Anat. Rev.* 85:285-87.

Erickson, A. B. 1946. Incidence of worm parasites in Minnesota Mustelidae and host lists and keys to North American species. *Amer. Midl. Natur.* 36:494-509.

Erlinge, S. 1974. Distribution, territoriality and numbers of the weasel *Mustela nivalis* in relation to prey abundance. *Oikos* 25:308-14.

_____. 1975. Feeding habits of the weasel *Mustela nivalis* in relation to prey abundance. *Oikos* 26:378-84.

_____. 1977. Spacing strategy in stoat *Mustela erminea*. *Oikos* 28:32-42.

_____. 1979. Adaptive significance of sexual dimorphism in weasels. *Oikos* 33:233-45.

Erlinge, S., B. Bergsten, and A. Kristiansson. 1974. Hermelinen och des bute-Jaktbeteende och flykreaktioner. *Fauna och flora* 69(6):203-11.

Erlinge, S., and M. Sandell. 1986. Seasonal changes in the social organization of male stoats, *Mustela erminea*: An effect of shifts between two decisive resources. *Oikos* 47:57-62.

Erlinge, S., and P. Widen. 1975. Hermilinens activitetsmönster under hösten. *Fauna och flora* 70(4):137-42.

Errington, P. L. 1943. An analysis of mink predation upon muskrats in north central United States. Agr. Exp. Sta. Iowa State Coll. Agr. & Mech. Arts Res. Bull. No. 320:797-924.

_____. 1967. *Of Predation and Life*. Iowa State University Press, Ames.

Ewer, R. F. 1973. *The Carnivores*. Cornell University Press, Ithaca, N.Y.

Farrell, D. J., and A. J. Wood. 1968. The nutrition of the female mink (*Mustela vison*). II. The energy requirement for maintenance. *Can. J. Zool.* 46:47-52.

Floyd, T. J., L. D. Mech, and P. A. Jordan. 1978. Relating wolf scat content to prey consumed. *J. Wildl. Mgt.* 42:528-32.

Fogl, J. G., and H. S. Mosby. 1978. Aging gray squirrels by cementum annuli in razor-sectioned teeth. *J. Wildl. Mgt.* 42:444-48.

Forthingham, E. H. 1915. The eastern hemlock. U.S.D.A. Bull. 152.

Fox, M. L. 1978. *The Dog: Its Domestication and Behavior.* Garland STPM Press, New York.

Fretwell, S. D. 1972. *Populations in a Seasonal Environment.* Princeton University Press, Princeton, N.J.

Fretwell, S. D., and H. L. Lucas, Jr. 1970. On territorial behavior and other factors influencing habitat distribution in birds. I. Theoretical development. *Acta Biotheoretica* 19:16-36.

Fries, S. 1880. Uber die Fortpflanzung von *Meles taxus*. *Zool. Anz.* 3:486-92.

_____. 1902. Zur Nahrung Fortpflanzung, sowie zur Schonzeit des duches. *Deutsche Jager-Zug.* 39.

Fritts, S. H., W. J. Paul, L. D. Mech, and D. P. Scott. 1992. Trends and management of wolf-livestock conflicts in Minnesota. U.S. Fish and Wildlife Service, Resource Publications 181.

Fyvie, A., and E. M. Addison. 1979. *Manual of common parasites, diseases and anomalies of wildlife in Ontario.* 2d ed. Ont. Min. Nat. Resources, Toronto.

Gambaryan, P. P. 1974. *How Mammals Run.* Halsted Press, Wiley, New York.

Gaughran, G. R. L. 1950. Domestic cat predation on short-tailed weasel. *J. Mammal.* 31:356.

Gause, G. F. 1934. *The Struggle For Existence.* Williams and Wilkins, Baltimore.

Gerell, R. 1970. Home range and movements of the mink *Mustela vison* Schreber in southern Sweden. *Oikos* 21:160-73.

Getz, L. L. 1961. Home ranges, territoriality, and movements of the meadow vole. *J. Mammal.* 42:24-36.

Gibilisco, C. J. In press. Distributional dynamics of American martens and fishers in North America. In S. W. Buskirk et al. (eds.).

Gillingham, B. J. 1978. A quantitative analysis of prey killing and its ontogeny in the ermine *Mustela erminea*. M.S. thesis, University of Montana, Missoula.

Giuliano, W. M., J. A. Litvaitis, and C. L. Stevens. 1989. Prey selection in relation to sexual dimorphism of fishers (*Martes pennanti*) in New Hampshire. *J. Mammal.* 70:639-41.

Glover, F. A. 1942. A population study of weasels in Pennsylvania. M.S. thesis, Pennsylvania State College, University Park.

_____. 1943. Killing techniques of the New York weasel. *Penn. Game News* 13(10):11.

Goldman, F. A. 1935. New American mustelids of the genera *Martes*, *Gulo*, and *Lutra*. *Proc. Biol. Soc. Wash.* 48:175-86.

Golley, F. B. 1960. Energy dynamics of a food chain of an old field community. *Ecol. Monogr.* 30:187-206.

Golley, F. B., G. A. Petrides, E. L. Rauber, and J. H. Jenkins. 1965. Food intake and assimilation by bobcats under laboratory conditions. *J. Wildl. Mgt.* 29:442-47.

Goszczynski, J. 1976. Composition of the food of martens. *Acta Ther.* 21(36):527-34.

Grafen, A. 1980. Opportunity, cost, benefit and degree of relatedness. *Anim. Behav.* 28:967-68.

Graham, M. A., and R. W. Graham. 1990. Holocene records of *Martes pennanti* and *Martes americana* in Whiteside County, northwestern Illinois. *Amer. Midl. Natur.* 124:81-92.

Graham, R. W., and M. A. Graham. In press. The late quaternary distribution of *Martes* in North America. In S. W. Buskirk et al. (eds.).

Grenfell, W. E., and M. Fasenfest. 1979. Winter food habits of fishers, *Martes pennanti*, in northwestern California. *Calif. Fish & Game* 65:186-89.

Griffin, K. A., and F. F. Gilbert. 1993. Heart rate of fishers (*Martes pennanti*) during exercise. *J. Mammal.* 74:285-290.

Grigoriev, N. D. 1938. On the reproduction of the stoat (in Russian). *Zoo. Zhur.* 17:811-14.

Grinnell, J., J. S. Dixon, and L. M. Linsdale. 1937. *Fur-Bearing Mammals of California: Their Natural History, Systematic Status and Relations to Man.* Vol. 1. University of California Press, Berkeley.

Grue, H., and B. Jensen. 1970. Review of the formation of incremental lines in tooth cementun of terrestrial mammals. *Danish Review of Game Biol.* 11:1-48.

Hagmeier, E. M. 1955. The genus *Martes* (Mustelidae) in North America, its distribution, variation, classification, phylogeny and relationship to Old World forms. Ph.D. thesis, University of British Columbia, Vancouver, B.C.

_____. 1956. Distribution of marten and fisher in North America. *Can. Field-Natur.* 70:149-68.

_____. 1959. A re-evaluation of the subspecies of fisher. *Can. Field-Natur.* 73:185-97.

_____. 1961. Variation and relationships in North American marten. *Can. Field-Natur.* 75:122-37.

Hahn, E. W., and R. C. Wester. 1969. The biomedical use of ferrets in research. Published by Marshall Research Animals, Inc. North Rose, N.Y.

Haley, D. 1975. *Sleek & Savage: North America's Weasel Family.* Pacific Search, Seattle.

Hall, E. R. 1926. The abdominal skin gland of *Martes. J. Mammal.* 7:227-29.

_____. 1942. Gestation period of the fisher with recommendation for the animals' protection in California. *Calif. Fish & Game* 28:143-47.

_____. 1951. *American Weasels.* University of Kansas Publ. Mus. Nat. Hist. No. 4.

_____. 1974. The graceful and rapacious weasel. *Nat. Hist.* 83(9):44-50.

_____. 1981. *The Mammals of North America.* John Wiley & Sons, New York.

Hamilton, G. T. 1957. Resurgence of the fisher in New Hampshire. *Appalachia* 31:485-90.

Hamilton, W. J., Jr. 1933. The weasels of New York. *Amer. Midl. Natur.* 14:289-344.

_____. 1943. *The Mammals of Eastern United States.* Comstock Publishing Co., Ithaca, N.Y.

Hamilton, W. J., Jr., and A. H. Cook. 1955. The biology and management of the fisher in New York. *N.Y. Fish & Game J.* 2:13-35.

Hamlett, G. W. 1935. Delayed implantation and discontinuous development in the mammals. *Quart. Rev. Biol.* 10:432-47.

Hardy, M. 1899. The fisher. *Shooting & Fishing* 25:526.

_____. 1907. The fisher. *Forest & Stream* 68:692-93.

Hargis, C. D., and D. R. McCullough. 1984. Winter diet and habitat selection of marten in Yosemite National Park. *J. Wildl. Mgt.* 48:140-46.

Harris, L. D., C. Maser, and A. McKee. 1982. Patterns of old growth harvest and implications for Cascades wildlife. *Trans. North Am. Wildl. Nat. Res. Conf.* 47:374-92.

Hawley, V. D., and F. E. Newby. 1957. Marten home ranges and population fluctuations. *J. Mammal.* 38:174-84.

Hayne, D. W. 1949. Calculation of the size of home-range. *J. Mammal.* 30:1-18.

Heidt, G. A. 1970. The least weasel, *Mustela nivalis* Linnaeus: Developmental biology in comparison with other North American *Mustela.* Publ. Mus. Michigan State University, Biol. Ser. 4(7):227-83.

Heidt, G. A., M. K. Petersen, and G. L. Kirkland, Jr. 1968. Mating behavior and development of least weasels (*Mustela nivalis*) in captivity. *J. Mammal.* 49:413-19.

Henderson, F. R., P. F. Springer, and R. Adrian. 1969. *The Black-footed Ferret in South Dakota.* South Dakota Dept. Game, Fish & Parks, Brookings.

Hendrickson, J., W. L. Robinson, and L. D. Mech. 1975. Status of the wolf in Michigan, 1973. *Amer. Midl. Natur.* 94:226-32.

Herreid, C. F., and B. Kessel. 1967. Thermal conductance in birds and mammals. *Comp. Biochem. Physiol.* 21:405-14.

Hibbard, C. W. 1970. Pleistocene mammalian local faunas from the Great Plains and Central Low-land Provinces of the United States. Pages 395-433 in W. Dort, Jr. and J. K. Jones (eds.), *Pleistocene and Recent Environments of the Central Great Plains.* University of Kansas Dept. Geol. Spec. Publ. No. 3.

Hildebrand, M. 1959. Motions of the running cheetah and horse. *J. Mammal.* 40:481-95.

———. 1974. *Analysis of Vertebrate Structure.* John Wiley & Sons, New York.

Hildebrand, M., D. M. Bramble, K. F. Liem, and D. B. Wake. 1985. *Functional Vertebrate Morphology.* Harvard University Press, Cambridge.

Hillman, C. N. 1968. Field observations of black-footed ferrets in South Dakota. *Trans. N. Amer. Wildl. Conf.* 33:433-43.

Hine, R. L. 1975. Endangered animals in Wisconsin. Unpubl. report, Wisc. Dept. Nat. Res., Madison.

Hixon, M. A., F. L. Carpenter, and D. C. Paton. 1983. Territory area, flower density, and time budgeting in hummingbirds: An experimental and theoretical analysis. *Amer. Natur.* 122:366-91.

Hodgson, R. G. 1937. *Fisher Farming.* Fur Trade J. Can. Toronto.

Holland, G. P. 1950. *The Siphonaptera of Canada.* Science-Service, Div. Entomol., Livestock Insect Lab., Kamloops, B.C.

Holling, C. S. 1959. Some characteristics of simple types of predation and parasitism. *Can. Entomol.* 91:385-98.

Holmes, T. 1980. Locomotor adaptations in the limb skeletons of North American mustelids. M.A. thesis. Humboldt State University, Arcata, Calif.

———. 1987. Sexual dimorphism in North American weasels with a phylogeny of the Mustelidae. Ph.D. thesis. University of Kansas, Lawrence.

Holmes, R., and R. A. Powell. In press. Morphology, ecology and the evolution of sexual dimorphism in North American *Martes.* In S. W. Buskirk et al. (eds.).

Ims, R. A. 1987. Male spacing systems in microtine rodents. *Amer. Natur.* 130:475-84.

———. 1988a. Spatial clumping of sexually receptive females induces space sharing among male voles. *Nature* 335:541-43.

———. 1988b. The potential for sexual selection in males: Effect of sex ratio and spatiotemporal distribution of receptive females. *Evol. Ecol.* 2:338-52.

———. 1990. Mate detection success of male *Clethrionomys rufocanus* in relation to the spatial distribution of sexually receptive females. *Evol. Ecol.* 4:57-61.

Ingram R. 1973. Wolverine, fisher and marten in central Oregon. Central Reg. Admin. Rep. No. 73-2. Oregon State Game Comm., Salem.

Irvine, G. W. 1960a. Preliminary report on the porcupine problem on the Ottawa National Forest. Unpubl. report, Ottawa National Forest, Forest Service, U.S.D.A., Ironwood, Mich.

———. 1960b. Progress report on the porcupine problem on the Ottawa National Forest. Unpubl. report, Ottawa National Forest, Forest Service, U.S.D.A., Ironwood, Mich.

———. 1961. Fisher restoration project, 1961. Unpubl. report, Ottawa National Forest, Forest Service, U.S.D.A., Ironwood, Mich.

———. 1962. Fisher restoration project: Progress report, 1962. Unpubl. report, Ottawa National Forest, Forest Service, U.S.D.A., Ironwood, Mich.

Irvine, G. W., B. J. Bradle, and L. T. Magnus. 1962. The restocking of fisher in lake states forests. Midwest Fish & Wildl. Conf. 24.

Irvine, G. W., and R. B. Brander. 1971. Progress report on a fisher-porcupine study on the Ottawa National Forest. Unpubl. report, N. Cen. For. Exp. Sta., Forest Service, U.S.D.A., St. Paul.

Irvine, G. W., L. T. Magnus, and B. J. Bradle. 1964. The restocking of fishers in lake states forests. *Trans. N. Amer. Wildl. Nat. Res. Conf.* 29:307-15.

Ivlev, V. S. 1961. *Experimental Ecology of Feeding of Fishes.* Yale University of Press, New Haven, Conn.

Jackson, H. H. T. 1961. *Mammals of Wisconsin*. University of Wisconsin Press, Madison.

Jedrzejewski, W., and B. Jedrzejewski. 1990. Effect of a predator's visit on the spatial distribution of bank voles: Experiments with weasels. *Can. J. Zool.* 68:660-66.

Jenks, J. A., R. T. Bowyer, and A. G. Clark. 1984. Sex and age-class determination for fisher using radiographs. *J. Wildl. Mgt.* 48:626-28.

Jenks, J. A., A. G. Clark, and R. T. Bowyer. 1986. Sex and age-class determination for fisher using radiographs: A response. *J. Wildl. Mgt.* 50:277-78.

Jense, G. K. 1968. Food habits and energy utilization of badgers. M.S. thesis, South Dakota State University, Brookings.

Jensen, A., and B. Jensen. 1970. Husmaaren (*Martes foina*) og maarjagten i Danmark. Danske Vildtundersøgelser, Hefte 15. Vildtbiologisk Station.

Johnson, S. A. 1964. Home range, movements, and habitat use of fishers in Wisconsin. M.S. thesis, University of Wisconsin, Stevens Point.

Johnson, W. A., and A. W. Todd. 1985. Fisher, *Martes pennanti*, behaviour in proximity to human activity. *Can. Field-Natur.* 99:367-69.

Joliceous, P. 1963a. The degree of generality of robustness in *Martes americana*. *Growth* 27:1-27.

_____. 1963b. Bilateral symmetry and asymmetry in limb bones of *Martes americana* and man. *Rev. Can. Biol.* 211:409-32.

Jones, J. L. 1991. Habitat use of fishers in northcentral Idaho. M.S. thesis. University of Idaho, Moscow.

Jones, J. L., and E. O. Garton. In press. Selection of successional stages by fishers in northcentral Idaho. In S. W. Buskirk et al. (eds.).

Jonkel, C., and R. P. Weckwerth. 1963. Sexual maturity and implantation of blastocysts in wild pine marten. *J. Wildl. Mgt.* 27:93-98.

Kebbe, C. E. 1961. Return of the fisher. *Ore. St. Game Comm. Bull.* 16:3-7.

Keith, L. B. 1963. *Wildlife's Ten-Year Cycle*. University of Wisconsin Press, Madison.

_____. 1966. Habitat vacancy during a snowshoe hare decline. *J. Wildl. Mgt.* 30:828-32.

Keith, L. B., J. R. Cary, O. R. Rongstad, and M. C. Brittingham. 1984. Demography and ecology of a declining snowshoe hare population. *Wildl. Monogr.* 90:1-43.

Keith, L. B., and L. A. Windberg. 1978. A demographic analysis of the snowshoe hare cycle. *Wildl. Monogr.* 58:1-70.

Kelly, G. M. 1977. Fisher (*Martes pennanti*) biology in the White Mountain National Forest and adjacent areas. Ph.D. thesis, University of Massachusetts, Amherst.

Kelsey, P. 1977. The return of the fisher. *N.Y. St. Environ.* 6(8):10.

Kenagy, G. J. 1987. Energy allocation for reproduction in golden-mantled ground squirrels. Pages 259-74 in A. D. S. Loudon and P. A. Racey (eds.), *Reproductive Energetics in Mammals*. Proc. Zool. Soc. Lond. 57. Clarendon Press, Oxford.

Keuhn, D. W. 1985. Calculating whole-body weights of fishers from skinned weights. *Wildl. Soc. Bull.* 13:176-77.

Keuhn, D. W., and W. E. Berg. 1981. Use of radiographs to identify age-classes of fisher. *J. Wildl. Mgt.* 45:1009-10.

King, C. M. 1975. The sex ratio of trapped weasels (*Mustela nivalis*). *Mammal Review* 5:1-8.

_____. 1989. *The Natural History of Weasels and Stoats*. Cornell University Press, Ithaca, N.Y.

Kleiber, M. 1975. *The Fire of Life*. 2d ed. John Wiley & Son, New York.

Kleiman, D. 1977. Monogamy in mammals. *Quart. Rev. Biol.* 52:39-69.

Klimov, Y. N. 1940. Data on the biology of the ermine (in Russian). *Trudy Biologischenkogo Instituta* 7:80-88. Also: Pages 108-17 in C. M. King (trans., ed.), 1975, *Biology of Mustelids: Some Soviet Research*. Brit. Libr. Lending Div. Wetherby.

Kodric-Brown, A., and J. H. Brown. 1978. Influence of economics, interspecific competition, and sexual dimorphism on territoriality of migrant rufous hummingbirds. *Ecology* 59:285-96.

Koford, C. B. 1978. The welfare of the puma in California. *Carnivore* 1(1):92-96.

Koteja, P. 1991. On the relation between basal and field metabolic rates in birds and mammals. *Functional Ecology* 5:56-64.

Kraft, V. A. 1966. Influence of temperature on the activity of the ermine in winter (in Russian). *Zool. Zhur.* 45:567-70. Also: Pages 104-7 in C. M. King, (trans., ed.), 1975, *Biology of Mustelids: Some Soviet Research.* Brit. Libr. Lending Div. Wetherby.

Krebs, R. J. 1973. Behavioral aspects of predation. Pages 73-111 in P. P. G. Bateson and P. H. Klopfer (eds.), *Perspectives in Ethology.* Plenum, New York.

Krefting, L. W., J. W. Stoeckeler, B. J. Bradle, and W. D. Fitzwater. 1962. Porcupine-timber relationships in the lake states. *J. Forest.* 60:325-30.

Krohn, W. B., S. M. Arthur, and T. F. Paragi. In press. Mortality and vulnerability of a heavily trapping fisher population. In S. W. Buskirk et al. (eds.).

Krott, P. 1959. Der Vielfrass (*Gulo gulo* L. 1758). *Monogr. Wildsäugeret* 13:1-159.

Kruuk, H. 1972. Surplus killing by carnivores. *J. Zool.* 166:233-44.

Kurtén, B. 1971. *The Age of Mammals.* Columbia University Press, New York.

LaBarge, T., A. Baker, and D. Moore. 1990. Fisher (*Martes pennanti*): Birth, growth and development in captivity. *Mustelid & Viverrid Conserv.* 2:1-3.

Laberee, E. E. 1941. *Breeding and Reproduction in Fur Bearing Animals.* Fur Trade J. Can. Toronto.

Larsen, J. A. 1965. The vegetation of the Ennadai Lake area, N.W.T.: Studies in subarctic and arctic bioclimatology. *Ecol. Monogr.* 35:37-59.

Latham, R. M. 1952. The fox as a factor in the control of weasel populations. *J. Wildl. Mgt.* 16:516-17.

Leach, D. 1977a. The forelimb musculature of marten (*Martes americana* Turton) and fisher (*Martes pennanti* Erxleben). *Can. J. Zool.* 55:31-41.

———. 1977b. The description and comparative postcranial osteology of marten (*Martes americana* Turton) and fisher (*Martes pennanti* Erxleben): The appendicular skeleton. *Can. J. Zool.* 55:199-214.

Leach D., and A. I. Dagg. 1976. The morphology of the femur in marten and fisher. *Can. J. Zool.* 54:559-65.

Leach, D., and B. K. Hall. 1982. Aging marten and fisher by development of the suprafabellar tubercle. *J. Wild. Mgt.* 46:246-47.

Leach, D., and V. S. de Kleer. 1978. The descriptive and comparative postcranial osteology of marten (*Martes americana* Turton) and fisher (*Martes pennanti*: Erxleben): The axial skeleton. *Can. J. Zool.* 56:1180-91.

Leonard, R. D. 1980a. Pages 15-25 in C. W. Douglas and M. A. Strickland (eds.), Trans. 1979 Fisher Conf. Ontario Min. Nat. Resources. Unpubl. report.

———. 1980b. Winter activity and movements, winter diet and breeding biology of the fisher in southeast Manitoba. M.S. thesis, University of Manitoba, Winnipeg.

Leonard, R. D. 1986. Aspects of reproduction of the fisher, *Martes pennanti*, in Manitoba. *Can. Field Naturalist* 100:32-44.

Lieberman, D. E., and R. H. Meadow. 1992. The biology of cementum increments (with an archaeological application). *Mammal Review* 22:57-77.

Lindström, E. 1989. The role of medium-sized carnivores in Nordic boreal forest. *Finnish Game Res.* 46:53-63.

Litvaitis, J. A., and W. W. Mautz. 1976. Energy utilization of three diets fed to a captive red fox. *J. Wildl. Mgt.* 40:365-68.

———. 1980. Food and energy use by captive coyotes. *J. Wild. Mgt.* 44:56-61.

Litvaitis, J. A., J. A. Sherburne, and J. A. Bissonette. 1985. Influence of understory characteristics on snowshoe hare habitat use and density. *J. Wildl. Mgt.* 49:866-73.

Llewellyn, L. M. 1942. Notes on the Alleghenian least weasel in Virginia. *J. Mammal.* 23:439-41.

Lockie, J. D. 1959. The estimation of the food of foxes. *J. Wildl. Mgt.* 23:224-27.

———. 1961. The food of the pine marten in West Ross-shire, Scotland. *Proc. Zool. Soc. Lond.* 136:187-95.

———. 1964. Distribution and fluctuations of the pine marten, *Martes martes* (L.), in Scotland. *J. Anim. Ecol.* 33:349-56.

_____. 1966. Territory in small carnivores. *Symp. Zool. Soc. Lond.* 18:143-65.

Łomnicki, A. 1978. Individual differences between animals and natural regulation of their numbers. *J. Anim. Ecol.* 47:461-75.

_____. 1988. Population biology of individuals. Princeton University Press, Princeton, N.J.

Long, C. A. 1969. Gross morphology of the penis in seven species of the Mustelidae. *Mammalia* 33:145-60.

Lund, H. M.-K. 1962. The red fox in Norway. II. The feeding habits of the red fox in Norway. Papers of the Norwegian St. Game Res. Inst. 2d Ser. No. 2:1-79.

MacArthur, R. H. 1972. *Geographical Ecology.* Harper & Row, New York.

McCord, C. M. 1974. Selection of winter habitat by bobcats (*Lynx rufus*) on the Quabbin Reservation, Massachusetts. *J. Mammal.* 55:428-37.

McMahon, T. 1973. Size and shape in biology. *Science* 179:1201-04.

Manville, R. H. 1948. The vertebrate fauna of the Huron Mountains, Michigan. *Amer. Midl. Natur.* 39:615-41.

Markley, M. H., and C. F. Bassett. 1942. Habits of captive marten. *Amer. Midl. Natur.* 28:604-16.

Marr, J. W. 1948. Ecology of the forest-tundra ecotone on the east coast of Hudson Bay. *Ecol. Monogr.* 18:117-44.

Marston, M. A. 1942. Winter relations of bobcats to white-tailed deer in Maine. *J. Wildl. Mgt.* 6:328-37.

Martell, A. M. 1983. Changes in small mammal communities after logging in north-central Ontario. *Can. J. Zool.* 61:970-80.

Maser, D., and R. S. Rohweder. 1983. Winter food habits of cougars from northeastern Oregon. *Great Basin Natur.* 43:425-28.

Matjushkin, E. N. 1974. Notes on the relationship of *Martes* Flavigula Bodd. and *Moschus moschiferus* L. in the middle Sikhote-Aline and evolution of the predator-prey relations. *Teriologia* 11:227-52.

May, R. M. 1973. *Stability and complexity in model ecosystems.* Princeton University Press, Princeton, N.J.

Mayr, E. 1963. *Animal Species and Evolution.* Belknap Press, Cambridge, Mass.

Mead, R. A. In press. Reproduction in the genus *Martes*. In S. W. Buskirk et al. (eds.).

Mech, L. D. 1966. The Wolves of Isle Royale. Fauna Natl. Pks. U.S. Fauna Ser. 7.

_____. 1970. *The Wolf: The Ecology and Behavior of an Endangered Species.* Natural History Press, Garden City, N.Y.

_____. 1977a. Population trend and winter deer consumption in a Minnesota wolf pack. Pages 55-83 in R. L. Phillips and C. Jonkel (eds.), Proc. 1975 Pred. Symp., Montana For. Conserv. Exp. Sta., University of Montana, Missoula.

_____. 1977b. A recovery plan for the eastern timber wolf. *Natl. Pks. & Conserv. Mag.* Jan.: 17-21.

Mellett, J. S. 1981. Mammalian carnassial function and the "Every Effect." *J. Mammal.* 62:164-66.

Mendall, H. L. 1944. Food of hawks and owls in Maine. *J. Wildl. Mgt.* 8:198-208.

Meyer, M., and B. G. Chitwood. 1951. Helminths from fisher (*Martes pennanti pennanti*) in Maine. *J. Parasit.* 37:320-21.

Miller, F. W. 1931. A feeding habit of the long-tailed weasel. *J. Mammal.* 12:164.

Monte, M. de, and J. J. Roeder. 1990. Histological structure of the abdominal gland and other body regions in olfactory communication in pine martens (*Martes martes*). *Z. Säugetierkunds* 55:425-27.

Moors, P. J. 1974. The annual energy budget of a weasel (*Mustela nivalis* L.) population in farmland. Ph.D. thesis, University of Aberdeen, Scotland.

_____. 1977. Studies of the metabolism, food consumption and assimilation efficiency of a small carnivore, the weasel (*Mustela nivalis*). *Oecologia* 27:185-202.

_____. 1980. Sexual dimorphism in the body size of mustelids (Carnivora): The roles of food habits and breeding systems. *Oikos* 34:147-58.

Morgan, B. B. 1942. New host records of nematodses from Mustelidae (Carnivora). *J. Parasit.* 29:158-59.

Morse, W. B. 1961. Return of the fisher. *Amer. For.* 64(4):24-26,47.

Mullen, R. K. 1970. Respiratory metabolism and body water turnover rates of *Perognathus formosus* in its natural environment. *Comp. Biochem. Physiol.* 32:259-65.

_____. 1971a. Energy metabolism of *Peromyscus crinitus* in its natural environment. *J. Mammal.* 52:633-35.

_____. 1971b. Energy metabolism and body water turnover rates of two species of free-living kangaroo rats, *Dipodomys merriami* and *D. microps. Comp. Biochem. Physiol.* 39A:379-90.

Mullen, R. K., and R. M. Chew. 1973. Estimating the energy metabolism of free-living *Perognathus formosus*: A comparison of direct and indirect methods. *Ecology* 54:633-37.

Murdoch, W. W., and A. Oaten. 1975. Predation and population stability. *Adv. Ecol. Res.* 9:1-125.

Murr, E. 1929. Zur Erklarung der verlangerten Tragdaur bei Säugetieren. *Zool. Anz.* 85:113-29.

_____. 1931. Experimentelle Abkurzung der Tragdaur beim Frettchen (*Putorius furo* L.). *Anz. der Akad. Wiss., Wien,* s.:265-66.

Nagy, K. A. 1987. Field metabolic rate and food requirement scaling in mammals and birds. *Ecological Monographs* 57:111-28.

Nellis, C. H., S. P. Wetmore, and L. B. Keith. 1978. Age related characteristics of coyote canines. *J. Wildl. Mgt.* 42:680-83.

Nishimura, K. 1991. Optimal patch residence time of a sit-and-wait forager. *Behavioral Ecology* 2:283-94.

Novak, M. 1987. Traps and trap research. Pages 941-69 in M. Novak, J. A. Baker, M. E. Obbard, and B. Malloch (eds.), *Wild Furbearer Management and Conservation in North America.* Ontario Ministry of Natural Resources, Toronto.

Nyholm, E. S. 1959. Stoats and weasels in their winter habitat (in Finnish). *Suomen Riista* 13:106-16. Also: Pages 118-31 in C. M. King (trans., ed.), 1975, *Biology of Mustelids: Some Soviet Research.* Brit. Libr. Lending Div. Wetherby.

Olson, H. F. 1966. Return of a native. *Wisc. Conserv. Bull.* 31(3):22-23.

O'Meara, D. C., D. D. Payne, and J. F. Witter. 1960. Sarcoptes infestation of a fisher. *J. Wildl. Mgt.* 24:339.

Ondrias, J. C. 1960. Secondary sexual variation and body skeletal proportions in European Mustelidae. *Arkiv. fur Zoologi.* 12:577-83.

_____. 1962. Comparative osteological investigations on the front limbs of European Mustelidae. *Arkiv. fur Zoologi.* 13(15):311-20.

Papke, R. L., P. W. Concannon, H. F. Travis, and W. Hansel. 1980. Control of luteal function and implantation in the mink by prolactin. *J. Anim. Sci.* 50:1102-7.

Paragi, T. F. 1990. Reproductive biology of female fishers in southcentral Maine. M.S. thesis, University of Maine at Orono.

Parmalee, P. W. 1971. Fisher and porcupine remains from cave deposits in Missouri. *Trans. Ill. Acad. Sci.* 64:225-29.

Parsons, G. R. 1980. Pages 25-60 in C. W. Douglas and M. A. Strickland (eds.), Trans. 1979 Fisher Conf. Ontario Min. Nat. Resources. Unpubl. report.

Parsons, G. R., M. K. Brown, and G. B. Will. 1978. Determining the sex of fisher from lower canine teeth. *N.Y. Fish & Game J.* 25:42-44.

Pearson, O. P., and R. K. Enders. 1944. Duration of pregnancy in certain mustelids. *J. Exp. Zool.* 95:21-35.

Pease, J. L., R. H. Vowles, and L. B. Keith. 1979. Interactions of snowshoe hares and woody vegetation. *J. Wildl. Mgt.* 43:43-60.

Pennant, T. 1771. *Synopsis of Quadrupeds.* J. Monk, Chester, England.

Penrod, B. 1976. Fisher in New York. *Conservationist* 31(2):23.

Petersen, L. R., M. A. Martin, and C. M. Pils. 1977. Status of fishers in Wisconsin, 1975. Wisc. Dept. Nat. Res., Rep. No. 92.

Petskoi, P. G., and V. M. Kolpovskii. 1970. Neck glandular structure in animals of the family Mustelidae (in Russian). *Zool. Zhur.* 49:1208-19.

Phillips, M. K., and W. T. Parker. 1988. Red wolf recovery: A progress report. *Conserv. Biol.* 2:139-41.

Pittaway, R. J. 1978. Observations on the behaviour of the fisher (*Martes pennanti*) in Algonquin Park, Ontario. *Le Naturaliste Canadienne* 105:487-89.

———. 1983. Fisher and red fox interactions over food. *Ontario Field Biologist* 37:88-90.

———. 1984. Fisher, *Martes pennanti*, scent marking behaviour. *Can. Field-Natur.* 98:57.

Poole, K. G., G. M. Matson, M. A. Strickland, A. J. Magoun, R. P. Graf, and L. M. Dix. In press. Age and sex determination in American martens and fishers. In S. W. Buskirk et al. (eds.).

Poole, T. B. 1970. The polecat. Grt. Brit. Comm. Forest. Rep. No. 76.

Possingham, H. P. 1989. The distribution and abundance of resources encountered by a forager. *Amer. Natur.* 133:42-60.

Powell, R. A. 1975. A model for raptor predation on weasels. *J. Mammal.* 54:259-63.

———. 1976. Compact carnivore. *Anim. Kingdom* 78(6):12-19.

———. 1977a. Hunting behavior, ecological energetics and predator-prey community stability of the fisher (*Martes pennanti*). Ph.D. thesis, University of Chicago.

———. 1977b. Return of the fisher. *Field Mus. Nat. Hist. Bull.* 48(2):8-12.

———. 1978a. A comparison of fisher and weasel hunting behavior. *Carnivore* 1(1):28-34.

———. 1978b. Zig! Zag! Zap! *Anim. Kingdom* 80(6):20-25.

———. 1979a. Ecological energetics and foraging strategies of the fisher (*Martes pennanti*). *J. Anim. Ecol.* 48:195-212.

———. 1979b. Mustelid spacing patterns: Variations on a theme by *Mustela. Z. Tierpsychol.* 50:153-65.

———. 1979c. Fishers, population models and trapping. *Wildl. Soc. Bull.* 7:149-54.

———. 1980a. Stability in a one-predator-three-prey community. *Amer. Natur.* 115:567-79.

———. 1980b. Fisher arboreal activity. *Can. Field-Natur.* 94:90-91.

———. 1981. Hunting behavior and food requirements of the fisher (*Martes pennanti*). Pages 883-917 in J. A. Chapman and D. Pursley (eds.), Proc., 1st Worldwide Furbearer Conf. Worldwide Furbearer Conference, Inc., Baltimore.

———. 1982a. The evolution of black-tipped tails in weasels: Predator confusion. *Amer. Natur.* 119:126-31.

———. 1982b. The Fisher: Life History, Ecology and Behavior. 1st ed. University of Minnesota Press., Minneapolis.

———. 1984. Marten. Pages 118-19 in D. Macdonald (ed.), *The Encyclopedia of Mammals.* Facts on File Publications, New York.

———. 1985. Fisher pelt primeness. *Wildl. Soc. Bull.* 13:67-70.

———. 1990. Final report: Part A, Small mammal occurrence in high elevation habitats of Great Smoky Mountains National Park, Part B, Feasibility of reintroducing fishers to Great Smoky Mountains National Park. Cooperative agreement CA-5000-3-8025, Sub-agreement No. 2, USDI National Park Service, Great Smoky Mountains National Park.

———. 1991. Thoughts on fishers and forests on the Olympic Peninsula. Unpub. report, U.S. Forest Service Pacific Northwest Forest and Range Experiment Station and National Park Service Olympic National Park.

———. In press a. Structure and spacing of *Martes* populations. In S. W. Buskirk et al. (eds.).

———. In press b. Habitat selection by fishers in Upper Peninsula, Michigan, in winter. *J. Mammal.*

Powell, R. A., and R. B. Brander. 1977. Adaptations of fishers and porcupines to their predator-prey system. Pages 45-53 in R. L. Phillips and C. Jonkel (eds.), Proc. 1975 Pred. Symp., Montana For. Conserv. Exp. Sta., University of Montana, Missoula.

Powell, R. A., and C. M. King. In preparation. Sexual size dimorphism of stoats (*Mustela erminea*) in New Zealand in relation to abundance of food.

Powell, R. A., and R. D. Leonard. 1983. Energy expenditure of a female fisher with kits. *Oikos* 40:166-74.

Prell, H. 1927. Uber doppelte Brunstzeit und verlangerte Tragzeit bei den einheimische Arten der Mardergattung *Martes* Pinel. *Zool. Anz.* 74,s.:112-28.

_____. 1930. Die verlangerte Tragzeit der einheimischen Martes-Arten. Ein Erklarungsversuch. *Zool. Anz.* 88,s.:17-31.

Pringle, L. 1964. Killer with a future—the fisher. *Anim. Kingdom* 67:82-87.

_____. 1973. *Follow a Fisher.* Thomas Y. Crowell, New York.

Pringle, L., and D. Mech. 1961. The fascinating fisher. *Field & Stream* 66(August):31,106, 107,109,111.

Progulske, D. R. 1969. Observations of a penned, wild-captured black-footed ferret. *J. Mammal.* 50:619-20.

Proulx, G., A. Kolenosky, M. Badry, R. Drescher, K. Seidel, and P. Cole. In press. Post-release movements of fishers reintroduced in March and June in the parklands of central Alberta. In S. W. Buskirk et al. (eds.).

Pulliainen, E. 1982. Scent-marking in the pine marten (*Martes martes*) in forest lapland in winter. *Z. Säugetierkunde* 47:91-99.

Pyke, G. H. 1978. Are animals efficient harvesters? *Anim. Beh.* 26:241-50.

_____. 1984. Optimal foraging theory: A critical review. *Ann. Rev. Ecol. Syst.* 15:523-75.

Pyke, G. H., H. R. Pulliam, and E. L. Charnov. 1977. Optimal foraging: A selective review of theory and tests. *Quart. Rev. Biol.* 52:137-54.

Quick, H. F. 1953a. Wolverine, fisher and marten studies in a wilderness region. *Trans. N. Amer. Wildl. Conf.* 18:513-33.

_____. 1953b. Occurrence of porcupine quills in carnivorous mammals. *J. Mammal.* 34:256-59.

Radinsky, L. B. 1968a. A new approach to mammalian cranial analysis, illustrated by examples of prosimian primates. *J. Morph.* 124:167-80.

_____. 1968b. Evolution of somatic sensory specialization in otter brains. *J. Comp. Neur.* 134:495-506.

_____. 1971. An example of parallelism in carnivore brain evolution. *Evol.* 25:518-22.

_____. 1973. Are stink badgers skunks? Implications of neuroanatomy for mustelid phylogeny. *J. Mammal.* 54:585-93.

_____. 1984. Basicranial axis length v. skull length in analysis of carnivore skull shape. *Biol. J. Linnean Soc.* 22:31-41.

Rahel, F. J. 1990. The hierarchical nature of community persistence: A problem of scale. *Amer. Natur.* 136:328-44.

Raine, R. M. 1979. Ranges of juvenile fisher, *Martes pennanti*, and marten, *Martes americana*, in southeastern Manitoba. *Can. Field-Natur.* 96:431-38.

_____. 1981. Winter food habits, responses to snow cover and movements of fisher (*Martes pennanti*) and marten (*Martes americana*) in southeastern Manitoba. M.S. thesis, University of Manitoba, Winnipeg.

_____. 1983. Winter habitat use and responses to snow of fisher (*Martes pennanti*) and marten (*Martes americana*) in southeastern Manitoba. *Can. J. Zool.* 61:25-34.

_____. 1987. Winter food habits and foraging behaviour of fishers (*Martes pennanti*) and martens *Martes americana*) in southeastern Manitoba. *Can. J. Zool.* 65:745-47.

Ralls, K., and P. H. Harvey. 1985. Geographic variation in size and sexual dimorphism of North American weasels. *Biol. J. Linnean Soc.* 25:119-67.

Rand, A. L. 1944. The status of the fisher (*Martes pennanti* Erxleben) in Canada. *Can. Field-Natur.* 58:77-81.

Rausch, R. A., and A. M. Pearson. 1972. Notes on the wolverine in Alaska and the Yukon Territory. *J. Wildl. Mgt.* 36:513-33.

Remington, J. D. 1952. Food habits, growth, and behavior of two captive pine martens. *J. Mammal.* 33:66-70.

Roberts, W. K., and R. J. Kirk. 1964. Digestibility and nitrogen utilization of raw fish and dry meals by mink. *Am. J. Vet. Res.* 25:1746-50.

Robinson, W. L., and G. J. Smith. 1977. Observations on recently killed wolves in Upper Michigan. *Wildl. Soc. Bull.* 5:25-26.

Romer, A. S. 1966. *Vertebrate Paleontology.* University of Chicago Press, Chicago.

Rosenzweig, M. L. 1966. Community structure in sympatric Carnivora. *J. Mammal.* 47:602-12.

———. 1991. Habitat selection and population interactions: The search for mechanism. *Amer. Natur.* 137(supplement):S5-S28.

Roy, K. D. 1991. Factors affecting fisher reintroduction success in the Cabinet Mountains of northwest Montana. In R. A. Powell, S. W. Buskirk, and J. Jones (eds.), Abstracts of presentations: Symposium on the biology and management of martens and fishers. University of Wyoming, Laramie.

Roze, U. 1989. *The North American Porcupine.* Smithsonian Institution Press, Washington D.C.

Roze, U., D. C. Locke, and N. Vatakis. 1990. Antibiotic properties of porcupine quills. *J. Chem. Ecol.* 16:725-34.

Rozhnov, V. V. 1991. Changes in the marking behavior in marten evolution. In R. A. Powell, S. W. Buskirk, and J. Jones (eds.), Abstracts of presentations: Symposium on the biology and management of martens and fishers. University of Wyoming, Laramie.

Rudnai, J. A. 1973. *The Social Life of the Lion.* Washington Square East Publishers, Wallingford, Penn.

Sandell, M. 1986. Movement patterns of male stoats, *Mustela erminea*, during the mating season: Differences in relation to social status. *Oikos* 47:63-70.

———. 1989a. The mating tactics and spacing patterns of solitary carnivores. Pages 164-82 in J. L. Gittleman (ed.), *Carnivore Behavior, Ecology, and Evolution.* Cornell University Press, Ithaca, N.Y.

———. 1989b. Ecological energetics, optimal body size and sexual dimorphism: A model applied to the stoat, *Mustela erminea* L. *Func. Ecol.* 3:315-24.

———. 1990. The evolution of delayed implantation. *Q. Rev. Biol.* 65:23-42.

Schaller, G. B. 1967. *The Deer and the Tiger.* University of Chicago Press, Chicago.

Schempf, P. F., and M. White. 1977. Status of six furbearers in the mountains of northern California. Calif. Reg., Forest Service, U.S.D.A.

Schmidt-Nielsen, K. 1971. Locomotion: Energy costs of swimming, flying and running. *Science* 177:222-28.

Schoener, T. W. 1969. Optimal size and specialization in constant and fluctuating environments: An energy-time approach. *Brookhaven Symp. Biol.* 22:103-14.

———. 1971. Theory of feeding strategies. *Ann. Rev. Ecol. Syst.* 2:369-404.

Schoonmaker, W. J. 1938. The fisher as a foe of the porcupine in New York State. *J. Mammal.* 19:373-74.

Schorger, A. W. 1942. Extinct and endangered mammals and birds of the Great Lakes Region. *Trans. Wisc. Acad. Sci., Arts & Letters* 34:24-57.

Scott, T. G. 1941. Methods and computation in fecal analysis with reference to the red fox. *Iowa St. Coll. J. Sci.* 15:279-85.

Scott, W. E. 1939. Rare and extinct mammals of Wisconsin. *Wisc. Conserv. Bull.* 4(10):21-28.

Seaman, D. E. 1993. Home range and male reproductive optimization in black bears. Ph.D. thesis. North Carolina State University, Raleigh.

Selwyn, S. 1966. Kestrel catching weasel. *Brit. Birds* 59:39.

Seton, E. T. 1926. *Lives of Game Animals.* Vol. 2. Doubleday, Doran & Co., New York.

———. 1937. *Lives of Game Animals.* Vol. 2. The Literary Guild of America, New York.

Shea, M. E., N. L. Rollins, R. T. Bowyer, and A. G. Clark. 1985. Corpora lutea number as related to fisher age and distribution in Maine. *J. Wildl. Mgt.* 49:37-40.

Silver, H. 1957. A history of New Hampshire game and furbearers. N.H. Fish & Game Dept. Concord, N.H.

Sokolov, I. I., and A. S. Sokolov. 1971. Some characteristics of locomotor organs of *Martes martes* L. associated with its mode of life (in Russian). *Byull. Mosk. O-va. Ispt. Priv. Otd. Biol.* 76(6):40-51.

Song, J. H., Y. Tong, and Y. Xiao. 1988. Effects of light on reproduction and molting of *Martes zibellina. J. Ecol. China.* 7:17-29.

Spencer, R. F., J. D. Jennings, D. E. Dibble, E. Johnson, A. R. King, T. Stern, K. M. Stewart, and W. J. Wallace. 1965. *The Native Americans: Prehistory and Ethnology of the North American Indians.* Harper & Row, New York.

Spencer, W. D. 1987. Seasonal resting-site preference of martens in the northern Sierra Nevada. *J. Wildl. Mgt.* 51:616-21.

Statistics Canada. 1978. Fur production, season 1976-1977. Can. Min. Indus., Trade & Comm. Ottawa.

Stevens, C. L. 1968. The food of fisher in New Hampshire. N.H. Dept. Fish & Game. Unpubl. report, Concord.

Strickland, M. A. 1978. Fisher and marten study, Algonquin region, progress report no. 5. Ontario Min. Nat. Res. unpubl. report.

_____. 1980. Pages 25-60 in C. W. Douglas and M. A. Strickland (eds.), Trans. 1979 Fisher Conf. Ontario Min. Nat. Res. unpubl. report.

_____. In press. Harvest Management of Fishers and American Martens. In S. W. Buskirk et al. (eds.).

Strickland, M. A., and C. W. Douglas. 1978. Some predictions for fisher and marten harvests in 1978-1979. *Can. Trapper* (December):18-19.

_____. 1981. The status of the fisher in North America and its management in southern Ontario. Pages 1443-58 in J. A. Chapman and D. Pursley (eds.), Proceedings of the Worldwide Fur-bearer Conference. Worldwide Furbearer Conf., Baltimore, Maryland.

Strickland, M. A., C. W. Douglas, G. R. Parsons, and M. K. Brown. 1981. Age determination of fisher by cementum annuli. *N.Y. Fish & Game J.* 29:90-94.

Tapper, S. C. 1976. The diet of weasels, *Mustela nivalis*, and stoats, *Mustela erminea*, during early summer, in relation to predation on gamebirds. *J. Zool.* 179:219-24.

_____. 1979. The effect of fluctuating vole numbers (*Microtus agrestis*) on a population of weasels (*Mustela nivalis*) on farmland. *J. Anim. Ecol.* 48:603-17.

Taylor, C. R. 1973. Energy costs of locomotion. Pages 25-42 in L. Bolis, K. Schmidt-Nielsen, and S. H. Maddrell (eds.), *Comparative Physiology.* North-Holland Publishing Co., Amsterdam.

Taylor, C. R., K. Schmidt-Nielsen, and J. L. Rabb. 1970. Scaling the energetic cost of running to body size in mammals. *Amer. J. Physiol.* 219:1104-7.

Taylor, W. P. 1935. Ecology and life history of the porcupine (*Erethizon dorsatum*) as related to the forests of Arizona and the southwestern United States. *Univ. Arizona. Bull. Biol. Sci.* 6.

Teplov, V. P. 1948. The problem of sex ratio in ermine (in Russian). *Zool. Zhur.* 27:567-70. Also: Pages 98-103 in C. M. King (trans., ed.), 1975, *Biology of Mustelids: Some Soviet Research.* Brit. Libr. Lending Div. Wetherby.

Thomasma, L. E., T. Drummer, R. O. Peterson. 1991. Testing the habitat suitability index model for the fisher. *Wildl. Soc. Bull.* 19:291-97.

_____. In press. Habitat selection by the fisher. In S. W. Buskirk et al. (eds.).

Travis, H. F., and P. J. Schaible. 1961. Fundamentals of mink ranching. Coop. Extension Serv., Mich. Agr. Exp. Sta. Bull. 229.

U.S. Fish and Wildlife Service. 1981. Standards for the development of suitability index models. Ecol. Serv. Man. 103. U.S. Fish and Wildlife Serv., Div. Ecological Serv., U.S. Government Printing Office, Washington, D.C.

_____. 1991. Notice of petition finding: 90-day petition finding for the Pacific fisher. Fed. Reg. 58:1159-61.

van Nostrand, N. 1977. Nova Scotia reports: Fisher. *Can. Trapper* 6(2):20.

Vaughn, M. R., and L. B. Keith. 1981. Demographic response of experimental snowshoe hare populations to overwinter food shortage. *J. Wildl. Mgt.* 45:354-80.

Watt, K. E. F. 1959. A mathematical model for the effect of density of attacked and attacking species on the number attacked. *Can. Entomol.* 91:129-44.

Weckwerth, R. P., and V. D. Hawley. 1962. Marten food habits and population fluctuations in Montana. *J. Wildl. Mgt.* 26:55-74.

Weckwerth, R. P., and P. L. Wright. 1968. Results of transplanting fishers in Montana. *J. Wildl. Mgt.* 32:977-80.

Weiner, J. 1989. Metabolic constraints to mammalian energy budgets. *Acta Theriologica* 34:3-35.

Weise, T. F., W. L. Robinson, R. A. Hook, and L. D. Mech. 1975. An experimental translocation of the eastern timber wolf. Audubon Conserv. Rep. No. 5.

Welker, W. I., and G. B. Compos. 1963. Physiological significance of sulci in somatic sensory cerebral cortex in mammals of the family Procyonidae. *J. Comp. Neur.* 120:19-36.

Welker, W. I., and S. Seidenstein. 1959. Somatic sensory representation in the cerebral cortex of the raccoon (*Procyon lotor*). *J. Comp. Neur.* 111:469-501.

Whitaker, J. O., Jr. 1970. The biological subspecies: An adjunct of the biological species. *The Biologist* 52:11-15.

White, G. C., and R. A. Garrott. 1990. *Analysis of Wildlife Radio-tracking Data.* Academic Press, New York.

Wiens, J. A. 1977. On competition and variable environments. *Amer. Sci.* 65:590-97.

Wilbert, C. J. 1992. Spatial scale and seasonality of habitat selection by martens in southeastern Wyoming. M.S. thesis. University of Wyoming, Laramie.

Williams, R. M. 1962. The fisher returns to Idaho. *Idaho Wildl. Rev.* 15(1):8-9.

Wilson, D. S. 1975. The adequacy of size as a niche difference. *Amer. Natur.* 109:769-84.

Wolff, J. O. 1975. The effects of over-winter food supply and habitat patchiness on seasonal movements and population densities of snowshore hare (*Lepus americanus*). Abst. Tech. Papers, 55th Ann. Meeting. Amer. Soc. Mammal:17-18.

Wood, J. 1977. The fisher is: . . . *Natl. Wildl.* 15(3):18-21.

Worley, D. E., J. C. Fox, J. B. Winters, and K. R. Greer. 1974. Prevalence and distribution of *Trichinella spiralis* in carnivorous mammals in the United States northern Rocky Mountain region. Pages 597-602 in C. W. Kim (ed.), *Trichinellosis.* Intext Educational Publishers, New York.

Worthen, G. L., and D. L. Kilgore. 1981. Metabolic rate of pine marten in relation to air temperature. *J. Mammal.* 62:624-28.

Wozencraft, W. C. 1985. A phylogenetic reappraisal of the Viverridae and its relationship to other Carnivora. Ph.D. diss., University of Kansas, Lawrence.

_____. 1989. The phylogeny of the recent Carnivora. Pages 495-535 in J. L. Gittleman (ed.), *Carnivore Behavior, Ecology, and Evolution.* Cornell University Press, Ithaca, N.Y.

Wright, P. L. 1948. Preimplantation stages in the long-tailed weasel (*Mustela frenata*). *Anat. Rev.* 100:593-608.

_____. 1950. Development of the baculum of the long-tailed weasel. *Proc. Soc. Exp. Biol. Med.* 75:820-22.

_____. 1963. Variations in reproductive cycles in North American mustelids. Pages 77-97 in A. C. Enders (ed.), *Delayed Implantation.* University of Chicago Press. Chicago.

Wright, P. L., and M. W. Coulter. 1967. Reproduction and growth in Maine fishers. *J. Wildl. Mgt.* 31:70-87.

Wunder, B. A. 1975. A model for estimating metabolic rate of active or resting mammals. *J. Theor. Biol.* 49:345-54.

Wynne, K. M., and J. A. Sherburne. 1984. Summer home range use by adult marten in northwestern Maine. *Can. J. Zool.* 62:941-43.

Ylönen, H. 1989. Zum einfluss det Musteliden *Mustela nivalis* und *M. erminea* auf zyklische Kleinnager am Beispiel von Clethrionomys-Populationen in Mittelfinland. Pages 553-62 in M. Stubbe (ed.), *Populationsökologie Marderartiger Säugetiere.* Wissenschaftliche Beiträge, Universität Halle.

Yocum, C. F., and M. T. McCollum. 1973. Status of the fisher in northern California, Oregon and Washington. *Calif. Fish & Game* 59(4):305-9.

Young, H. C. 1975. Pequam the fisher. *Fur-Fish-Game* 71(11):16-17, 48-50.

Youngman, P. M., and F. W. Schueler. 1991. *Martes nobilis* is a synonym of *Martes americana*, not an extinct Pleistocene species. *J. Mammal.* 72:567-77.

Yousef, M. K., W. D. Robertson, D. B. Dill, and H. D. Johnson. 1973. Energetic cost of running in the antelope ground squirrel *Ammospermophilus leucurus*. *Physiol. Zool.* 46:139-47.

Yurgenson, P. B. 1947. Sexual dimorphism in feeding as an ecological adaptation of a species (in Russian). *Byull. Mosk. Obsh. Lsp. Prirody* 52:33-35. Also: Pages 79-83 in C. M. King (trans. and ed.) 1975, *Biology of Mustelids: Some Soviet Research*. British Library Lending Div. Wetherby.

Zielinski, W. J. 1981. Food habits, activity patterns and ectoparasites of the pine marten at Sagehen Creek, California. M.S. thesis, University of California, Berkeley.

Zimmerman, J. W. 1990. A critical review of the error polygon method. *Intnatl. Conf. Bear Res. and Mgt.* 8:251-56.

Index

Den: natal, 55-57, 155, 188; sleeping, 125, 157, 159, 162-64; snow, 162-63

Dentition. *See* Teeth

Description, 3-11

Development, 42-73; behavioral, 68-70; fetal, 49; physical, 62-68

Disease, 71, 208

Dispersal, 43, 70

Distribution, 74-77; and noble marten, 76-77

Dog: and porcupine quills, 147; as predator on fisher, 71

Domestic animals, as food for fisher, 101, 102-3, 104, 127

Ducks, as food for fisher, 127

Eating behavior, 31, 125; and muscles of jaw, 31-33

Elevation, 96

Elongation, 4-6, 22, 193

Endangered species petition, 84-85

Energy acquisition, 181-183; optimal foraging models of, 195-199

Energy availability: from food, 181-83; optimal foraging models of, 195-99

Energy expenditure, 183-91; and optimal foraging for porcupine, 195-99; for reproduction, 188, 191-93

Energy models, 2, 184-99; for optimal foraging, 195-199; for reproduction, 191-93

Energy requirements, 183, 184-185; of carnivores, 180; and elongation, 193; and sexual dimorphism, 193-195

Eocene, 15

Euro, delayed implantation in, 58-59

Evolution, 15-17

Extermination, 78-80; and population model's predictions, 151-52. *See also* Population, decline

Eyes, 3, 67

Family breakup, 69-70

Farming, and habitat destruction, 79

Ferret, classification of, 12

Ferret, black-footed, 136

Ferret, European, 38, 65, 136; glands of, 38. *See also* Polecat, European

Fire, and habitat destruction, 205

Fish, use of as trap bait, 2

Fisher, 11

Fitness, 88-89, 179

Food, 100-116; analysis, 104; caching, 125; requirements, 184, 188-90; by season, 113-15; by sex, 115; webs, 17

Foraging. *See* Hunting behavior

Forest management, 204-5, 206, 208; and future of the fisher, 209

Fox, red: as competitor with fisher, 18, 207; and food analysis, 104; hunting behavior of, 119-20; nutritional and energy requirements of, 181, 183; as predator on weasel, 121

Fox, silver, pelt value of, 77

Fur, 6-8; color, 6; of kit, 63-64; molt, 6, 7; seasonal changes in, 6; and value of fisher, 201

Furbearer, value of fisher as, 208

Fur farm, 201; and problem with delayed implantation, 207; as source of scientific data, 42

Fur trade, 77-79; by American Indians, 75

Future of the fisher, 208-9

Gait, 9-11, 23, 25-27

Genet, 126

Gestation, 42, 48-50, 53, 61-62

Gland, 37-38; abdominal, 38; anal, 37; chin, 38; hind paw, 9, 38, 171

Grouse, ruffed: effects of fisher on population of, 201; and fisher hunting behavior, 122; as prey for fisher, 101, 102-3, 104, 113, 161

Habitat, 88-99; and activity, 95; destruction, 77, 84-85; differential use of by sexes, 96; and distribution, 76; and elevation, 96; and future of fisher, 204-5, 209; and home range, 89; and hunting behavior, 94-95, 122, 195-99; old-growth, 84, 92, 94, 97, 205, 207; open space avoided, 92-94; and population recovery, 80; preference, 89-95; and prey diversity, 95; quality, 88-89; recovery and reintroduction of fisher, 80; and rest sites, 96; scale, 89; second-growth, 91-92, 97, 204-5; and snow, 95-96; structure, 89, 96-97; Suitability Index, 97-99

Hare, snowshoe: attacked by European ferret, 136; effects of hunting on population of, 201; energy available in, 181-83; energy required to kill, 186-87, 196-97; fisher eating behavior for, 31, 125; and fisher food requirements, 189; fisher hunting behavior for, 117-23, 196-99; fisher killing behavior for, 68-69, 123-27; habitat, 92, 108-9; population cycles of, 86, 106, 205; in population models, 150-52; as prey for fisher, 18, 68-69, 101, 105, 106-9, 117-

18, 119; range of, 92, 107; sign of, 161; trophic level of, 18

Henhouse syndrome, 127

Holocene, 76

Home range, 167-79; and activity, 157-58; and elevation, 96; overlap, 172; by season, 169-70; sex differences in, 169-70, 172; size, 157, 167-70

Hunger, 126

Hunting behavior, 117-52; climbing used in, 120, 135, 138, 139, 142-43; energy expenditure in, 184-85, 191; evolution of, 2, 109, 135-38; and habitat, 90-91; for high-density prey, 117-18, 118-23; and optimal foraging, 122-23; for porcupine, 135-38; and snow, 95-96; for snowshoe hare, 117-18, 120-22; success, 119; two techniques, 117-18; when female has young, 57

Identification: from bones, 22; from teeth, 29-30

Jay, as prey for fisher, 102, 113

Killing behavior, 123-27; development, 68-69; energy expenditure for, 184-85, 186-87, 191; evolution of, 2, 109, 125-27; for mouse, shrews, snowshoe hare, squirrel, 123-27; and movement of prey as stimulus, 126-27; parental instruction in, 69; for porcupine, 135-39

Kits: development of, 62-70; energy models for, 191-93; in natal den, 55-57; weaning of, 67

Lactation, energy cost of, 191-93

Length, 4

Life history, 42-73

Litter size, 50-53

Live-trapping, as source of scientific data, 85-87

Locomotion: of adult, 9-11, 25-27; of kit, 66-67

Logging: and biological control of porcupines, 80-81, 208; effects of on fisher habitat, 77, 84-85, 201, 204-5; effects of on fisher populations, 77, 79-80, 204-5; and future of fisher, 204-5

Longevity, 70-71

Lynx, 18, 19, 77, 135

Management, 201-9

Marking. See Scent marking

Marsupials, delayed implantation in, 58-59

Marten: anatomy of, 22; brain of, 36; classification of, 12-13; climbing ability of, 164-65; delayed implantation in, 58, 59;

fossil remains of, 17; locomotion of, 25-27; as predators on weasels, 121; range of, 13; sexual dimorphism, 38

Marten, American: age and sex determination, 33; arboreal adaptations, 25, 164-65; classification of, 12-13; as competitor with fisher, 18; delayed implantation in, 58, 59; and development of kits, 65, 68, 69; and fisher's name, 2; glands of, 38; hunting behavior of, 121; identification of, 22; killing behavior of, 69; pelt value of, 77; range, 13, 76; reproduction of, 46; resting sites, 163-64; sexual dimorphism in, 41, 65; skeleton, 22; social organization and aggression, 166; spacing pattern, 166

Marten, beech, 12. See also Marten, stone

Marten, European pine: classification of, 12; climbing of, 22; glands of, 38; habitat of, 207; hunting behavior of, 121; scent marking of, 38

Marten, house, 12. See also Marten, stone

Marten, Japanese, 12

Marten, noble, 76-77

Marten, stone, 12, 14, 25, 38; reproduction of, 46

Marten, yellow-throated, 12, 13, 38, 111

Martes: anderssoni, 17; divuliana, 17; palaeosinensis, 17. For living species, see Marten, American; Marten, European pine; Marten, Japanese; Marten, stone; Marten, yellow-throated

Mating, 54-55; energy expenditure in, 191-92; pattern, 54. See also Reproduction

Miacidae. See Miacids

Miacids, 2, 15, 16, 126; hunting behavior of, 118, 120; killing behavior of, 126

Mink: classification of, 12; delayed implantation in, 59, 60; jaw joint, 33; nutritional and energy requirements of, 180-81, 183; reproduction in, 43; sexual dimorphism in, 65; skull, 31

Miocene, 17

Molting, 6-8

Mongoose, 126

Moose, 102, 119

Mortality, 70-73; due to disease in zoos, 70; due to porcupine quills, 71; due to predation, 18, 71, 73, 121-22; trapping as a factor in, 86-87, 203

Mountain lion, 135; controversy over, 208

Mouse: and fisher food requirements, 189; fisher hunting behavior for, 119-20, 122;

fisher killing behavior for, 123; as prey for
fisher, 18, 101, 104, 111-12; as prey for
weasel, 69, 121; smelled by fisher, 161;
trophic level of, 18
Movement, 155-62; circuital, 159; and energy
expenditure, 185-91; by habitat, 159;
during lactation, 57; by season, 155-57
Muscle, 21
Muskrat, as food for fisher, 102
Mustelidae. *See* Weasel family
Mustelinae. *See* Musteline
Musteline: classification of, 12; evolution, 17;
glands of, 37-38, 68; hunting behavior of,
118, 120, 197; killing behavior of, 126;
and optimal foraging, 197; reproduction of,
46, 55, 191-93
Myth, 19, 127, 128, 134, 135, 145, 164

Name, 2, 11
Neck bite, 123-26
Nutritional requirements: and optimal
foraging, 195-99. *See also* Energy
requirements

Oligocene, 15
Optimal foraging, 123, 195-99
Otter, 12, 78; brain, 37; jaw joint, 33
Owl, 135

Parasites, 71, 72
Parturition, 42, 49-50, 53-54, 55; and delayed
implantation, 61-62
Paws, 8-9
Pekan, 2
Pelt, 8; value of, 77-78; and value of fisher,
208
Placental scar, 52-53
Play, 68
Pleistocene, 17, 76, 134-35
Pliocene, 17
Polecat: classification of, 12; European, 2, 22,
68; and fisher's name, 2. *See also* Ferret,
European
Population, 77-87; cycles, 78, 79, 86, 106,
150-52, 203; decline, 77-80, 81, 148;
effects of logging on, 79-80; effects of
trapping on, 77-79, 86-87, 202-4; density,
85-87; dynamics, 86-87, 150-52, 202-03,
206; management, 202-4, 208, 209;
models, 2, 148-52, 202-3; recovery,
80-84; stability, 86, 148-52, 202-3
Porcupine: coevolution of with fisher, 109,
134-35; defense against predators, 134,
140-43; den, 131, 132, 138, 141, 142;
description of, 130-31; energy available in,
181-83; energy required to kill, 186, 196-
97; and fisher food requirements, 189;
fisher hunting behavior for, 120-22, 143-
45; fisher killing behavior for, 69, 135-39;
and fisher sexual dimorphism, 143; life
history of, 131-34; population density of,
80-81, 148-50; in population models, 150-
52; population stability of, 148-52, 206;
predation on by fisher of different sexes,
143; as prey for fisher, 18, 19, 69, 80-81,
101, 106, 109, 128-52, 206; as prey for
Martes divuliana, 17; range, 128-30;
road-killed, 149; and trees, 81; trophic
level, 18; and value of fisher, 208; weight
of and predation by fisher, 148-49. *See
also* quills, porcupine
Posture, 8-9
Predation: effects of on prey populations,
205-6; on fisher, 18, 71-72; and optimal
foraging, 195-99; teeth used, 31
Prey, 3, 18, 100-116, 119, 122, 123, 127,
134-52, 161; energy available in, 182. *See
also* Deer, black-tailed; deer, white-tailed;
Hare, Snowshoe; Mouse; Porcupine;
Shrew; Squirrel

Quail, Coturnix, 68, 182, 183, 189
Quills, porcupine: antibiotic qualities, 147;
avoidance of by fishers when eating, 140;
as defense against predators, 128, 129,
133, 134, 135, 136, 138, 141, 150;
description of, 129, 130-31; in fishers,
138; fisher's adaptations to, 145-47; and
infection, 145-47; at kill sites, 138, 139,
140; as source of fisher mortality, 147

Rabbit, 101, 102, 123, 125, 201
Raccoon, 5, 37, 102
Radiotelemetry: description of techniques of,
20; problems, 91; as source of scientific
data, 20, 56-57, 85, 153-59, 167-69, 187-
88, 191-93
Range: original, 74-77; present, 74-77, 83-84
Raptors, as predators on weasels, 121
Ratel, 12
Reintroduction, 81-83, 148
Reproduction, 42-57; and age, 46; in energy
models, 191-93; female, 47-48, 53-54;
male, 44-46, 54. *See also* Mating
Resource depression, 173
Resting site, 96, 157, 162-64

Sable, 12, 14; glands of, 38; predation on musk deer, 111; reproduction of, 46, 47

Scavenging, 101, 102-3, 104, 105, 110-11, 161; energy acquisition from, 190-91; of road-killed animals, 105

Scent marking: and breeding season, 43; development, 68; and spacing patterns, 170-71

Sea lions, delayed implantation in, 58, 59-60

Seals, delayed implantation in, 58, 60

Sex determination, 22, 33

Sex ratio, 87

Sexual dimorphism, 3, 33, 65; and behavior, 69-70, 155-57, 165; effects of on porcupine population density, 193-95; and energy requirements, 193-95; evolution, 39-41, 54; and food, 115-16; and foraging behavior, 195-99

Shape, 22

Shrew, 112, 119, 123

Size, 3, 41

Skeleton, 21-28; using to determine age and sex, 22

Skull, 29-35; crests in, 29, 33-34; use of for aging, 33-34

Skunk, 12, 38

Snow: and gait, 10, 11, 26; and foraging, 95-96, 189; and habitat preference, 95-96; resting site, 162-63

Snowshoe hare. *See* Hare, snowshoe

Spacing patterns, 166-79

Squirrel, 101; energy available in, 181-83; fisher eating behavior for, 125; and fisher food requirements, 189; fisher hunting behavior for, 119-20, 122, 196; fisher killing behavior for, 69, 123; as prey for fisher, 18, 69, 101, 112-13; as prey for *Martes divuliana*, 17

Stoat. *See* Weasel, short-tailed

Study techniques, 18-20

Subspecies, 14

Surplus killing, 127

Swimming, 165-66

Tail, 22

Tayra, 25

Teeth, 29-35; carnassials, 29-32; eruption of, 67; in evolution, 15-17, 126; sexual dimorphism in, 39; use of for aging, 34-36; use of to determine sex, 34

Territoriality, 167-79; change with food abundance, 177-78; model, 173-79

Thermoregulation, 185, 191-92

Tracking, as source of scientific data, 85, 18-20, 104, 158, 159-62, 167

Tracks, 9-11; and breeding season, 43; sexual differences in, 11; as source of scientific data, 85, 18-20, 104, 158, 159-62, 167; use of to determine gait, 9

Trapping: closure of to protect fisher, 78-79; and fisher's name, 2; and future of fisher, 201-4, 209; and population decline, 77-79, 80, 201-4; and population recovery, 82-84; as source of scientific data, 19, 85-87, 105; and value of fisher, 201-4, 208

Value of fisher, 207, 208

Vegetation, as food for fisher, 102-3, 115

Weaning: age at, 67; and delayed implantation, 58, 60; parental activity before, 57

Weasel: classification of, 12; as competitor with fisher, 18, 191; delayed implantation in, 59-61; and development of kits, 63, 64, 65, 67-68, 69; elongation of, 5-6; glands of, 38, 68; hunting behavior of, 120-22; killing behavior of, 69, 126, 136; predation on, 121; as prey for fisher, 102-3; as prey for raptors, 121-22; sexual dimorphism in, 38, 41, 65; skull, 31

Weasel, least: energy acquisition by, 183; energy requirements of, 181; reproduction of, 47; sexual dimorphism in, 65, 193-94

Weasel, long-tailed, 27, 136

Weasel, short-tailed, energy requirements of, 181

Weasel family: anal glands in, 37; classification of, 12; curiosity and reaction to humans, 201; delayed implantation in, 60-62; elongation in, 4-6, 22; evolution of, 15-17; henhouse syndrome in, 127; locomotion in, 22; reproduction, 47; teeth in, 31

Weight, 3, 5; and energy expenditure, 187-88; and energy requirements, 193-95; of kits, 63, 64-65, 66; and sexual dimorphism, 3, 193-95; variation in, 3

Wolf: controversy over, 208; and food analysis, 104; hunting success of, 119; malnutrition in, 180; as porcupine predator, 135

Wolverine, 12, 18, 135

Wraparound assist, 69, 124, 125

Zoo, and captive fisher, 207-8

Roger Powell is an associate professor in the Departments of Zoology and Forestry at North Carolina State University at Raleigh. He received his B.A. from Carleton College in Northfield, Minnesota, and his Ph.D. from the University of Chicago. He is the coeditor of books on mammal morphology and on the biology and conservation of martens and fishers and is the author of numerous professional and popular articles on members of the weasel family and other mammals.